Here's to more clients and sweeter ~~Carrie~~

CURRENCY

STRIKING
NETWORKING GOLD
IN A RELATIONSHIP
ECONOMY

CARRIE PERRIEN SMITH

A Publisher Driven
by Vision and Purpose
www.soarhigher.com

*Currency: Striking Networking Gold
in a Relationship Economy*

Copyright © 2008 by Carrie Perrien Smith. All rights reserved.

ISBN-13: 978-0-9771403-8-1
Library of Congress Control Number 2008907463

No part of this book may be reproduced, stored in a retrieval system, or transmitted in any form or by any means, electronic, mechanical, photocopy, recording, or any other — except for the inclusion of brief quotations in a review — without written permission from Soar with Eagles.

First Edition

Published by
Soar with Eagles
1200 North Mallard Lane, Rogers, AR 72756, USA
http://www.soarhigher.com

Printed in the United States of America

Contents

Introduction ix
   This Isn't Just Another Book on Networking ix

Expose Yourself 1
   Promotional Strategy 3
      Overview of Promotional Strategy for the Rest of Us 4
      The Art of Shameless Self-Promotion 5
      Creating a Promotional Strategy Based on Networking 6
      Finding the Right Networking Events 11
      Design Your Own Networking Opportunities 17
      Capitalizing on the Networking Gold Zone™ 20
      Always Be Prepared 20
      Start Your Own Networking Group 21
      Boost Your Exposure through Social Networking 23

   Promotional Tools 29
      Crafting a Memorable Sixty-Second Commercial 29
      Features versus Benefits 33
      Business Cards: Valuable Networking Currency 34
      Managing Your Business Cards 36

   Tips and Techniques to Get The Most from Networking 39
      Networking: The Gift That Keeps Earning Dividends 39
      Marketing Lessons from My Dog Jazmin 41
      Know Your Product, Love Your Product, Use Your Product 43
      Twenty-One Ways to Stay In Front of Your Target Client 46
      Marketing Yourself and Your Company
      Through Community Involvement 50
      What I Learned About Business While Working for Free 52

Word Power 57

   Leading Meaningful Conversations 59
      Creating Meaningful Conversations: It's All About Them 61
      Creating Meaningful Conversation with New People 64
      So I Met Someone New. Now What? 67
      Caution: Slippery Conversation 67
      What If You Forget a Name? 68

   The Importance of Speaking Skills 71
      The Road to Speaking Confidently 73
      Listening: The Most Powerful Communication Tool of All 74

   Why Don't People Listen? 77
      Types of Communicators 78
      Understanding the Roadblocks to Communication 79
      Clues You Can See 85

   Communicate So People Will Hear You 91
      Using a Multi-Dimensional Approach to Communication 92
      Designing the Multi-Dimensional Communication Strategy 93
      Types of Communication Vehicles 97

Transactions **115**

   Creating Meaningful Customer Dialogue...117
      Understanding Who Your Customer Is 118
      Customer Service versus an
      Extraordinary Customer Experience 119
      Face Time and Revealing Questions..124
      Meaningful Customer Dialogue Paves the
      Way for Extraordinary Stories of Customer Service 127
      Exceptional People Make It Possible to
      Overlook a Multitude of Flaws 130
      Hospitality Takes the Chill Off a Travel Experience..............................131
      Customers Reward a Great Customer
      Experience with Repeat Business...133

   The Value of the F Word..137
      The Inevitable Confrontation..139
      The Power of Being Nice 140
      Feedback Isn't the Enemy — It's the Answer 140
      The Benefit of Asking the Right Questions..141

   Be a Sales Consultant 145
      We're All in Sales 146
      Buyers Want a Consultant — Not a Salesperson..................................146
      Choose to Be a Sales Consultant 148
      What If All Employees Learned to Sell? 148

   Pit Bull Follow-Up 153
      Keep in Touch with Customers..153
      Making Mass E-Mail Contact Meaningful...159
      Is E-Mail Contact Becoming an Endangered Species?..........................162
      Meaningful Content Can Cause
      Your E-Mail to Rise to the Top of the Inbox 163

Brand Equity 165
   The Hard Skills Necessary for Becoming A Person of Influence 167
      Your Experience and Expertise 167
      Set Kick-Butt Goals 175
   The Unspoken Rules for Becoming a Person of Influence 187
      Willingness to Maintain Personal Contact with Your Customers 188
      Knowing and Living Your Calling 190
      Carrying Yourself with Grace and Humility 191
      Acting Consistently and Dependably 191
      Defining Your Values and Living by Them Courageously 192
      Speak and Live with Truth and Honor 195
      Making Decisions with a Sense of Urgency 198
      Acting on Requests with a Sense of Urgency 201
      Adopting an Attitude of Servant-Leadership 208
      Helping People Discover Their Personal Genius 209
      Possessing a Genuine Interest in
      Serving Something Bigger Than Yourself 211
      Becoming Extraordinary through Passion and Vision 214
   The Secret to Being Attractive 219
      The Law of Attraction 223
      Becoming an Attractive Person through Conversation 224
      Make a Powerful, Confident, and Memorable First Impression 229
   Getting What You Want, Need, and Deserve 237
      Making Requests with Warmth and Sincerity 237
      Gratitude 238
      The Chemistry of Conflict 245
      Staring Conflict in the Face: What to Do When Conflict Happens 251
      Resolving Conflict 254
      Prayer: Not the Least We Can Do 258
   Brands and Legacies: Not Such Different Creatures 261
      Build the Right Brand and Your Legacy Will Come 262
      What Will Your Legacy Be Worth? 262
      Eight Belles: The Price of Winning 263
      Some Examples of Lasting Legacies 265
      Your Legacy is Your Choice 267

Exercises and Bonuses

Who Needs to Be in Your Network? 8
Building a Network That Benefits Your Current Professional Role 9
Networking Truths and Survival Tips 14
Eleven Essentials to Effective Networking 18
Create Your Own Sixty-Second Commercial 30
Networking is Not Network Marketing 45
Brainstorm Some Questions for People You'd Like to Know Better 66
The Value of Writing at the Eighth-Grade Reading Level 102
Identifying Your Customers 120
Questions That Create the Foundation for
Meaningful Customer Dialogue 125
Raise the Bar on Customer Service 128
Questions That Will Provide Meaningful Feedback 142
Three Steps to Being a Great Sales Consultant 149
Follow Up on Leads You Receive 157
Expertise Inventory 169
Expertise to Develop 170
Experience Inventory 173
Experiences You Want to Have 174
Goal Worksheet 183
Professional Image and Interpersonal Skills
Make a Big Impression on Customers 189
Ten Ways to Change Your World by Changing Your Point of View 204
Change Your World by Changing Your Environment 212
Questions for Each Stage in Life 227
Mastering the Winning Attitude:
Be Someone People Can't Wait to Be Around 231
Five Tips for Making an Organized Impression 232
Upgrade Your Appreciation 241
Ideas for Showing Your Appreciation 243
Conflict Resolution Formula 256
Reality Check to Test Your Priorities 264

INTRODUCTION
This Isn't Just Another Book on Networking

After devoting years of research on the art of networking, I began to ask myself, "Is this all there is?" I sensed an enormous need to connect the art of meeting people to an outcome other than building a big contact list. No one can survive on contacts alone.

Well, my search for the answer to the question brought me to a gold mine — a networking gold mine. If I took networking a step beyond the typical techniques and provided the tools to communicate more effectively, deliver an unforgettable customer experience, and build a personal brand, I could empower people to create more clients, bigger paydays, and sweeter success.

This book contains four sections focused on the objective of building lifelong business relationships:

- **Expose Yourself:** Building a Solid Business Referral Network through Shameless Self-Promotion
- **Word Power:** Using Your Verbal Assets to Accumulate Relationship Capital
- **Transactions:** Delivering an Unforgettable Customer Experience
- **Brand Equity:** Building a Lasting Brand That Grows in Value and Leaves a Legacy

This book takes the topic of networking and turns it into the study of building lifelong business relationships. The benefit is less expense on marketing and less time spent learning the needs and interests of new customers. That equates to more profit, more energy to put into improvements with guaranteed outcomes, and more quality time in your personal and professional life to invest in things that really matter.

You can read this book from

front to back. It's designed so that each section can stand alone if you only want to read one section. Feel free read it in any order. However, if you're like me, I want to know how books end so I like to start with the last chapter. If you read the last chapter in this book, you'll understand the purpose of the whole journey — should you choose to take it — I lead you through in *Currency*. The final chapter sums up what I really believe to be so compelling about this process. Building our legacy through relationships during the course of our life will make us proud of a life well-lived.

When you dig deep into the client list you already have, you realize you are sitting on a gold mine of information and relationships from people who already have chosen to do business with you.

This isn't just another book on networking, and I'm not just another expert on networking — building lifelong business relationships is my passion, and I want you to have what I've achieved too.

Go get 'em, Tiger. It's time to dig deeper in your gold mine. More clients, bigger paydays, and sweeter success await you there.

Carrie Perrien Smith
Networking Junkie and Business Relationship Expert
www.soarhigher.com

Expose Yourself

Chapter 1   Promotional Strategy
Chapter 2   Promotional Tools
Chapter 3   Tips and Techniques to Get the Most from Networking

Building a Solid Business Referral Network through Shameless Self-Promotion

You bought this book to become a better networker, right? Whether you are a business owner, salesperson, or employee in a company looking for a competitive edge, strong networking skills will open doors for you that no degree, certification, or award could. In today's relationship economy, success is not achieved by WHAT you know as much as it is through WHO you know.

The next three chapters discuss the core skills for becoming a good, solid networker. You'll learn how to approach your networking endeavors with purpose and planning so you can make the most of your time and your contacts. You'll learn how to define your target market. We'll also cover where to find the people you need to add to your network. You'll even learn why the Networking Gold Zone™ is the most important part of any networking event. Before you leave this section, you'll have a memorable sixty-second commercial.

Shameless self-promotion utilizes the best of marketing and public relations tools and places an emphasis on increasing your exposure through networking. What makes networking so powerful is that a good referral from a trusted colleague can carry more weight than thousands of dollars spent on advertising. Just make a great impression on the people you meet and provide excellent care with the leads you receive, and you'll earn a place in the hearts and minds of the people you know.

If you want to become a great networker, you must commit to becoming more than just a shameless self-promoter. The next step is to turn your networking contacts into lifelong business relationships that will provide more clients, bigger paydays, and sweeter success. To make that happen, you'll need to become a student of communication, customer relations, and branding. The three sections that follow this section will help you do that. Don't be afraid to skip around in the book but above all, make sure you read the section on branding. It is one of the more important skills of all for the new millennium networker.

CHAPTER 1
Promotional Strategy

When you run a business today, you are really in the marketing business — regardless of what kind of product or service you sell. Even when you work inside a company and want to improve your visibility, you need to become an expert in marketing because you are in the business of marketing you! The concepts that you have available whether you are marketing your business or just marketing yourself are not that different. Think about it — when you open a store, you have to get the word out about your location, product selection, special offerings, and hours, right? When you are networking for upward mobility, you need to get the word out about your experience, expertise, desired next steps in your career, character, and work ethic. Circulating a résumé via e-mail can't do all that.

Since I started my first business in Dallas in 1992, I've been a student of marketing and publicity — I didn't have a choice. By default, I was the chief marketing officer. I became most fascinated by networking and have devoted years of research to it. Today, I'm considered an expert in the science of building a strong business referral network. However, I didn't realize for many years that I was a gifted connector like Malcolm Gladwell talks about in *The Tipping Point*. I was deathly shy, and I was perfectly happy working alone behind a computer. I didn't even LIKE meeting new people! How the heck was I ever going to overcome the shyness so I could become a successful entrepreneur? You needed to be good at sales and that meant being a social butterfly, right?

I chose to pursue a laser-focus commitment to learning to network because it was a gateway to prospects for my business. When you work for yourself and your survival matters, it's amazing what kind of adversity you can overcome. I developed the skills and strategies for building a strong network of contacts. With that behind me, I was able to use my God-given talent for connecting to help my company and others in my network. I share my networking secrets in this book. You'll find they are relevant to whatever stage of life you are in.

Because I've learned that networking isn't enough to achieve promotional success quickly, I'm providing you a blended approach to exposing yourself that utilizes networking but also incorporates common street marketing and public relations tools.

Overview of Promotional Strategy for the Rest of Us

People who specialize in marketing and public relations will tell you they are two completely different animals. To the rest of us, the lines become blurred. Our eyes glaze over when the pros talk about unique selling propositions, eyeballs, Four Ps, and Seven Ps. According to marketing guru and Harvard Business School Professor E. Jerome McCarthy, a marketing mix contained four elements: product, price, place, and promotion — the Four Ps. To the average person, marketing has come to mean simply promotion.

In this chapter, I'll focus on the use of promotional strategy instead — specifically shameless self-promotion. In marketing, promotion generally refers to the various methods of promoting the product, brand, or company through publicity, advertising, sales promotion, and personal selling. Shameless self-promotion uses all those with an emphasis on increasing exposure though networking.

As you become busier because all your networking efforts are paying off, you'll need to complement them with advertising and sales promotion. Networking and personal selling require one-on-one attention and that acquires a tremendous amount of time. When you get busy, your ability to do those two tasks drops off. If networking and personal selling stops, you'll find yourself with periods without work. You'll need to find ways to keep your client pipeline full. Balancing your networking and personal selling with an advertising and sales promotion plan will help you avoid the promotional peaks and valleys that create ups and downs in your success.

The Art of Shameless Self-Promotion

No one tells your story like you can. Most of us are modest about our skills and abilities, and we just stand in a crowd waiting to be discovered through our hard work and expertise. In a world where we deal with tyranny of the urgent, immediate gratification, and a fire hose spewing thousands of marketing and information messages each day, do the undiscovered really stand a chance without a promotional strategy? NO!

If you want to be successful, your promotional strategy has to consist of a blended approach that includes publicity, advertising, sales promotion, and personal selling. However, some of these approaches carry more weight than others. People know that advertising — whether it's in a newspaper, on television, or on Monster.com in the form of a résumé — is initiated and/or paid for by the promoter. If we are selling ourself or our company, we are telling our own story, and our effort is sometimes considered biased.

However, when an article appears about someone in the newspaper or she is quoted in a magazine, somehow that changes everything — even though the promoter probably received the initial exposure because of a publicity effort that she initiated. One of the things I learned after I wrote my first book, *Networking Zone: The Business Referral Network Construction Guide,* was that I was suddenly elevated to the level of guru the day my book was published even though I had the same knowledge the day before. Perception shouldn't be discounted when developing your own promotional strategy.

That's why I love networking. It uses a combination of promotional tools. You are putting yourself out there so people can get to know you, and you are telling your own story in your own words. If you are likeable and sincere in addition to having the right product available at the right price, you have a great start. Networking allows you to multiply your reach. You have the chance to educate the people you meet about your product or service so they can educate the people they know. Good for you if you have many chances to tell your story to your target buyer but that's generally rare.

If you are telling your story in the right way so those people you meet can educate those in their network, suddenly the magic of word-of mouth kicks in. When someone else tells your story and recommends or refers you, it establishes the same level of respect as if you were quoted in a magazine. No matter how knowledgeable, ethical, and hard working you are, your perceived level of validity is always elevated when someone else says so.

Creating a Promotional Strategy Based on Networking

Networking is generally regarded as the art of meeting new businesspeople. It's a great way to meet prospects and can be a great alternative to cold calling. No smart salesperson should operate without a networking strategy. However, networking can benefit literally everyone. We don't realize that when we play softball on the church team that we are part of a network. When we join a professional association, we become part of a network. As the member of a family, you are part of a network. Your networks can create a common foundation upon which to build a relationship. When you engage in a series of meaningful conversations with people in those networks, you build solid business relationships with people who are willing to introduce you to others and refer you to people they know.

To begin the process of creating a promotional strategy, evaluate your goals and build relationships with the network you have. It might not be strong enough to help you accomplish your goals, but someone in your network can probably connect you to a new network.

Networking isn't just for business. A new mom may want to meet other new moms to create a support system as she transitions from working woman to stay-at-home mom. A coordinator of a charity event can use networking to recruit volunteers for his committee. Networking is a fantastic resource for a human resources manager who is looking for talented job applicants. You just need to know who you want to meet.

Identifying Your Target Market

One of the most important things to consider when you embark on your journey to build a business referral network is who you want to meet — your target market. It's never a bad thing to meet a lot of people because everyone crosses our path for a reason. However, you only have so much discretionary time. Creating a strategy for building your network will move you to success faster.

Connections can create a personal power grid — the more quality connections you have, the more "in demand" you are among your peers. A strong network can create a list of preferred suppliers and offer those you know quick access to a trusted peer network. Anything you need will be just a phone call away. You'll become known as the "go to" person whenever anyone needs something, and you'll find that people count on you to connect them.

Who you need to meet has a lot to do with your objectives. As a business owner, I want to meet people who could become my customers. However, as a corporate employee, my motivation to network was to facilitate my job duties — knowing people in other departments definitely helped. It also made it easier to job search because I found out about job openings before they were made public. When I started volunteering with charity organizations, meeting people in the community connected me to sponsors, volunteers, and other people necessary to helping my charities.

If you don't know who you need to meet, complete the exercise on page 8.

Defining Your Niche: Finding Treasures in Your Current Gold Mine

Identifying your target market is a powerful exercise in defining a niche. If you are in sales, you wouldn't turn anyone away just because they aren't in your target market. However, networking is a marketing activity and it's impossible to market yourself to everyone. Time and money considered, you only have a limited supply of each. You'll spread them too thin trying to reach too many different markets. It's like spraying a cup of water over a large area. It won't benefit anything because there is too little to go around. However, if you take the same amount of water and use it on just one plant, you can sustain a strong, healthy plant.

Choosing one or two target markets to go after allows you to work smarter instead of harder. The quicker you determine your niche, the faster you'll reach your promotional goals. The nice thing about niching is that you can invest time getting to know one group of people. You'll learn their preferences, needs, and interests. You'll also discover how to find them. As you work with the people in your target market, you'll learn even more about them. They also tend to know people just like themselves. If you do a great job serving them, then you stand a good chance of them referring you to their peers as well.

Know Who Your Customer Is

If you are prospecting to build your business, look at the companies you presently serve, and go after more companies just like them. You most likely already know their needs and desires, where they network, and what motivates them. Over time, you even learn what types of advertising they respond to and where they get their information. You probably have created success stories among their peers. Focus your promotional efforts on that market segment. It will allow you to increase your visibility in front of your target client with greater success.

That is the hardest advice for me to take. I give it all the time, but I'm like everyone else — always looking for ways to increase my client base. I'm not saying that you shouldn't look for unserved parts of the market. What I'm suggesting is that you take a more focused approach to your business.

Any novice will say, "Everyone is my target customer." Okay, repeat after me, "Everyone is NOT my target customer." While there is some chance

Who Needs to Be in Your Network?

What are three of your goals that could benefit from knowing the right people?

1. _____
2. _____
3. _____

For those goals, write down the types of people you need to meet.

_____
_____
_____

Where could you go to meet those people? Do a little research on the local professional associations, intercompany organizations, and volunteer opportunities for ideas.

_____
_____
_____
_____

that anyone could be your customer, you'll get more market awareness and success if you'll focus on particular market segments. Only initiate calls to those types of customers, and customize your marketing approach to their interests and terminology.

Of course, you should follow a lead to another type of company, and consider working with anyone who approaches you. You can always determine if you are the right fit for the potential customer by engaging in some meaningful conversation. Narrowing your marketing focus will allow you to maximize your marketing dollars and exposure to your target client. The added focus will prevent you from spinning your wheels.

Building a Network That Benefits Your Current Professional Role

Make a list of the information, products, or services you need.

_____
_____
_____
_____

Write down everyone you know who provides those items.

_____
_____
_____

If you don't have at least two providers for each link in your network, make a list of those deficiencies. Who do you need to meet?

_____
_____

Where will you find those people to add to your support network?

_____
_____
_____

Another expert I recommend is Thomas J. Stanley, PhD and his *Networking with Millionaires* CD box set. He suggests that you target a single type of client. Join affinity organizations where that target client may network, hold membership, and serve in leadership roles. You will benefit by better understanding their needs, interests, and concerns. Do a great job for someone in that affinity group, and they will refer you to their friends within the same group — probably people just like them. When you get to know their area of interest well, they grow to understand that you are sincerely interested in helping them.

Here is an example. Say your target clients are home builders. You would benefit from joining the Home Builder's Association and getting involved in the organization. You should definitely volunteer for a position on the board or as committee leader. You'll get to know people while you serve alongside them. Thomas Stanley suggests becoming an advocate for their industry and writing letters to political leaders who can affect legislation that eases their industry challenges. You'll become their hero.

My database list is loaded with over 2,100 contacts. Those are people I have developed relationships with over the years. I am a customer, friend, family member, peer, or service provider to those contacts. I can open up the local business journal or newspaper to find names of people I need to add to that list. Not all those people are my target customer but a sizeable number of them are. I would venture to guess that a number of people who know me don't know everything they should know about my company.

Decide first who your target customer is — that customer you can help the most, who is most profitable, and who is most likely to want to pay for your services. Then, decide who fits that description in your current list of contacts. Pull those folks aside into a special target customer list. After that, you can add people who fit that list who are not in your database yet. You should always be on the lookout for potential customers. In addition to your local media publications, use chamber of commerce and professional association membership lists to find contact information for other potential clients.

Is Any Networking Function a Waste of My Time?

In networking, you must not focus on selling directly to the people you meet. Your mission is to educate them about your company and your ideal potential customer only *after* you invest the time in getting to know them.

Find out about them and their ideal potential customer before you allow the focus of the conversation to transfer to you.

A common excuse for not investing time in a particular networking group is, "My prospective client isn't in that group of people." If you have a big-picture view of the world, you already understand that few people get a lot of business from people they meet this first time and speak to directly. However, if you do a great job of preparing them to speak to others in their network on your behalf; you will have access to their networking contacts as well as your own.

People give excuses for not networking because they do not understand the process and need to learn the skill. Too many people use lack of time and client appointments as an excuse to avoid the potentially uncomfortable experience of meeting new people. They are missing out.

Finding the Right Networking Events

Networking is a process and not a place. Newbie networkers think they have to find networking events and if there aren't any available, they can't network. It's great if networking groups and mixers are available. However, that's not always the case and in general, they consist of mixed groups of people instead of focused groups of your target market. Mixed networking activities contain people from many walks of life. Pure groups, on the other hand, consist of a single type of field or industry, such as a professional association for construction professionals. Both are fine options but you need to understand the nuances of each so you can adjust your promotional strategy.

Mixed Groups

Mixed networking groups are the most widely available. They consist of people from all walks of life who are interested in coming together to promote their business and meet other businesspeople. Because networking is about educating others about your business so they can connect you to people they know, this is a viable networking vehicle. To be most successful, you have to be a master at telling your story and educating people about your target customers. You'll generally find the mixed groups to be inexpensive. They are normally open to the public or at least everyone within a membership group.

Your local chamber of commerce is often regarded as the first stop for networking events in your community. Because their membership base is mixed, their networking events will normally be mixed as well. Depending on their sub-committees or particular focus, you might see events that have more of a certain profession than others do, but generally, they are mixed events. Civic clubs also provide a wide variety of mixed networking choices. You may find affinity groups such as professional women's groups and Hispanic business organizations provide mixed networking opportunities as well.

Many of the exclusive networking groups are also mixed. One advantage that they offer is there is only one member of each profession in the group. That ideally means that every insurance lead that group members get will automatically go to the one insurance professional in the group. Another advantage they offer is that members are often held accountable to introduce other members to people in their network and bring leads on a regular basis. There are attendance requirements as well so you have a greater ability to get to know people better through the forced exposure. That matters because people are more likely to refer people that they know better. The structure of the exclusive groups can benefit people who won't create their own networking strategy, need to be held accountable, and required to attend a networking event. Many groups also vote on members so you have some control over who you network with.

One reason people don't join exclusive groups is because of the cost. Some of the membership fees are expensive, but if you have the type of business that benefits from these groups, that's a modest investment. Not all professions benefit from closed groups, and you need to evaluate where you make most of your money and who your target market really is. Don't judge the group based on whether the members are your target client because you really aren't selling to the members. Base your decision on who they know — do they know your target client and would they feel comfortable recommending you?

One of the dangers is that some people join an exclusive group as their only networking activity. They don't really know a lot of people and don't do anything to build their personal network outside of the group. Because the strict attendance requirements can be demanding on a busy professional, they don't have time to explore other groups and expand their network outside the exclusive group they've joined. How many good leads could this type of person bring? Member selection is very important, and you can't always pre-screen someone to discover whether they are going to be duds in the lead-generation department. Networking is about giving leads as much or more as it is about gaining leads. For any type of group to experience true networking success, everyone has to be a lead-generating machine.

Networking through community involvement will provide mixed networking as well. You'll rub shoulders with people from all walks of life who will share a common interest. To derive the most value from these activities, you'll need to do more than show up and participate. You'll receive the most benefit from volunteering for extra activities such as serving on the board or chairing a subcommittee. The more responsible role you take on, the more exposure you'll gain. Do a great job, and it will earn you an excellent reputation as a mover and shaker.

Pure Groups

If you live in a larger metropolitan area, you'll find some excellent choices for pure networking. These are generally membership-driven groups that serve the needs and interests of a particular profession or industry. If you work in that professional field or serve that industry, you'll find a great network to hang your hat on.

If your objective is to become upwardly mobile within your organization, you'll find professional associations to be a great place to gain a professional edge. The programs are often focused on professional development and continuing education. Just being a member shows that you are interested in furthering your profession. You'll meet people at every meeting who are also interested in the profession and will connect you to opportunities within other organizations you might not hear about otherwise.

If you want the biggest benefit from your professional association membership, serve on the board or chair a committee. You'll find the more frequent contact creates a rich environment for building deeper relationships in a way that is less threatening than walking up to total strangers. You get a chance to show off your work ethic and your values through service to the organization.

If you sell products or services to a particular industry, you'll definitely want to explore professional associations that contain members of your

Networking Truths and Survival Tips

There you are — ready to walk into a networking function armed with your sixty-second commercial and your business cards. You know you have to do this because it beats cold calling, but why are you screaming on the inside? Does this ever get any easier? Relax. There are some things you can do to make your networking worth your time and effort. These tips are meant for protecting your safety as well as your professional image. Many of these rules apply to both genders, but some are extremely important for women.

Truth #1. Your purpose is to make new contacts. The nervous feeling will probably always be there and most everyone has it — but resist the urge to talk to people you already know. Harness that nervous energy and turn it into enthusiasm for your business and the new people you meet. Set a goal to meet five new people, and spend six to seven minutes with each of your new contacts. After you meet that goal, feel free to talk with the people you already know and catch up on the latest news about them.

Truth #2. When you dress so that you look good on the outside, you feel good on the inside, and the result is greater confidence. Stand tall and smile — a lot! Be conscious of the setting and dress accordingly. If you are attending a lake party with business acquaintances, resist showing too much skin. My rule: don't mix business with bathing suits or cleavage.

Truth #3. You are the only one who thinks you are a goober. Yes, it's awkward to know very few people in a networking setting. Put on your best smile and introduce yourself to people who are standing alone. You'll know them because they are the frowning people standing against the wall clutching a beverage. You will be their hero! Of all the people you meet, those are the ones who never forget you. The food line is another great place to strike up a conversation. Try walking up to a person you know if they are talking with someone casually — if they don't introduce you to the person they are talking with, introduce yourself. My favorite technique is to walk into a networking function, meet someone who is obviously new, introduce them to someone I know, and help them get their conversation started.

Truth #4. You must banish phrases like these from your vocabulary: "I just hate to speak in front of a group." "I'm a terrible public speaker." "This is my first time to speak in front of a group." "I'm really not very prepared for this." "I didn't get much notice so I'm not very prepared." "Sorry I didn't dress very well this evening." "I'm having a terrible morning." "I apologize for these tacky brochures." Phrases like these discredit you and waste valuable time that you could spend talking about your business. Concentrate instead on how much you love what you do for a living. People pay little attention to your appearance, speaking, or the quality of your marketing material if you are excited and genuine.

Truth #5. Listening sincerely is a genuine act of kindness that goes a long way with people. Spend more time asking questions about the other person's business than talking about your business. Generally, the other person will return the favor and ask questions about your business. Be sure to get a business card. You can always send a follow-up note with some more information about your business. By learning about the other person, you'll be able to come up with many excuses to follow up later.

Truth #6. Personal questions are okay as long as you ask the right ones. Ask people which community they live in, how long they've lived there, and how they like it. Most of the time, people will offer information about their family life. If you learn they are married, you can ask where their spouse works. You can safely ask about hobbies and current events. Part of building a good network is making new friends. Talking business is fine, but people are more likely to refer people they know personally.

Truth #7. Some people are networking to enhance their business and their personal life. Avoid conversation that is overly friendly with the opposite sex. Never complain about your spouse because this easily transitions from business to intimately personal. If someone of the opposite sex begins to talk negatively about their spouse or share too much intimately personal information, end the conversation quickly and walk away. Your willingness to engage in conversation that is too personal can signal a predator that you are an easy target. Regardless of how much you need to make that contact for your business, walking away from unacceptable conversation reveals your professionalism. Be ready to tell someone that they are giving you too much information. Here's a warning especially for women: women often leave networking functions alone. Avoid becoming a victim to someone who gets the wrong idea. Make sure someone knows where you are, and don't hesitate to ask someone to walk you to your car.

Truth #8. Combining alcohol and networking is a recipe for disaster. Networking functions give you many opportunities to make a good first impression. Your professional image is too important to compromise. A good rule of thumb is to avoid drinking alcohol in a business setting or to limit it to just one glass. A drink may make you feel looser, but sometimes that thing that makes you feel more comfortable makes those around you feel uncomfortable. You never know who is watching you, and it would be a terrible shame if a person who could be your next big client doesn't look fondly on alcohol consumption. Besides, if you drink too much, you override Truth #3, and everyone will think you are a goober.

target market. For instance, if you run a recruiting company or agency that sells health insurance, you should consider joining your local human resources association. There are several organizations to choose from but a widely known national organization is the Society for Human Resources Management (SHRM). You can find a local chapter of a national association by visiting the national chapter's website. They will provide links to local chapters around the country. That will provide you a chance to meet people who could buy directly from you. It probably won't include everyone in that industry in your area; however, you'll find professionals tend to know other professionals just like them.

If you sell to the particular industry the association serves, you will often be required to join as an affiliate member which can result in an additional cost. Organizations vary widely on their policy in regard to limitations and benefits for the extra cost. The real purpose of joining is to gain exposure and get to know members of the association on a personal level. Some industries treat these affiliate members as if they have body lice and cringe when they sit down next to them. To the members' defense, they've probably been attacked by hard-core salespeople at these meetings who have a very diligent sales follow-up process. Some people just don't like to tell others no, so they find dealing with sales people uncomfortable. Affiliate members are sometimes considered guilty of the same hard-sell tactics until they prove themselves innocent. Launching into a sales pitch when you first meet someone at a networking event is the kiss of death for an affiliate.

If you plan to sell to members of the association you join, you'll benefit by serving on a committee. This will provide more frequent contact with people who are your target client or are at least connected to your target client. Don't hide what you do for a living but give a great sixty-second commercial about what you do, who your target clients are, and how they benefit. Spend the bulk of any transaction leading meaningful conversation that focuses on what he does. That will put him at ease, make him feel honored, and give you the information to judge whether he is connected to your target market. Not everyone in an industry should be your target client.

If you serve in a leadership role in a professional organization, understand that affiliate members are a tremendous source of revenue outside your typical members, and they are an excellent source of willing volunteers. Give them opportunities to serve in chapter leadership. You can provide them opportunities to support the organization financially through advertising and sponsorship. Many of those benefits will have high value to the affiliate but will cost the chapter little or nothing to provide.

The Best Type of Pure Networking Group Ever

Another type of pure group that I love is a networking group made up of members who sell to the same target client — brides for example. They may be exclusive (limited to one type of profession) or non-exclusive (open to anyone). Their whole purpose is to exchange leads and connect their clients to other companies they trust. The beautiful thing about a group like this is that they do more than exchange leads. They also learn from each other about how to market to that target audience, and they can pool their advertising resources to reach the same group. They all have a client list and can build a targeted direct mail list that benefits all the members of the group.

When you know exactly who your target client is, this is absolutely the best use of your networking resources. Remember though that you will be expected to provide an exceptional customer experience and bring leads to other members of the group. People who are lead-generating machines often keep a mental running tally of how many times you return the favor by bringing leads to the group.

If you tend to provide the kind of service or product that is purchased somewhat later in the process that your target client (like a bride) is going through (such as catering for a wedding), you'll need to have a good promotional strategy to generates prospects.

Design Your Own Networking Opportunities

Remember I said that networking is a process and not a place? There are many reasons that the typical networking meetings aren't effective for us. They might not contain the right people, are run in a sloppy manner, or don't fit our schedules, lifestyle, or personality. Networking opportunities, on the other hand, are everywhere. Networking is an important skill that will never seem out-of-place and self-serving as long as you network sincerely by showing interest in the other person.

There are formal networking events that you should attend such as professional association and chamber of commerce events. The problem with relying on those events is they often occur once a month, and it is difficult to build a relationship with people you see so infrequently. In addition, you need to maximize your time and meet as many people as possible. That means limiting yourself to a few short minutes with your new friend.

The answer to the dilemma is to create more opportunities. Look at these ideas and think about your own daily activities to identify other networking opportunities.

Charity Events. You can attend charity balls or fund-raisers and meet people whose path you might not otherwise cross. Better yet, volunteer to serve on a planning committee. You'll visit with committee members on a regular basis and build a trusting, personal relationship.

Fitness Center. If you can be flexible, exercise at different times of the day. Look for people you would like to get to know better and work out regularly at that time. Many influential people work out the same time each day. Seeing them frequently will help you gradually get to know them.

Eleven Essentials to Effective Networking

Use these tips to make the best use of networking as a communication and promotion medium.

- **Show up early for the best networking.** The beginning of an event is the Networking Gold Zone™. It's the time when attendees have not yet settled into their regular groups with people they know. The Networking Gold Zone is the first 20 percent of any meeting. Actively networking during that period will yield the most new relationships.
- **Make the other person the focus of the conversation.** They will remember your interest in them. It's also a great way to cure the anxiety you might feel while networking because you put the focus on them. You can quit worrying about what you're going to say next and focus on getting to know the other person better.
- **Listen actively, and ask questions.** Listening is a genuine act of kindness and helps build trust because it shows you care about the other person. Don't worry if you don't get that much time to talk about your business. Your new networking friend will remember more about your sincere interest than anything else you can tell them about your business. For techniques for connecting with others through conversation, check out Chapter 4: Leading Meaningful Conversations.
- **Always carry your business cards.** If you get caught without cards, be sure to get business cards from people you meet. You can always drop them a personal note with your business card inside later.

Church. Here is a group of people you see at least once a week. Get involved in projects, Bible studies, or fund-raisers where you meet with people on a regular basis.

Shopping Centers. You have a captive audience when standing in the checkout line at Wal-Mart, Barnes and Noble, or Kroger. Never rule anyone out. You never know when you are talking to the grandfather of the local manufacturing plant manager or the wife of a retail executive. They can be a good source of leads because family and friends often discuss business at the dinner table or on family outings.

Airport. This is an excellent source of contacts who have long stretches of time with no one to interact with but their computer and their cell phone. The airport is full of potential clients during the business week. Be sure you pack your promotional materials in your carry-on bag.

Ballpark. During the summer, the ballpark is full of parents who see each

- **Wear your company logo.** Wear a custom name badge, embroider it on your clothes, and have it put on your vehicle with window decals or magnetic signs.
- **Set goals for each networking event.** Determine how many new people you will meet before you start visiting with people you already know.
- **Give more leads than you receive.** Part of networking is finding leads for fellow networkers. Find out as much as possible about the people you meet so you understand what leads they need. There's no greater thrill to a business owner than to receive the gift of a new customer.
- **Treat networking functions as you would a customer appointment.** Dress and conduct yourself as though you were meeting with a customer. Avoid alcohol and inappropriate discussion.
- **Display a winning attitude.** People want to do business with people who energize them and lift them up.
- **Banish negative phrases from your vocabulary.** Don't waste valuable time talking about how you are a terrible public speaker, how nervous you are, how bad you think your marketing materials look, etc. Most people don't notice those things if you don't tell them.
- **Use your manners.** Simple courtesies like saying please and thank you and shaking hands never go out of style. A fine set of manners make you look better than the finest clothing. Watch your driving etiquette, especially when you display your company logo on your vehicle. And remember to silence your cell phone when networking.

other at least once a week. That is an excellent opportunity to strike up a conversation while you watch your kids play ball together.

Family Gatherings. When you attend a wedding, funeral, or family reunion, spend time catching up with people you haven't seen in many years and make an effort to meet people who are new to you. While those events may not be a great place to talk business, you can build a relationship and renew others that you can follow up on later.

Capitalizing on the Networking Gold Zone™

The best networking is at the beginning of an event. I call this segment of any meeting or conference the Networking Gold Zone™. That is where you have the best opportunity to meet new people because attendees have not yet settled into conversation groups. Arrive early at meetings before people start walking in and settling into their regular groups. If you frequently attend a networking group, scope out the new people and be the first to greet them and make them feel welcome. They will never forget you because you eased the tension that comes with attending an unfamiliar function.

The Networking Gold Zone is the first 20 percent of any meeting. If it's a five-day conference, it's the first day. It's is a two-hour social, it's the first twenty-five minutes. Arrive late, and you'll miss it! Actively networking during the Networking Gold Zone will reap the most new relationships. After that period, attendees will start to hang out with people they've already met. It then becomes a little more difficult to break into those groups.

Always Be Prepared

Carry your promotional materials with you at all times. At the very least, never go anywhere without your business cards. Women can carry a purse that can store brochures. Inspect the quality of the marketing materials that you carry with you on a regular basis. Check for tattered edges, crumples, and smudged ink. If you can't pull out a clean marketing piece to hand to someone, it's better to exchange business cards and mail them a brochure later. That is also a great reason to follow up.

If you don't have materials that are compact enough to store in a clean, safe place, get some made. People get into a rut and think only of trifold brochures, full-size résumés, or items with your logo on them such as pens and notepads. These can be costly to produce. Besides, they travel home to the pile of papers on your new friend's office desk and then later to the trash. Few people read the brochures they pick up.

By far, the most frequently saved promotional piece is your business card. You don't have to settle for the traditional business card though. Make a larger fold-over business card or print on both sides to make effective use of the real estate available.

Postcards are an excellent alternative to a letter mailed in an envelope. Not only is it cheaper to produce and mail, it is more effective because your message is in your contact's face when they remove it from the mailbox.

Here is a great example of the magic of being prepared to network anytime. Gerald Taylor is a concrete artist from El Dorado, Arkansas who specializes in engraved floor murals. He always carries his portfolio and sample photos to give away. One cold December day, he drove seven hours to Rogers, Arkansas just to attend one networking party. He was trying to build his business in the area before he relocated there in eighteen months, and he thought this party was worth the journey.

Okay, so Gerald is late for the party because he is lost. He stops in a parking lot to look at his map. A man pulls up beside him and asks if he needs help. It turns out that man is Joe, a local bank president and prominent member of the community. Joe gives him directions and they visit for a while and talk about what they each do. Joe asks to take sample photos of Gerald's work so he can give it to some people he knows and open up a few doors for him. How cool is that? God sometimes chooses your networking opportunities for you. Be ready!

Start Your Own Networking Group

Perhaps you don't have many formal networking events in your area. Organize one of your own that works for your fellow business owners. Here are two examples.

Coffee Groups

In Northwest Arkansas where I live, a group of us was standing at a monthly chamber of commerce social discussing the need for more frequent networking groups. In May 2002, five people gathered around a table at a local coffee shop and started a weekly morning coffee group that was free and open to anyone. Here is the format: they meet at 8:00 a.m., feature a five-minute presentation from a group member, go around the table and each give their sixty-second commercial, share public service announcements, and then break up for more casual networking.

In just eighteen months, this group inspired six other similar groups in the area as well as two monthly women's luncheon-style groups. They regularly draw twenty to thirty people each week. They each have two to three people who coordinate each group and handle tasks such as sending out e-mail reminders and leading the meeting. Roughly 50 percent of the group's members attend regularly. Even though the groups are not part of the chamber of commerce in their area, the chamber is wise to stay involved. When chamber of commerce staff members are actively involved in the group, the networking group members are more supportive of the chamber and more likely to purchase a chamber of commerce membership. Their involvement in the groups is an indicator of how interested in small businesses the local chambers are.

The availability of networking groups has changed the way we do business in our area. These groups make it possible for people to network in ways that work for their schedule. Volunteers dedicate countless hours to run these grassroots networking groups with an open attitude to networking that defines the way business is done in Northwest Arkansas — on a sincere handshake, a meaningful conversation, and a warm smile. There are many people in the background with these groups that help with coordination, database management, inviting new people, and many other details. Networking isn't about capturing market share (although that happens if you do it right) — it's simply about creating a bigger pie and caring enough about other businesspeople in the community to pass along leads and referrals. Networking is more about giving than receiving really — the *gift of networking*. I can't think of any business gift I'd rather have more than a nice warm gift-wrapped lead.

Focused Networking Parties

One of the key purposes of networking is to gain referrals from people who are in complementary businesses. For example, if you are in the building trade, you could host a party and invite anyone in the building and home improvement industry. This could include interior decorators, carpet and window covering companies, plumbers, mortgage companies, and more.

Try this format with a group of professional services providers such as accounts and business consultants. You could also host one with people who are involved with non-profit fund-raising in a professional or volunteer capacity.

I have used this format in stand-up mixers and in a smaller dinner party format. Either way, I facilitate a time when we all give our sixty-second commercial. In the more intimate setting of the dinner party, I invite each person to share personal details because that connects people faster and takes some of the formal edge off the setting. Stronger relationships are forged in a relaxed atmosphere.

I've found that people who would never consider attending a large networking social will gladly attend a dinner party. I put the early arrivals in charge of things like greeting the guests as they arrive, taking coats, and pouring drinks so they have a reason to engage with the other guests.

Boost Your Exposure through Social Networking

If I had one regret from my corporate life, it was that I didn't understand the power of a social network. Now that I run a company, I sure could use a few more corporate contacts in my network. Back then, I thought networking was something you did only if you owned a business or performed a sales role in your company — it is, after all, a great way to create prospects.

When I made my final departure from the corporate world in 2001, people were just starting to talk about the importance of networking to career futures. Just a few years before, the buzz about mentoring rose to a deafening roar. In truth, people with mentors have a better link to their next job. That is because mentoring creates a foundation of social networking inside companies — face-to-face interaction over meaningful conversation. Somewhere along the way, people began to understand that you didn't need a formal mentoring relationship to benefit from networking.

Now I know a few people pooh-pooh networking's usefulness. I think they aren't doing it right or maybe they have less-polished interpersonal skills. I know that sounds harsh but the two most important rules in networking are to take a genuine interest in the other person and listen more than you talk. Not everybody is wired that way, but anyone can learn those two skills.

It's pretty rare that the employee gets noticed on a large scale who keeps his nose to the grindstone and works through lunch everyday. If that's you,

you are going through life undiscovered. You're doing yourself a major disservice when you don't actively boost your social network by scheduling lunch with someone besides your cubicle mates. You practically live with them — meet someone new! You probably support people within your company who aren't in your department — schedule a meeting with them to find out what needs they have and see if you are meeting them adequately. Find out what changes they see in the business so you can be a partner in their success. Once you meet with them, you can make a little casual conversation by asking them about their family, hobbies, or charity work. If you want to approach it as a consultant, ask them, "What keeps you up at night?" Then just sit back and listen. You just have to try this — it works to like magic!

Here are a few tips for expanding your social networking possibilities — AKA exposing yourself.

Tuck your business cards in the airplane seat pocket. Nervous about your privacy? Okay, there's some risk involved with this but you never know who will pick up your card. My friend, Maxie Carpenter of MVC Advisory Resource, a retail and small business-consulting firm in Bentonville, Arkansas is the author of *I Didn't Ask You to Dance! I Asked You to Talk!* He carries business cards designed to promote his book. He routinely leaves his business cards in airport terminal waiting areas. These strategic card drops have garnered book orders.

Get a mentor. Your mentor can help you meet other people as well as guide you as you work on your strengths and weaknesses. They'll even facilitate the introduction and help you brainstorm what you'll talk about when you meet with new acquaintances. Your mentor should be someone who is advanced enough in their career because they will have a strong professional network as well. Choose someone besides your supervisor to mentor you, but be sure to talk to your supervisor about helping you select a mentor. Don't be afraid to ask your supervisor to help you meet people as well. The same goes for people you volunteer with. Learn who is in their network, and ask them to connect you.

Build an online presence on social networking websites. Are social networks really replacing face-to-face networking? Uh, no! However, social networking sites such as LinkedIn, Plaxo, Facebook, MySpace, and Classmates.com are starting to get traction. Should you have a presence on those sites? Yes — Internet presence is a valuable networking currency. In fact, if you google my name, my LinkedIn page will come up number one in the search engine. Now truthfully, I haven't received many new connections from total strangers, but I get connection requests from people I haven't spoken with in a long time. It's always good to catch up with old friends and find out how we can help each other.

No matter how popular Internet social networking sites get, they will never replace the value of one-on-one contact over a meaningful conversation where you can read someone's facial expressions, study their body language, and listen to the inflection in their voice. And just a reminder, if you are using theses social networking websites, make sure they present you in a professional manner. Potential employers and clients use your web presence to judge your character and professionalism before they make the decision to interview you.

Make a point to spend face time with your friends. We all live in a crazy busy world and nailing our tails to a chair long enough to make an appointment with our friends is tough. We always say we'll do it next week — we'll get together for coffee, play a few rounds of golf, or go work out together soon! It's a lot easier to ask your friends for help when you've stayed in contact. You never know when you are going to need a job reference, a connection with a potential client, or even a volunteer for a fund-raiser. When you stay genuinely interested and engaged with friends, you'll earn the love and respect of a group of people who would walk through fire for you. I don't know about you, but I would prefer that as opposed to my friends saying, "Here's Carrie calling — I wonder what she wants now!"

If you can spare some time for a professional association that supports your industry, get involved. I mentioned this earlier, but it bears mentioning again. It's a great way to meet great people who have similar interests. Don't just go to meetings though. Get as involved as you can without burying yourself in administrative work. Yes, serve your association, but make sure you leave some time for meeting with others in the association outside regular meetings. That's a new "aha" experience for me as I tend to volunteer for things that require a lot of hands-on work. If you volunteer, you can use your involvement as a reason to strike up conversations with others in the industry. If you serve in leadership, offer to speak to the association's member companies about the association. Don't be humble or secretive about what you do for a living. You're volunteering your time, and that tiny mention might be the best repayment for the time you invest. You never know whose spouse or best friend is sitting in the audience and would be willing to open a door for you with them.

If you are in sales or run your own business, consider choosing a niche in which your target client is easily accessible through a professional association. Speaking to associations and civic clubs can open you up to a whole new network. If you own a company or sell a product or service, put together an informational program that showcases your expertise and experience. People are more likely to buy from someone they know as an expert. People don't buy products and services — they buy solutions. If you work for a company, put together a presentation about what your company or department does. It's great experience, and people in your industry or company appreciate getting a snapshot of your world. You never know — your next boss could be in the audience. Just remember to get your presentation approved by key players in your organization and your legal team if your company has one.

If you don't feel comfortable speaking in front of a group, look for a Toastmasters Club in your area (www.toastmasters.org). It's inexpensive and gives you a great opportunity to work on your speaking skills on a regular basis. They provide exercises and activities to guide you along your self-paced, self-development journey. Whether it's speaking to groups, learning to speak off the cuff, socializing one-on-one, or expressing your ideas at a meeting, it will build your confidence and your personal presence. I can't think of anything that has done more for me than investing in my speaking skills. I was the shyest person ever — the poster child for scared public speakers — so if I can do it, you can too!

Ask for the business card! The key to creating lifelong business relationships is follow-up. An acquaintance can forget you easily in twenty-four hours. Don't wait to be called — even if they said they'd call you. Peoples are easily distracted. Make notes on the business cards about your conversation so you have a way to start a conversation next time you see the person. If you are speaking to a group, collect business cards to draw for a special prize you've purchased.

Likewise, find an inconspicuous way to get your cards into the hands of others. Some people put calendars or tip charts on the back of their cards so they earn a long-term place in a billfold versus the stack of business cards that pile up on our desks. I put my "Leading Meaningful Conversation" template on the back of my card. When you speak to civic clubs, they often frown on passing out your business card. Instead, mine becomes a learning tool because I incorporate that in my talks. It's extremely rare to find one left on a table after the meeting is over.

If you are visiting with someone one-on-one, wait until they ask for your card. Asking for their card will prompt them to ask for yours in return. If they don't, you still have their card. You can always enclose your business card in a simple handwritten note card the next day.

If you travel, always dress for business even if it's a nice blazer over jeans and polished boots — even on Saturday and Sunday! Pack your toothbrush in your carry-bag and skip the cocktail at the airport sports bar. Always be ready! You never know when you're going to meet someone in an airport who can impact your future. You can be comfy and still dress professionally.

Final Thoughts on Promotional Strategy

Whether you run a business or you work inside a company and want to improve your visibility, you need to become a marketing expert because you are marketing you! In marketing, promotion generally refers to promoting the product, brand, or company through publicity, advertising, sales promotion, and personal selling. Shameless self-promotion uses all those with an emphasis on increasing exposure though networking.

- Balancing your networking and personal selling with an advertising and sales promotion plan will help you avoid the promotional peaks and valleys that create ups and downs in your success.
- Networking allows you to multiply your reach because you can educate people you meet about your product or service so they can tell people they know. If you tell your story in the right way, suddenly the magic of word-of mouth kicks in.
- When you engage in a series of meaningful conversations with people, you build solid business relationships with people who are willing to introduce you to others and refer you to people they know.
- Choosing one or two target markets to go after allows you to work smarter instead of harder. The quicker you determine your niche, the faster you'll reach your promotional goals.
- Decide first who your target customer is — that customer you can help the most, who is most profitable, and who is most likely to want to pay for your services. Then, decide who fits that description in your current list of contacts, and put those folks into a target customer list.
- Mixed networking activities contain people from many walks of life. Pure groups consist of a single type of field or industry such as a professional association for construction professionals.
- Networking is a process and not a place.
- The Networking Gold Zone™ is the first 20 percent of any meeting. Arrive late, and you'll miss it! Actively networking during the Networking Gold Zone will reap the most new relationships.
- Always be prepared. You never know who you will meet.
- You're doing yourself a major disservice if you eat lunch alone.

CHAPTER 2
Promotional Tools

You are going to need a few promotional tools for your promotional strategy. Key tools that no shameless self-promoter should be without are a memorable sixty-second commercial, business cards, and a plan for managing all the new contacts and leads you are going to have.

Crafting a Memorable Sixty-Second Commercial

The most important thing you'll need is your sixty-second commercial. You've probably heard it called an "elevator statement." It is the answer to the question "What do you do?"

It's not always sixty seconds long. It could be thirty seconds or it could be five minutes based on the situation. Your sixty-second commercial consists of your positioning statement and something that differentiates you from your competition.

You can change it up, but you need to make it repeatable. Repeatable? What for? Here's why: You probably aren't selling to the person you are speaking to when you give your sixty-second commercial. Instead, you are helping them understand what you do and educating them on your ideal prospect. If your sixty-second commercial is clear, concise, memorable, AND REPEATABLE, they will tell someone who they consider to be your ideal prospect next time they get a chance.

Follow the process on the next three pages. If you'd rather have a separate downloadable version, you'll find one at the Soar with Eagles website at www.soarhigher.com/networkingtools.htm.

Create Your Own Sixty-Second Commercial

Part 1: Developing Your Positioning Statement

Use this positioning statement formula:

> "I'm [your name] and I'm with [your organization's name]. I provide [list the services you provide] so that [the benefit to your client]. A good client for me is [your ideal client]."

Here is a positioning statement for a SCORE counselor:

> "My name is Dana Jones. I'm a volunteer with SCORE, Counselors to America's Small Business. SCORE provides free counseling and mentoring services to people who want to start a small business or improve aspects of their existing business such as profitability, customer service, visibility, and overall success. A great lead for me is someone who is starting a business or has questions about making their small business more successful."

Your positioning statement should be simple, memorable, and repeatable. It seems a lot like a mission statement, and it often contains many of the same elements. However, a mission statement is written for the people inside your organization while a positioning statement is written for your target client. It should appear on all your promotional materials.

Fill in the components of your positioning statement below.

Your Name _____

Your Organization's Name_____

Services You Provide_____

_____

Benefit to Your Client _____

_____

_____

Your Ideal Client _____

_____

_____

Using the positioning statement formula from the previous page, write your own positioning statement below.

_____
_____
_____
_____
_____
_____
_____
_____
_____
_____

Part 2: What Makes You Different?

When looking for something that makes you a better choice than your competitors or differentiates you, think of a key service or product that your competitors don't offer. Think of something that will make your potential client's life so wonderful that they have to know more. Some people use this portion of their sixty-second commercial to share product knowledge which helps position them as an expert. Know what differentiates you from your competitors, but never speak negatively of the competition.

List all the things that differentiate you.

_____
_____
_____

How can you make your client's life better?

_____
_____

What product knowledge can you share with people you meet?

_____

_____

_____

Write your statement about what differentiates you from your competitors.

_____

_____

_____

_____

Put the Two Elements Together

Without mentioning anything about your competitors, develop a statement from the information you've written that will build on your sixty-second commercial.

_____

_____

_____

_____

_____

_____

Revise and Refine as Needed

Use it every chance you get. Practice will make it seem much more natural. Study the reactions to your sixty-second commercial. It should make people want to know more by inspiring them to ask questions. If they look confused after listening to your sixty-second commercial, you should consider refining it.

Features versus Benefits

It's easy to spend too much time talking about the features you offer when you give a sixty-second commercial. When we are experts in our field, we forget that people may not really understand the features. People understand the benefits you offer if they are the right client for you.

When I bought paint for a room in my house, I was presented with many different paints with varying price points and features. I could get them all in the same color. What the decision came down to was my needs. I needed something that was scrubbable and I wanted one-coat coverage. I plan to sell my house in a couple of years so I didn't need something with a twenty-five-year warranty. Knowing what benefits I really needed and wanted helped me sift through the features and make a decision.

Features often create confusion. Too many features create a fog. A confused prospect does not buy. By creating meaningful conversation, you can determine what benefits the prospect really wants, and you can base your sixty-second commercial on those. You may find that the product or service you offer doesn't offer the right benefits for the person and they aren't even your target client.

What this sometimes looks like is when someone gives their sixty-second commercial and they only talk about their degrees, certifications, past jobs, awards, or big deals. What those things do is reinforce why that person is important or qualified. While a potential buyer probably wants to know that eventually, those just waste valuable time in the initial conversation.

Worst of all, they can make the person seem like they feel overly self-important. Perhaps you've known people who won't take the next step in their career because they don't think they have enough experience, degrees, or credentials. You'll meet people who spend all their time getting those credentials because they think it will make others think they are more important or knowledgeable. If you get to know those people well, you'll sometimes find they don't believe in themselves or they have low self-esteem.

The first sale you make is to yourself. If you believe in yourself and focus on your client's needs, you'll find there is rarely a need to present your credentials or your résumé. You'll also find that you'll have more business than you can handle, and you'll be able to raise your price tag. That is a beautiful thing.

So instead of talking about your features, talk about the benefits of working with you or buying your product or service. If you are selling personal services such as lawn maintenance or house cleaning, mention the benefit of having extra time to relax or spend with family and friends. If you are selling consulting services, talk about results other clients have achieved after working with you on similar projects. If you are interviewing for a career move, focus on the results you've achieved on past projects. Benefits are where your perceived value lies in the eyes of the prospect.

Aren't credentials, degrees, awards, and certifications important features? Absolutely, but those are what earned you the right to do what you do for a living. Most prospects aren't that excited about features initially. Prospects don't care so much about what you have. They are far more interested in what you can do for them to improve their current condition — benefits.

Business Cards: Valuable Networking Currency

Business cards are the most popular currency of the networking transaction. I have a stack on my desk of all the recent cards I've acquired. I bet you do too. I have another larger stack in the drawer of the important ones I thought I should keep. I toss most of the other marketing materials I receive, but I can't seem to bring myself to throw away a business card. It's a compact advertising medium and has all the information I need to know about the person. I even make notes on the back if there is additional information about them that I need to remember.

Of all the marketing materials you will create, your most important tool is your business card. Because of its compact size, it is the promotional piece that people most often keep. They tuck it in their pocket, billfold, or business card holder if you impressed them.

A business card can say so much about your business, and nice ones don't have to be expensive. If you can afford it, have a talented graphic designer create one — and a logo if you don't have one already. Don't be afraid to put your photo on it — you are the business image. People do business with your company because of you. Throw away those business cards you printed at home on your printer, and make an important investment in your business image.

I know many people are cost-conscious. There are affordable, high-quality, full-color options that are available online. Check out the Soar with Eagles website at www.soarhigher.com/networkingtools.htm for affordable business card options. Online printing solutions have come a long way in the last few years with easy-to-use templates for professional-looking designs. You can even download your design that your graphic designer created, and order your cards whenever you are ready.

Details Make the Difference

Your business card is the passport to everything needed to contact you. It should have these components.

Company Name and Logo. This is your identity. People may not remember your name, but they will remember something that is visually different from all the other text on your business card. You don't necessarily need a logo, but your company name should appear in a visually distinctive typeface.

Name You Wish to Be Called. You could list your formal name but the point of networking is to build relationships with friends who will refer you because they know you well enough to call you by your casual, everyday name.

Title (optional). You don't need to put your title on your card. People are more impressed by your interest in them than by your title. A significant number of people don't put their title on their business card — a practice common among female business owners.

Tagline or Slogan. Sometimes your company name may not do enough to describe what your business does. A carefully crafted tagline can convey your mission and clarify your company's product or service.

Mailing Address. When I see a card without a mailing address, I tend to wonder why it's missing. Are they working out of their home? Are they a fly-by-night operation? Do they live in the city park? A small number of people who have their office in their home are worried that potential clients will think they are unprofessional or stop by unannounced. Today, the ability to work at home is respected and prized because of the quality of life and low overhead it can provide. You don't have to meet with clients at your home if you aren't comfortable. A restaurant or coffee shop can provide the perfect meeting place away from your home office.

Office Phone Number. This is vital information for your clients. If your phone number changes, get new cards printed. Scratching out information on your business card appears sloppy and unprofessional.

Cell Phone Number. If you have a cell phone, put that information on your business card. Also include your cell phone number on your office voice mail recording. Plans can change at the last minute, and your client will appreciate the ability to reach you if they need to cancel an appointment due to an emergency.

E-mail Address. If you don't have an e-mail address, get it. In this high-tech, instant messaging, 24-7 world, some potential clients will prefer to make their appointment with you or request more information via e-mail.

Website Address. While not critical to the marketing success of many businesses, a website can be your living brochure. It has unlimited space, is graphic, and is inexpensive to update and distribute. If you have a website, display your website address on every marketing piece and in the signature line of your e-mails, and include it in your voice mail message.

Managing Your Business Cards

Besides having your own business cards, you will need a way to manage all the great business cards you will collect while networking. A great organizational tool can help you keep your leads at your fingertips. The more effective you are at locating contacts quickly, the more helpful you will be to others. Here are two popular tools. It doesn't matter which you choose as long as you organize them for mobility. Your networking friends will marvel at your ability to provide a needed lead quickly and effortlessly.

Business Card Holder

The handiest holder is a notebook-style folder with individual card slots. You will want to get one that holds the most cards in the least amount of space and carry it with you. Here are three ways to organize them.

Alphabetically by Name. You can organize them by the person's first or last name or the company name.

Alphabetically by Type of Business. It's common for effective networkers to have several contacts for one type of business. Consider organizing cards by type of business such as "Bookkeeping" or "Interior Design."

By Type of Networking Relationship. If you are in a networking group, you may find it easier to organize those contacts in one section.

Personal Data Assistant (PDA)

If you use a computer, consider using a PDA such as a Palm® Treo™, BlackBerry®, or Hewlett-Packard® iPAQ™. These data organizers allow you to create backups because you can synchronize your data and updates between the PDA and your computer. However, don't use a PDA unless you plan to synchronize your PDA with your computer regularly. Your PDA can fall victim to disasters such as dead batteries, damage from a fall, or loss. Without a backup on your computer, these disasters spell total loss of your valuable database.

A great way to remember names is to enter your new networking friends in your e-mail program as soon as you return to your office. Just typing all their contact data into your database helps imbed their information in your mind. They will be so impressed when you remember their name and company the next time you see them.

If you want to manage your leads better, consider using a contact-management software program such as Act! that will synchronize with your PDA. Along with providing advanced tools for organizing your data, you can send a mass e-mail to a group of individuals that looks like you sent a single e-mail to a single individual. That can be a major time saver, and it looks much more personal.

The benefit to using a PDA and computer database setup is that you can use your Find function to sort for contacts you are looking for by first or last name, company name, city, or type of business.

Final Thoughts on Promotional Tools

Key tools that no shameless self-promoter should be without are a memorable sixty-second commercial, business cards, and a plan for managing all the new contacts and leads you are going to have.

- The most important thing you need is your sixty-second commercial. You've probably heard it called an "elevator statement." It answers the question "What do you do?" It consists of your positioning statement and something that differentiates you from your competition.
- A positioning statement is like a mission statement only it is written for your target client. It should appear on all promotional materials.
- Know what differentiates you from your competitors, but never speak negatively about them.
- Features often create confusion. Too many features create a fog. A confused prospect does not buy. By creating meaningful conversation, you can determine what benefits the prospect really wants, and you can base your sixty-second commercial on those.
- The first sale you make is to yourself. If you believe in yourself and focus on your client's needs, you'll find there is rarely a need to present your credentials or your résumé. You'll also find that you'll have more business than you can handle, and you'll be able to raise your price tag.
- Because of its compact size, the business card is the promotional piece that people most often keep. In addition to the usual contact information, your business card should include your tag line or slogan, cell phone number, website, and e-mail address.
- Your PDA is only as good as your last synchronization.
- A great way to remember names is to enter your new networking friends in your e-mail program as soon as you return to your office.
- A contact-management software program such as Act! that will synchronize with your PDA can help you manage your leads better.

CHAPTER 3
Tips and Techniques to Get The Most from Networking

Here are some more ideas for getting the most out of the time that you invest in networking. It will also give you some new ideas. Warning: The advice in this section is most useful to people who operate a business or perform a sales role. Should you read it if you work for a company and don't really affect the sales and marketing of your company? Heck yes! A Gallup survey reported that only one in four people is truly engaged in their jobs. That means that on any given day, a huge chunk of people marching into their corporate job are planning their exit strategy. A large number of them want be self-employed. It's never too soon to learn these lessons. Besides, you may find some nuggets that will help you promote the projects you're working on to high-level decision makers or open your own door to your next corporate move.

Networking: The Gift That Keeps Earning Dividends

One of the most special things about networking is what you get in return for your investment of time. Now, most folks think of networking as this great marketing activity where they raise awareness about their business and meet other people who can buy from them. However, they are ignoring the most important and satisfying aspects — the gifts!

"What kinds of gifts?" you ask. Try these on for size. Are there some listed here you've overlooked?

Referrals. Wondering what to get that special business owner or sales professional in your life? You won't have to write a check or swipe you credit card. You won't even have to gift wrap it. It's worth far more than you would ever consider spending. Stumped? It's a nice warm lead. You know the kind where someone says, "I'm looking for someone who does this? Do you know anyone?"

The beautiful thing is that these referrals and leads for others are trinkets you stumble across while networking. A new customer for one business may result in a single $300 purchase. For another business, a $30 first-time purchase can lead to a regular customer who spends that amount weekly.

It just doesn't stop at business though. Think about the people you meet who are new to business or new to your area. How many people are out there looking for jobs? How many charity fund-raisers need volunteers, silent auction donations, sponsorships, and participants? When you spend more time asking questions than talking about your business, you open your mind and heart to the needs of the other person. Regardless of who you are, you have something that someone needs.

Building Your Reputation. Once you hand off that nice warm lead to a trusted associate, they hopefully do something wonderful — provide extraordinary customer service. That builds your reputation as someone people can trust for reliable referrals. You shouldn't hand off leads to someone because he is in your leads group or is your buddy. Send them to the business who will take the best care of them.

Friendship. By investing time learning about others, you'll discover they want to know more about you. You'll learn you have common interests and, through repeated contact, become friends. People are more likely to refer their friends than people they barely know. Your life is enriched by your new friends and your business benefits through more referrals.

Stronger Community. When you provide leads to your fellow businesspeople in your community, it increases their sales. More sales mean they may need additional employees and will purchase additional supplies to provide their product or service. More sales often mean more sales tax revenue in your community which provides better city services, roads, parks, and more.

Serving Something Bigger Than Yourself. The most gratifying gift of all is the opportunity to serve one small part of the bigger plan. When you are networking, don't overlook those times when unmistakably God has used you to connect two businesspeople together. You were chosen for the task, so don't miss the opportunity to celebrate your participation in that one little miracle.

Next time you are networking, relax and remember that it's not all about you and promoting your business. **In leads as well as in life, strive to give more than you receive.** The more you try it, the more impossible it seems because people will want to repay your kindness. Then, sit back and let the gifts roll in.

Marketing Lessons from My Dog Jazmin

There are lessons to be learned about business marketing from unassuming sources. My dog, Jazmin, for instance, understands well the concept of marketing aggressively — especially gaining market share.

Jazmin is forty pounds of black furry sunshine and is my favorite little power networker. No one I know works a room quite like she does. She sells a variety of services that include companionship, happiness, and the ability to touch her incredibly soft fur. In exchange for that service, she gets hugs, pets, or — the Holy Grail of the canine world — belly rubs!

Here are the lessons we can learn from Jazmin.

Look for the part of the market that is unserved and go after it first before you take on the competition. When my husband and I adopted her in January 2003, she decided that she would sleep with us at night. Consider the available area on the top of the bed as "the market." Before Jazmin, ideally my husband and I each had 50 percent of the market share.

Now there's a new competitor in the marketplace. When we hear her toenails clicking down the hall, we race to get our share of the space on the bed before she gets there.

Jazmin jumps up on the bed, kisses us good night, and settles into the available space on the bed that is not occupied — the unserved share of the market. Next, she moves in to start snatching up market share, getting closer and closer to our market share and edging us out. Pretty soon, Jazmin has reduced our market share to the edges of the bed.

You don't have to be the first one in the market to establish yourself quickly and be successful. We have two other dogs that have been around much longer than Jazmin. They are also twice her size. Jazmin understands the disadvantage of being the smaller newcomer but she uses it to her

Currency: Striking Networking Gold in a Relationship Economy   41 advantage. At the dinner table, she positions herself under my chair (a space too small for the other competitors) to make sure she that she's close to any morsels of food (potential business) that drop on the floor. Another lesson to learn here: location is important.

Be the first one to check out new developments in the market. As businesspeople, the market in which we operate changes quickly and we have to pay attention. This can range from the opening of the new bag of dog food or treats to the arrival of a new dog toy. Jazmin is always first in line to try new things. That doesn't mean that she will eat raw carrots twice, but she always gives new things a fair shake. Sometimes new developments are as insignificant as waiting for one of the other dogs to drop the bone she's been watching and moving in quickly to snatch it.

Differentiate yourself from your competitors. Jazmin adores people. Our other two dogs are very shy and scatter when visitors (Jazmin's potential customers) come to our home. Perhaps you have some competitors like that. The other two will sometimes warm up to visitors after awhile. Guess which dog gets the most attention (business) — the one who actively seeks out the visitors.

Aggressively search for new clients or ways to establish a competitive advantage. Jazmin, a shameless self-promoter, is always the first one to the door to greet newcomers to the market — her potential customers. She doesn't wait for them to discover there's a dog waiting to serve them; she jumps on them as they walk in the door. As they settle into our home, she sits next to them and reminds them often that she is there in case there is anything she can do for them. Folks who visit my home rarely leave without giving Jazmin belly rubs — Bingo! Jazmin scores another sale! Another satisfied customer: visitors get to play with the happy black ball of fur, and Jazmin gets the sales she wants.

Stay out in front of your potential client. Once Jazmin has market share, she hangs on to it. She constantly checks with her customers to make sure they are satisfied. She understands that just because no one needs her services right now doesn't mean that they will remember she's there later. Being in the right place at the right time is important to the busy people in her life. She always makes sure she's available when it's the right time.

It's important to always be nice to your competitors. The nice competitors get to stay in the market. As I mentioned previously, Jazmin shares the

Smith home with two larger older dogs who can whoop her at any time. She understands how important it is to show respect for others and play fair.

Business doesn't usually magically appear at your door. Our home is an abundant place for our spoiled pets with plenty of love and food (business and customers). Even though the food bowl is full, Jazmin still has to know where the food bowl is and go after it. The food isn't going to follow her around and jump in her mouth. It's a lot like business. Even though the potential clients are there, you have your chamber of commerce membership, and your yellow pages ad is in the telephone book, you still have to actively seek out the clients and be easy to do business with.

Know Your Product, Love Your Product, Use Your Product

People want to know how to make more sales. Here's my easy answer: get passionate about what you sell! I love to see people give their sixty-second commercial about their product or service when they are passionate about it.

One of the big differences between those who are successful and those who are not is their passion for and confidence in their product. You can appeal to your target audience more passionately and sincerely if you'll follow three simple rules:

>Know your product
>Love your product
>Use your product

Know Your Product

Image that you sell something like toilets. Now really, how excited can you get about toilets? Truthfully, there is really a lot to know about picking the perfect toilet that goes way beyond color and shape. If you strive to become an expert on all the toilets you offer in your product line, you can pass along that product knowledge to potential customers. An expert will understand the frustration of toilet buyer regret when customers realize they bought the wrong one — like when they sometimes have to flush the bargain toilet twice because the water conservation feature keeps it from completing the flush the first time. It's not that easy to return a toilet that didn't work out.

There's a pretty big difference between the product knowledge of someone who works at a big-box home improvement store — you know the one whose experience is limited to sitting on a toilet — and a plumbing sales professional who can tell you distinctive differences between product choices.

If you know your product, you can provide customers all the information they need to make the right buying decision so they get the toilet that meets their unique needs. Your customer gets a perfect fit and is grateful for your willingness to share your knowledge. Customers get excited about that regardless of what they are buying.

Love Your Product

Potential buyers can sense a sales professional's lukewarm feeling about a product or service. When you love your product and feel that your company provides excellent value (the perfect combination of price, quality, and service), it is easy to be passionate.

Mention the features but focus on the benefits. This applies to the company you work for. If you love your company, their values, and practices, and you are proud to work there, it's easy to be passionate. Companies have a culture and reputation whether they take an active part in shaping it or not. Their business practices inside the walls of their business follow their employees out the door and into the community. If you work for an organization you aren't proud of, RUN!

Use Your Product

It is easy to be passionate about a product that has personally benefited you. When you use your company's products, you send a strong message to your customer. What message does that send when an Old Navy apparel buyer doesn't buy any of her clothes at Old Navy? What if your State Farm insurance agent buys his personal insurance from Farmers Insurance Group? What if your investment advisor suggests you should buy REITs but doesn't invest her own money in them? If you have the occasion to use your company's products but don't, can you really sell the company?

A Special Note for People in Direct Sales

Some of the best products in the world are marketed by network marketing (direct sales or multi-level-marketing) companies such as Tupperware, Pampered Chef, Nikken, and Mary Kay. They offer business opportunities where people can sign up to sell the products or just the business opportunity. There is some income potential in selling the products, but the real money is made in getting others to sign up to sell the products or business opportunity too — also known as "building your team."

The unfortunate fact is that these companies attract the "something for nothing" people of the world who are looking for a get-rich-quick scheme.

Networking is Not Network Marketing

As an expert on networking, I recommend different types of networking to business and non-profit professionals. I find it humorous when I run into someone who thinks a networking group is an informational meeting where you bring six to eight nice warm prospects — people who you just want to help — to sign up for a multi-level marketing (MLM) company such as Prepaid Legal Services.

Then there are others who mistakenly call the process of building your business referral network "network marketing." It makes some sense — you are creating a *network* of contacts and that is a form of *marketing*.

I don't want to alienate all those devoted and successful people who have built great careers in MLM companies. Even those most successful will agree that multi-level marketing attracts a fair number of "something for nothing" people who give the companies a bad name.

Let's get the terminology straight once and for all.

Networking is the process of building a network of business contacts who can refer each other.

Network marketing is a type of business. You may hear them called direct sales companies or, most commonly, multi-level-marketing companies. *Wikipedia* defines network marketing as "a business model that combines direct marketing with franchising." It goes on to say, "Multi-level marketing businesses function by enrolling unsalaried salespeople (also labeled by MLM companies as distributors, independent business owners, franchise owners, sales consultants, consultants, independent agents, etc.) to sell products and meanwhile earn additional sales commissions based on the sales of people enrolled into their down line, an organization of people that includes direct recruits, recruits' recruits, and so on."

Then there are the others who spend a few months with one company and then jump to another company looking for yet a better deal. Business relationships are formed over time and require a level of trust. The most successful people in multi-level-marketing companies chose the right company for their needs and then stuck with it. Regardless of what kind of sales pitch a company gives, long-term financial success takes years to build and a consistent effort to maintain.

One of the greatest mistakes that direct sales people make is spending valuable time telling people about the business opportunity who really aren't interested. While few people are interested in another business opportunity, a larger number are interested in superior products that could improve their lives. For these people, we need to add another rule: *know your product, love your product, use your product, and understand who is interested in buying your product.*

Twenty-One Ways to Stay In Front of Your Target Client

Show me business owners who believe, "I'll just open my doors and customers will flock in," and I'll show you business owners who are scratching their head wondering where the customers are thirty days after they open their doors. Promoting your business is a constant struggle. If you take a break from it, your potential customers forget you're out there. Passive and active promotional activities are critical to creating top-of-mind awareness.

Here are twenty-one ways to reach a wide variety of potential clients — some for little or no money. Successful businesses don't utilize just one or two promotional methods. Businesses that are new or are in a competitive market should practice ten or more of these methods. The more you practice, the more customers you reach.

1. **Network.** Of course, you should seek out the normal venues (chamber of commerce events, networking coffees, or civic clubs) but you can network anywhere if you approach it as relationship building. Initiate conversations with people who you'd like to know better at church, youth sporting events, and fund-raisers.

2. **Purchase logo graphics for your vehicle.** Your local sign shop or banner company has options that include permanent graphics on your vehicle

windows or body, magnetic signs, and license plates. Don't forget to shine up your car and your courteous driving habits.

3. **Invest in logo apparel.** If you have a work-shirt kind of business, hire a local embroidery or screen-printing shop to put your logo on shirts and hats for you and your employees. Make sure employees know that a clean, pressed appearance is vital no matter how dirty your work is.

4. **Put your logo on a name tag.** If you prefer a more flexible or dressy wardrobe, invest in a name tag with your name and company logo. Look for these at print shops and trophy stores.

5. **Launch a website.** Businesses today should have a website. Make sure your website reflects the same look and image as your printed promotional materials. Be extremely cautious when selecting a web development company. Make sure they understand website coding, design, and marketing. Don't expect people to find you with a search engine. Put your website address in your e-mail signature, on business cards, and on all advertising.

6. **Send permission-marketing e-mails.** Internet spam has forced new regulations and tools to combat it. To protect yourself, make sure you build a permission-marketing database. To do that, invite people to sign up to receive reminders, updates, or information from your company. This will also allow you to include links to information on your website. Think of a website as a bulletin board in your closet — people aren't inclined to visit websites without some compelling reason. The right invitation in your e-mail will drive traffic to your website.

7. **Include your website address on your voice mail message and e-mail signature.** Your website will be waiting for them if they need more information before you can contact them personally.

8. **Write articles.** Many newsletter editors are starving for free content that is relevant and interesting to their readers. Your local business journal or community magazine may be willing to publish your article as a guest commentary or in a regular column. Ask them about free advertising space for your company in exchange for a free article. Better yet, ask them to trade you their subscriber list so you can follow up with a direct mail piece.

9. **Contact people you know.** You probably have a stack of business cards on your desk that you've been meaning to follow up with. Schedule some time each week to call or send notes or e-mails to those people.

Remind them where you met them and invite them to visit over coffee so you can get to know each other better. People are more likely to refer others to people they know well.

10. **Send e-mails and leave voice mails after hours.** Just because your business hours are filled with business duties doesn't mean your promotional activities have to stop at 5:00. You can send e-mails anytime (remember to personalize them). Don't be afraid to call your contacts and leave voice mails after hours.

11. **Utilize direct mail.** You can create your own database or purchase mailing lists from professional organizations, chambers of commerce, and direct-mail companies. Send information to your database regularly. Letters are easy but postcards can be more effective because recipients don't have to open an envelope to see your message. A postcard smaller than 4" x 6" is cheaper to mail too. Be selective — don't mail to everyone on the mailing list. For recommendations for online printing companies to order cost-effective, high-quality promotional materials, visit the Soar with Eagles website at www.soarhigher.com/networkingtools.htm.

12. **Get involved in the community.** Charity events are a great way to show off your work ethic and attention to detail while doing something wonderful in the community. Find a cause that moves you and get involved on a planning committee.

13. **Get involved in professional organizations or special interest groups.** Look for an organization that supports the field that you are in. Better yet, look for one that supports an industry you serve through your business. For instance, a training company benefits from joining an organization for training professionals or human resources professionals because many companies outsource their training needs.

14. **Tell friends, relatives, and neighbors.** Many people fail to inform those closest to them about what they do for living. Send them an e-mail, let them know what you do, and tell them you want their referrals. If you send out a holiday newsletter, be sure to include information and a progress report on your business.

15. **Informational seminars.** You are probably an expert in your chosen field. Put together an hour-long seminar on a topic that showcases your expertise and educates your audience. Potential customers will attend a free seminar if it's a topic that will improve some area of their life. It establishes a relationship of familiarity and trust that no advertising

campaign can match. When attendees decide they need help with your area of expertise, they will remember you. Make sure your seminar is 90 percent informational content and 10 percent sales pitch. If you don't think you can fill a whole hour, partner with two or three other people who sell different services to the same target audience to share the time with you. You can share expenses and merge your client lists to boost the size of your guest list.

16. **Speak at civic clubs.** Program coordinators for civic clubs are faced with the daunting task of scheduling as many as fifty-two free speakers a year. Make their job easier by contacting them and proposing a twenty-minute speech about your topic of expertise.

17. **Host a party.** Host a casual gathering at your home for a group of people who you would like to know better. Small gatherings such as dinner parties allow you to enjoy your guests and make the rounds to everyone. Consider hiring a caterer so you can concentrate on your guests rather than cooking or washing dishes.

18. **Participate in expos.** Check out expos carefully — who is their target attendee? How are they promoting the expo? How long is it? How many people attended last year? For instance, if your ideal customer is another business, you want to invest your time and money in expos that attract the greatest number of businesspeople. Don't forget to network with the other expo exhibitors. Create your own pre-expo marketing promotion by inviting your potential clients to visit your booth at the expo.

19. **Get active in your chamber of commerce.** Do more than join or you are just wasting your money. Your local chamber has a variety of committees that would allow you to invest time in a topic of interest as well as build relationships with other chamber members.

20. **Seek out sponsorships.** Local charities, chamber of commerce functions, and professional organizations offer sponsorship opportunities to raise funds for their projects and operations. In exchange, they offer the sponsor exposure to the members of the organization and the community.

21. **Advertise.** The most expensive of all promotional options is paid advertising. Unfortunately, many advertising representatives are more worried about their commission than making sure you will benefit from their advertising medium. If you like the medium but think you're getting poor customer service from your advertising representative, ask for a different one at the same company. Ask about their demographics and

shop around. You probably can't afford all the options so pick one target market to go after and invest in top-of-mind awareness — advertising that is frequent and consistent. It will prevent you from throwing your marketing dollars to the wind and getting nothing in return.

Marketing Yourself and Your Company Through Community Involvement

Volunteering as a promotion al strategy makes smart business sense. There are right ways and wrong ways to do it, and I've done both. These ideas will help you develop your promotional strategy through community involvement.

Follow your heart. Find an organization that matches your interests and serves the community in a manner you admire. Finding time to volunteer can create long days as you scramble to make up the time you take away from your workday. You will feel less burdened by the extra time crunch if you have a heart for the organization's mission and the cause it serves.

Volunteer strategically. Consider organizations with board members whose businesses serve the same clients you do. For instance, your target client may include building contractors, so you may choose to volunteer with an organization such as Habitat for Humanity, Rebuilding Together, or your local Home Builders Association. Working alongside your target client is a great way to build a solid relationship, and people are more likely to do business with someone they know well.

Do your homework on the organization. Are they using donations wisely, and are they well run? Will it be good for your business to align with them? What does the general public think about that organization? Your potential customer may choose to do business with you (or not) depending on who you align yourself with. The last thing you need is to align your reputation or company image with an organization that gets caught in a scandal.

Volunteer in roles that will show off your character and abilities. Will they use your time and talents the way you want them used? If you hate to ask for donations and that's all they want you to do, you will be miserable. On the other hand, if other committee members or board members see you doing your best work in a role you love, they will be more likely to recommend you. There are plenty of volunteer opportunities out there. Pick one where you shine.

Make sure you are a good fit. Organizational dynamics have everything to do with your success as a volunteer. If you like a collaborative type of leadership style, an executive director who makes all the decisions for you will dampen your spirit. However, some people prefer to be told what the direction is and what to do. It's okay if you don't know which style you prefer at first — feel free to experiment. If you find out that you aren't a great fit due to personalities, philosophical differences, leadership styles, or whatever, RUN! Be honest with the organization, but most of all, be true to yourself. Volunteering in the right organization is rewarding, but the wrong fit for you will be pure punishment.

Make sure that you meet all your commitments. People make judge how we operate professionally by how they see us work as a volunteer. If you accidentally overcommit, get help quick. It's not a crime to ask for help — it's a tragedy if you let your commitments slip and damage your reputation.

Give the organization a time limit. Set a length of time that you will work with the organization. Consider committing for one year at a time if you are working at a board, leadership, or committee level. Revisit your commitment at the end of the year. Planning your volunteer time on an annual basis when you are making other life plans and goals helps you achieve balance in all the aspects of your life.

Volunteer where you are valued and appreciated. Not every organization deserves you. Smart volunteer organizations understand that volunteers like to contribute where their ideas are valued. They are likely to stay where they believe in the mission and are actively included. Organizations retain volunteers by creating buy-in, and that means allowing them to participate in the decision-making and planning processes.

If you have a family, make sure they are understanding and supportive. While it is ideal for a husband and wife to volunteer together, that's not always possible because of different interests, preferred types of roles, and family responsibilities. Volunteer responsibilities can put pressure on a family when the hours increase close to an event or when meetings take place during normal family time. Always discuss the volunteer role's tasks and time commitments with your family before you volunteer. When they buy in and understand why you feel compelled to participate in the community, they are more understanding and supportive. Deep down, they are proud of what you're doing, and you should be too!

Not plugged into an organization you love? Start shopping for one now. The sooner you find an organization that aligns with your professional goals, the happier and more successful you'll be professionally.

What I Learned About Business While Working for Free

Year-round, I invest time in my community in volunteer roles that I feel benefit others. One of these is my commitment to supporting the local networking groups. However, I spend a good portion of the second quarter of my year in what I call my fund-raising season. For six years, a time-intensive piece of that time was devoted to coordinating a motorcycle show and poker run called the Cancer Road Challenge. It is just one part of the Cancer Challenge (www.cancerchallenge.com), a three-day annual cancer fund-raiser in Northwest Arkansas where I live. Other events include a massive golf tournament, tennis tournament, run, silent auction social, and trap shoot. This isn't any normal fund-raiser — it raised over $735,000 in 2008 and continues to grow each year.

You may ask, "Why would you sacrifice valuable time from your already packed schedule for this event? You don't even own a motorcycle!" Close to the June event each year, I even asked myself that question when I was working late hours in my office trying to make up all the time I spent on the event during normal office hours.

Here are the reasons that I did it and why I encourage you to volunteer in your community as well.

It's good experience to personally invite people to attend your fund-raiser. The ability to extend a personal invitation is an important business skill. Customers don't invest their time and dollars with organizations that are apathetic about doing business with them. Many customers jump from one business to another because they were personally invited to do so.

Charity involvement is a smart part of your marketing strategy. Whether you realize it or not, you are your brand. There is no better way to promote yourself, your company, and your abilities than by getting out there face-to-face with the community and being a good corporate citizen. When all things are equal between you and your competitors, your passion for community service can become a deciding factor for your potential clients.

You can learn a lot about business from a well-run non-profit event. You not only learn about budgeting and projections, you learn about building teams and managing relationships. I'm proud of my ability to recruit the right volunteers. Some of the most effective volunteers I've met were stay-at-home moms running major fund-raising activities at their children's schools. They were running lean organizations with high profit margins and rolling out programs in record time. They could teach the corporate executives a thing or two.

Business success is often about who you know. People are more likely to do business with someone they know well. I locate professional speakers, celebrities, and trainers for organizations. While working on the Cancer Challenge, I rubbed shoulders with people who hire professional speakers and celebrities and purchase training for their organization. Because I have gotten to know some of them over the years, we have been able to form good relationships. It makes it nice when I have something to talk about when we see each other instead of "So, are you ready to do business with me yet?"

Volunteering is a great way to add influential people to your business referral network. Some of the most influential people are involved with charities. Instead of watching the news to find out what is happening in their community, they are out making news working alongside people like you. They are most likely to be deeply involved in event planning or boards. That normally means that they meet regularly with the people they volunteer with as they fulfill the group's mission. When you see people more often, you build deeper relationships. The best referrals come from people you know well.

Sure, you meet people by volunteering. More importantly, you make friends. Some of my closest friends are people who volunteer on the same projects that I do. The moments that we spend together in service are the fibers that make up a life worth living. We learn about each other and ourselves as we discover our strengths. I have a group of people I love to volunteer with and our relationships are richer because we experience the challenges of life together.

Some of the best stuff on my résumé is my volunteer service. The exciting thing about volunteer work is that you don't need a certain number of years of experience or a particular degree to tackle anything you think you're big enough to try. For many people, they volunteered for organizations to explore their talents and dreams and ended up working for the charity. Some like to do what they are experienced at, but others feel a freedom to explore activities they've never tried. There is a reduced risk when your performance is not connected to your next promotion or raise. There is a deeper desire to excel because you are serving a higher cause. I worry less about making a mistake. Besides, what are they going to do — fire me?

Sometimes you get a little publicity for your volunteer work that sparks some interest in your professional life. Reporters get bored writing about all the money you're going make for charity, what kind of food you're going to have, and how many people are going to be there. Most reporters prefer a human-interest story so they write about the people behind the event. The local paper did an article on me as a human interest story. Okay, it was nice to be recognized and score some sincere publicity for my charity event. However, over the next three days, I had 1,500 hits to my website where people learned more about my company. At least ten people who I had never met contacted me that I can do business with. People I had never met asked about my book and my training programs. Not only that, but when people do a search for my company or my name in the future, the online article will come up in the search engine results.

Here is the most important thing of all — you get a chance to make a difference by serving others. At the end of the day, you make a difference to someone in your community. At the end of your life, you will have served something bigger than yourself. How much better does it get?

Final Thoughts on Getting the Most from Your Networking

The whole point of a promotional strategy is to get the most out of the time you spend networking. Determining what you want and how you can achieve it will help you say no to activities that waste your time.

- There is no better gift you can give your fellow businesspeople than a nice, warm gift-wrapped lead. The only thing it will cost you in most cases is being in the right place at the right time.
- Don't hand off leads to someone just because he is in your leads group or is your buddy. Send leads to businesses who will make you proud.
- One of the keys to successfully marketing yourself or your business is to be able to communicate how you are different from your competitors.
- Staying out in front of your target client or employer ensures they will remember you when they have a need for your product or service.
- One of the big differences between those who are successful and those who are not is their passion for and confidence in their product. You can appeal to your target audience more passionately and sincerely if you'll follow three simple rules: know your product, love your product, and use your product.
- Mention the features but focus on the benefits. What if you only had a few words to share with someone? The benefits are the best use of that valuable commodity.
- If you love your company, their values, and their practices and you are proud to work there, it's easy to be passionate. Companies have a culture and reputation whether they take an active part in shaping it or not. Their business practices inside the walls of their business follow their employees out the door and into the community. If you sell a product or work for a company you aren't proud of, RUN!
- Personal exposure is key to your success. Charity events are a great way to show off your work ethic, character, abilities, and attention to detail while doing something wonderful in the community.
- Speeches and informational seminars showcase your expertise.
- Business success is often about who you know. People are more likely to do business with someone they know well.

Word Power

Chapter 4   Leading Meaningful Conversations
Chapter 5   The Importance of Speaking Skills
Chapter 6   Why Don't People Listen?
Chapter 7   Communicate So People Will Hear You

Using Your Verbal Assets to Accumulate Relationship Capital

Imagine for just a minute what it would be like to be a highly regarded leader — someone who is respected, transparent, sincere, and genuine. Can you picture everyone wanting to talk with you because you are a great conversationalist? What would it mean to your career if you could use your voice — in both the written and spoken sense — to make a difference in the world?

Seem a little like a fairy tale? It's not. It can happen to you. You can become more dynamic whether you are speaking one-on-one, writing an e-mail to one or many people, or speaking to a group. All it takes is the ability to connect with others.

This section is devoted to making you a powerful communicator regardless of what stage in life you are in or what your role in your career is. By capitalizing on the power of words, you can position yourself as someone who is influential, engaging, and in high demand.

Chapter 4 provides techniques for making meaningful conversation that is based in the fine art of asking questions — the kind that creates the threads of conversation that begin to weave together a relationship. You'll also learn the secret to being memorable, the most powerful communication tool of all, and what to do if you forget a name.

Chapters 5 and 6 are full of information that your communications teacher never told you. They include the three most important mysteries that prevent people from listening to you. You'll be surprised to learn that it has little to do with you. You'll learn to identify the roadblocks and find a way to navigate around them.

This section closes by helping you understand how to use the communication tools available to accommodate any communication need. Using the techniques, you'll be able to design a communication strategy that will help you whether you are looking for a job, organizing a fundraiser, speaking to a client, or working with a team at your office.

Utilizing all the tools in this section will help you garner the respect you've earned. It's easier than you ever imagined. Does this mean that you'll never make a verbal mistake? Of course not, but you'll have the knowledge to make fewer mistakes, overcome them quicker, and make a difference in the lives of others so you enjoy sweeter success.

CHAPTER 4
Leading Meaningful Conversations

I was getting ready to leave for a business trip. I had made plans with my husband, Tom, to drive me to the airport. We went to dinner the night before and we started that familiar "What's for dinner?" conversation.

> Her: What would you like for dinner, dear?
> Him: Oh, I don't know. What would you like?
> Her: I don't have a preference tonight. What are you hungry for?
> Him: I don't care where we go. You decide.
> Her: Okay, let's go get Chinese food.
> Him: No, anything but that.
> Her: How about barbeque?
> Him: No, not that either.
> Her: [in a disgusted tone] I thought you didn't care.
> Him: I don't care. You decide.

And so goes the conversation.

At our house, that conversation is followed next by the question about who is driving to dinner. On that particular evening, when I asked which car we were taking to dinner, Tom said that we had to take mine because his gas tank was empty.

The next morning, I needed to be at the airport at 6:30 a.m. to catch my flight. When I dragged my bags into the living room at 6:15, Tom tells me in a his best "frustrated husband" tone that we have to stop for gasoline, and we were now going to be late.

Not leaving time for that, I assumed that we'd take my car instead. To my surprise, he announced that taking my car wasn't an option. When I asked why, he explained that he didn't like to drive my car, and we needed to take his. Hmmm ... I'm thinking out loud, "So what — be flexible for a change." Oops! Did I say that out loud? At 6:00 in the morning, I'm not great at solving problems or being tactful and he isn't flexible. The frustration escalated.

As we loudly discussed the gasoline problem while loading my luggage into his car, I quizzed him about *when* he told me that we would need to stop for gasoline in the morning. It sure seemed like the first time that I had heard it. He assured me that he told me the night before. I asked "When?!" and he said, "When we were going to dinner!"

It finally dawned on me — his words on the way to dinner were, "My car is out of gas. You'll have to drive yours." From that, I was supposed to deduce that we would have to allow time to stop to put gas in his car because he didn't like to drive my car and that meant leaving at 6:05.

What I got was an encrypted message. We seldom get lucky enough to work with, marry, or give birth to people who communicate the same way we do. We live in a fast-paced world of encrypted messages, and we don't all communicate the same way. Life requires a focused approach to communication.

The words we choose are important. The quality of the relationships we possess depends on the delicate balance of the spoken word and the implied intention. And when you get to the core of the cause of social anxiety, you'll find a good deal of the cause is rooted in a lack of ability to communicate effectively and confidently.

People in general struggle with making conversation and stating their opinion. Too commonly, people will not engage in conversation because they are unsure how to state their opinion without risk. For many people, the risk of being misunderstood, controversial, or different is too great. Instead, they mutter to themselves inside. This chapter is about understanding what to say and how to say it.

The scarcest commodity today isn't time — it's attention. Ask anyone who has ever organized a meeting with someone who pulled out their Blackberry in the middle of the meeting. Or ask someone who's been to dinner with a friend who took a phone call at the table.

What are you doing when you answer the phone at your desk? Are you paying full attention or scrolling through your e-mail? Ever heard someone clicking away while you talk to her on the phone? They can hear you type!

And speaking of overhearing things while you're on the phone, one of today's most dangerous additions to the home office is the cordless phone. It offers you the ability to do business from your patio or the luxury of fixing yourself a cup of tea while you participate in a conference call. It also provides you the opportunity to use the restroom while you talk on the phone. You might be thinking — what kind of person talks on the phone while they use the toilet? You probably aren't asking that question if you've ever been in a public restroom and had someone in the next stall answer her cell phone when it rang.

This chapter will give you some tools to wade through the world of encrypted messages, misunderstandings, and attention-deprived people.

Creating Meaningful Conversations: It's All About Them

Your mission, should you choose to accept it, is to create meaningful conversations. Life seems to be full of small talk and shallow conversations. We ask, "How are you?" not because we care but because it's a habit. We talk about what was on television the night before instead of what is in our heart. Conversations aren't made up of questions and answers; they are comments people take turns interjecting without stopping to ask why the other person holds that opinion.

If you broke down every relationship transaction, you'd find that the single element that determined the success of that transaction was your ability to communicate. If you are struggling in a relationship, take a hard look at your ability to get and convey your information. With the right information, you know exactly what that person needs, who they know, how they prefer to receive their information, and how you need to proceed with them next.

The Art of Asking Questions

When I say that you should lead meaningful conversation, what I'm really suggesting is that you take responsibility for leading the conversation. That means asking a series of open-ended questions.

Now there are good open-ended questions such as, "How would you like for me to handle this?" There are also bad examples of open-ended questions such as, "What kind of a fool do you think I am?" and "What were you thinking?"

My daughter is one of those people who can take any open-ended question and turn it into a closed-ended question. Here are some examples:

| Mom: | "Where would you like to eat supper? |
| Daughter: | "I don't care." |

| Mom: | "What did you do at school today?" |
| Daughter: | "Nothing." |

| Mom: | [Watching as her daughter stomps by avoiding eye contact] "How was school today?" |
| Daughter: | "Fine!" [Punctuating the sentence with a slamming bedroom door.] |

Sigh. Not everyone is ready to communicate when we are. Closed-ended questions are those that can typically be answered with a short answer. They are difficult to create a discussion with. Open-ended questions are asked in such a way that they require more information to answer. They normally give you enough details to be able to ask another question.

Here are some examples:

| Closed-ended: | How was your weekend? |
| Open-ended: | What did you do this weekend? |

Closed-ended:	How is your daughter?
Open-ended:	What does your daughter enjoy doing these days?
Open-ended:	What is your daughter doing over the summer?

| Closed-ended: | What was your first car? |
| Open-ended: | Tell me how you got your first car. |

Open-ended questions are the fibers that you can use to weave together a meaningful conversation. If you are a budding conversationalist, don't be discouraged if you feel like your questions are goofy. Like attempting a new language in a foreign country, it's the thought that counts. Besides, the more you use it, the easier it will become.

The Value of Meaningful Conversation

There are several benefits of leading meaningful conversation. First, it places the other person at the center of the conversation. It puts them at ease because they can relax and just answer questions. It also puts you at ease because you're not worried about what to say next.

It also enables you to mine for information that you need. Through a series of open-ended questions, you can also determine if your new acquaintance is a potential client for you or someone else you know. Leading the conversation allows you to find out who is in someone's network. Their network includes family, friends, volunteers, and professional contacts.

If you are in a sales role, remember that you are not always selling to the people you meet. Instead, you are teaching them how to sell you to the people who are in their network.

Meaningful conversation also helps you find reasons to follow up. Every good relationship is forged over a series of meaningful conversations. Sometimes you have to be creative to find reasons to contact someone later. If you've asked the right questions, it's much easier. Besides, people don't do business with us the first time they meet us for all kinds of reasons. They may not need our product or service yet or be able to afford what we offer. They may have a good supplier already. However, needs and relationships change, and we need to maintain top-of-mind awareness so they remember us when the time is right.

Another benefit of meaningful conversation is that it allows you to check your customer service level. Your customer may love you but may have some feedback that will help you serve him and other customers better. We sometimes dread feedback but we shouldn't. Even if it's tough feedback, it's better for you to hear it than for the customer to vent to other people. Make sure you are asking questions that provide insight on how you can serve your customer better.

With your customers, it's important to use the Golden Rule AND the Platinum Rule. Just because you are following the Golden Rule by treating them the way *you* want to be treated does not mean that *they* want to be treated that way. Create some meaningful conversation to learn more about them and follow the Platinum Rule: treat them the way they want to be treated.

Allot enough time in each conversation to build rapport. Listen to their responses, show genuine interest, and give them your full attention. They will feel honored that you took the time to talk with them.

Creating Meaningful Conversation with New People

So what do you say when you meet someone new? Part of the anxiety of meeting new people comes from not knowing what to say. Networking is a key first step in forming business relationships because it fills a pipeline with people we need to meet and possibly get to know better. Networkers often default to talking about themselves because they don't know how to initiate meaningful conversation. Relationships aren't forged in one conversation. A foundation of familiarity and trust requires multiple contacts. Creating meaningful conversation gives you the information you need to follow up later to deepen the relationship.

Enter a conversation with a new contact with the purpose of finding out as much about him as possible. Ideally, you want to learn his name, role, and organization he works for. Then, you want to get to know him at a personal level because that is where we discover ways to follow up to form deeper relationships. For instance, if your new acquaintances are businesspeople, you ideally want to know many of these critical details:

- Their name and company (or department if you both work for the same company)
- Role they play in the organization
- Details about their organization
- Their typical customer
- The city they live in
- Information about their family
- Community activities

This is a general list to get you started. Some of these items may seem nosy, but they have genuine value. Everyone you meet has a network that includes his or her family members, friends, and volunteer and professional contacts. Of course, you want to know all the details about their company so you can provide good referrals. However, knowing information about their network will help you discern what you tell them about your company. If we told people everything possible about our company, their eyes would glaze over. Asking questions allows you to create a logical balance between too much information and not enough.

Using the Meaningful Conversation Template

I teach this template in all of my business communication and networking programs because I found that far too many people are terrified of making conversation. It's perfect to use with new acquaintances and is easy to modify for people from all walks of life. I encourage you to use it as the foundation for your own meaningful conversation.

> **Hi! I'm Danny Mason.** [They will respond with their name. If they don't, it is okay to ask them their name.]
> **What company are you with?**
> **What is your role with your company?**
> **How long have you been there** [or owned it, etc.]?
> **Tell me more about what your company does.** [Listen to understand; ask questions about the company until you understand their business.]
> **Who is a good prospective client for you?**
> **Are you from this area?** [They usually offer information that tells you where they are from, and you can ask about their family located in other geographical areas.]
> [If not from your area] **What brings you to this area?**
> [If the last question yields information about their spouse]
> **What does your spouse do?**
> **Do you have family here in the area?** [May reveal children, spouse, or parent information.]
> **Are you involved in any local charities?** [Question further if they answer yes. They may also reveal they want to volunteer but don't know where they fit in. Make sure you keep up with local charity activities so you can offer ideas.]
> [Begin your close] **"It was great to meet you. Do you have a business card so I can refer you if I come across anyone who needs to know about you?"**

Normally at this point, they want to know more about you or your company because you have been attentive. If they don't, it's probably because they are just nervous or not very skilled in conversation. In a rare case, they may be self-centered and don't care about anyone else. Those people soon disappear off the business landscape. Think the best of those people anyway.

Here's why this works: You aren't just leading the conversation to gather the information you need — you are placing the other person in the spotlight. They feel flattered that you care enough to get to know them. You appear genuine, interested, and gracious — all virtues of the kind of person people like to do business with.

> ## Brainstorm Some Questions for People You'd Like to Know Better
>
> It's amazing how we march into the same office day after day but don't get to know the people we work with on a deeper level. Questions can help team members feel understood and valued. It creates an opportunity for you to find out if they are having challenges and need help in their personal or professional life.
>
> List three of your customers or coworkers.
>
> 1. _____
> 2. _____
> 3. _____
>
> Write five open-ended questions you can ask any of those people. If you need ideas, check out "Questions for Each Stage in Life" on page 227.
>
> 1. _____
>   _____
> 2. _____
>   _____
> 3. _____
>   _____
> 4. _____
>   _____
> 5. _____
>   _____

So I Met Someone New. Now What?

Once we meet someone, it's time to figure out what we are supposed to do with that person. In order to figure that out, we have to make contact with them. In Chapter 11: Pit Bull Follow-Up, I suggest techniques for following up once you meet someone new. People forget they've met us in as little as twenty-four hours. Once that happens, establishing a solid, useful relationship is more difficult. Many of the ideas in that chapter are well-suited for the business owner or sales professional, but they are easily adapted to anyone in any walk of life.

Humans were meant to engage in relationships. They enrich our lives, teach us how to interact with others, and connect us to others in ways that make us stronger as a group than we could ever be alone. Everyone crosses our path for a reason. Our challenge is to get to know them well enough to figure out why they've entered our life. Perhaps they can help us or maybe we can help them by connecting them to someone we know.

The magic of networking is that we have the opportunity to help others simply by getting to know the people that enter our life at a deeper level.

If you are self-employed or perform a sales role for your company, you already know that meeting a steady flow of new people is crucial to creating prospects. Of course, those prospects aren't normally ready to transition into customers. The only way we learn where they fit is to prequalify them through conversation and get to know them better.

If you work for a company, business relationships can provide the platform for showing your value to those who hold your destiny in their hands. They can also connect you to mentors, next steps in your career, and valued friends.

Caution: Slippery Conversation

Networking and most business relationship transactions are not the place for some types of conversation. Use extreme caution on certain topics.

Nosy Questions. There is a fine line between using meaningful dialogue to find out more about someone else's network and just being nosy. It depends on your intent and wording. If you are sincere in your conversations, you'll be fine in most cases. Just proceed carefully and evaluate the reaction to each question. Sometimes people don't want to reveal recent disappointing events such as the death of child or a divorce. Learn to ask questions gracefully so you can pay more attention to the reaction and hidden meaning in your new friend's responses.

Politics and Volatile Current Events Topics. A networking event is about meeting people. While you'll see campaigning politicians at networking events during an election year, avoid locking into a debate. Set up an appropriate time later to meet with them.

Gossip or Negative Opinions. Your reputation and positive outlook are necessary equipment when talking business. Nothing tarnishes your image faster than negative, destructive attitudes.

What If You Forget a Name?

Have you ever met someone and wondered if you've met them somewhere before? What if that man looks familiar, but you forgot his name? Unfortunately, few networking opportunities involve name tags. Relax! This is a problem almost everyone faces. Here are some ways to handle it.

Method 1: Introduce Them to Someone You Know

If you are afraid to admit that you don't remember someone's name, introduce him to someone you know (it should be to someone whose name you do know!).

Here's how it works when you are talking with that person whose name you've forgotten. Your friend, Jason Lane, walks by. Motion Jason over and ask your acquaintance, "Have you met Jason?" Jason will intuitively put out his hand and respond, "Glad to meet you. I'm Jason Lane." Your nameless contact will say, "Hi Jason, I'm Kay Donahue. What do you do?" You are no longer in the dark about Kay's name.

When I'm out at dinner or shopping with my husband and run into someone but blank out on their name, I use my husband. I warn him first when possible. I simply walk up to them and greet them. I immediately introduce them to my husband. The nameless person responds with an outstretched time and his name. My husband will typically ask him his name if he doesn't offer it right away.

And yes, I know this isn't exactly proper etiquette, but I'd rather break a rule of etiquette than make someone feel they are forgettable.

Method 2: Admit You Can't Remember Their Name

This is my preferred method these days. Method 1 is normally successful, but I can't concentrate on what they say because I'm racking my brain trying to remember their name. I just say, "I'm sorry, I have forgotten your name." If I'm lucky, they are having the same problem, we share a little chuckle, and it lightens up the conversation. If you use this method, I guarantee you will only forget their name once.

Method 3: Ask, "Have We Met?"

When you ask someone if you have met them, they automatically respond with an outstretched hand and their name. If you have indeed met before, usually one of you can remember where you met. If not, you have a new friend.

Method 4: Introduce Yourself Even If They Don't Know You

If you pay attention to what is going on in your community, you'll often recognize people who have never met you. Even though these people seemingly live on a pedestal because they are always in the public eye, most of them are just folks like you and I.

When you encounter someone like that, just walk up to the person and introduce yourself. "Hi, Hillary Clinton, my name is Donna Alexander. Welcome to our chamber banquet. Is this your first time here? Are you enjoying yourself? I read your book last month, and I found it insightful. Are you happy with the sales of the book?"

Obviously, you don't want to linger too long. End the conversation in a few minutes unless she keeps initiating more conversation. Be gracious and let her know you were glad to meet her.

Final Thoughts on Leading Meaningful Conversations

The words we choose are important. The quality of the relationships we possess depends on the delicate balance of the spoken word and the implied intention. If you broke down every relationship transaction, you'd find that the single element that determined the success of that transaction was your ability to communicate.

- The scarcest commodity today isn't time — it's attention.
- Open-ended questions — those that can't be answered with a simple one-word answer — are the fibers that you can use to weave together a meaningful conversation.
- Using a template for creating meaningful conversations will take your mind off what you're going to say next so you can focus on what the other person is saying.
- Allot enough time in each conversation to build rapport. Listen to their responses, show genuine interest, and give them your full attention. They will feel honored that you took the time to talk with them.
- Relationships aren't forged in one conversation. A foundation of familiarity and trust requires multiple contacts. Creating meaningful conversation gives you the information you need to follow up later to deepen the relationship.
- Humans were meant to engage in relationships. They enrich our lives, teach us how to interact with others, and connect us to others in ways that make us stronger as a group than we could ever be alone.
- Everyone crosses our path for a reason. Our challenge is to get to know them well enough to figure out why they've entered our life. Perhaps they can help us or maybe we can help them by connecting them to someone we know.
- The magic of networking is that we have the opportunity to help others simply by getting to know the people who enter our life at a deeper level.

CHAPTER 5
The Importance of Speaking Skills

Our ability to speak to others — one-on-one, small group, or in front of an audience — is critical to our success in life. As a teenager, I wasn't really unpopular. Actually, I'd call it "undiscovered." I was deathly shy and simply afraid to speak up. I didn't think I had anything to offer anyone and sure didn't know how to tell anyone about it if I did. I was afraid that if I opened my mouth to speak, people would think what I had to say was stupid. Worse yet, I was afraid that I would say it in a stupid way. Then, the unthinkable might happen next — everyone would laugh at me.

The only oral communications class I was required to take in high school was a semester in a torture chamber. The popular people did well, and they got chances to speak in front of the whole school. People looked up to them because they were able to speak to groups. Simply being on the stage in front of a microphone positioned them as a leader. I knew I could never make a difference because I was scared to death to speak in front of a group. I was convinced I would never be a leader.

I wish the teacher had recognized my fear and talked to me about the source of my fear. She just treated it as if a little practice was all any student needed. If she had spoken to me, she would have broken into my vault of misconceptions related to why popularity had eluded me and why I thought I would never be a leader.

If she had pulled me aside and told me that butterflies were okay and those pesky winged insects just needed training, maybe I would have learned to embrace my anxiety instead of letting it cripple my future. She knew why the popular kids were good speakers — they had taken several classes that focus on oral communication. More importantly, she might have explained that every time one of the popular kids stepped in front of an audience to speak, they took a huge risk. However, that risk provided an experience that grew their ability to speak more than just practicing in front of their bedroom mirror.

She never asked about my fear of speaking, and I never offered to talk about it. In fact, I'm not sure she and I even exchanged twenty words the whole semester outside of roll call. Perhaps that teacher could have used a little lesson in becoming the kind of person that people are attracted to. I felt like a necessary evil — one of those pesky students who doesn't want to apply herself. If she had spent a few minutes breaking down my internal barriers to speaking, it would have helped me along my road of self-development.

Could one simple conversation overcome all the negative self-talk I had about my perceived obscurity? Who knows? However, one thing is for sure, learning to take a few more chances and overcome my fears would have positioned me for quicker success in every area of my life.

Here's what I wished I had known then.

- Speaking in front of a group positions you as a leader.
- You can make a bigger difference in the world if you are willing to speak what is on your heart and mind.
- It's acceptable and natural to be nervous in front of a group.
- You don't have to be articulate to be a great speaker. It's more important to be passionate about your topic.
- You will learn more from your failures and mistakes in front of a live audience than you will from rehearsing in front of the bedroom mirror.
- The popular people were good speakers because they were willing to take a risk and speak in front of groups when they got the chance.
- Avoiding public speaking was the most detrimental thing I could do to my future success.
- Learn to speak in front of an audience, and you will improve in all areas of speaking — one-on-one, small group, family settings, larger group, and more.

I look back now and can't believe no one saw through me and pulled me aside to teach me that. My dad had been in Toastmasters International (it was only for men in those days) but I really didn't understand what it was about. My mom just comforted me and said, "It's okay. I was terrified of speaking in front of groups too." What I really needed was for someone to reach out and help me create the desire to overcome my fear of public speaking.

The Road to Speaking Confidently

It's been more than twelve years since I decided that I wanted to do whatever it takes to be a good public speaker. Even though I practiced, the first few times were dreadful, and I was mortified. Over time, I started speaking up at meetings at work and taking small roles in meetings. The more I practiced, the easier it got.

I found other ways to lead in the meantime. I volunteered in leadership roles in the community and found myself speaking to committees of people. My role was to coordinate activities, but I found my role as one where I asked questions and shared my vision for the task we were working on. Somehow, that didn't seem like public speaking. I started a business and had to meet with clients and promote my business. That didn't really seem like public speaking either. I was just sharing my knowledge and vision with others. The audiences gradually grew larger.

One day, Darren LaCroix, a Toastmasters World Champion of Public Speaking and close friend, urged me to join a Toastmasters Club in my city (www.toastmasters.org). There, he said, I could get "stage time." As I had learned already, nothing catapults your speaking ability like working in front of a live audience. It was a supportive environment, and it was okay to fail there because the organization's mission was to improve speaking skills. I can't believe it took me almost ten years to join a club. It's been one of the most meaningful investments in my success.

The ability to speak is revered by people everywhere because so many people fear it. My speaking skills have attracted people to me. I have more important things to say than I did years ago. However, I think I had many of the same things the popular people had all along. This difference is that I'm no longer "undiscovered." My speaking experience has given me the courage to step out of the crowd, actively expose myself to new experiences, and meet new people.

A combination of things — the ability to speak to groups, make a confident first impression, attract good things into my life, be more friendly and approachable, and lead meaningful conversations — have all helped me develop my ability to make a difference in the world. In fact, the less I worried about being popular and focused on learning the fundamentals of communicating with others in a meaningful way, the bigger difference I made in the world. How cool is that?

Listening: The Most Powerful Communication Tool of All

Listening accounts for 70 percent of all communication. You've probably heard the saying, "God gave you two ears and one mouth so you could listen twice as much as you talk." There's a huge amount of truth in that. Unfortunately, we get more training in speaking our thoughts than listening to the messages we encounter. The perceived meaning is where strong relationships are made or broken.

There is no substitute for two-way communication — live and in person. We can ask for clarification, read the speaker's facial expressions and body language, and hear their tone of voice.

When I worked for Wal-Mart in their training area, one of the last projects that I worked on was a video-based leadership program that chronicled the twenty-three leadership principles founder Sam Walton used to build and lead Wal-Mart. We interviewed fifty people who had worked with Sam Walton. The leadership principle that they commented on most often was his ability to communicate. Mr. Sam, as he was known, was a wise man who said many profound things. However, when I questioned the interviewees further to drill down into what made him a legendary communicator, I discovered that they were talking about his ability to listen.

Mr. Sam was an unassuming man with a laser focus on details. He gathered a great deal of information through research, and his chosen method of research was leading a meaningful conversation. When he went into a company facility, he opened up conversations — and launched relationships — by asking a series of questions. He would walk around stores — both his Wal-Mart stores and those of his competitors — and talk with customers and employees. He wanted to know what they thought because he truly believed that the best ideas about improving merchandise assortment and sales came from those who bought and sold merchandise.

Mr. Sam wanted to engage with the company's employees (they call them "associates") who worked in the Wal-Mart stores, Sam's Clubs, and distribution centers. He would show up with donuts at 3:30 a.m. to talk with the company's truck drivers and loaded trailers with the associates — all while checking the health of the organization. He would walk into company facilities unannounced and mingle with the associates. He would ask them how their manager was treating them. He often asked them about their families. He was a legend for remembering details of conversations and often asked for updates when he ran into the same associates years later. He was known for "having a mind like a steel trap."

Sam Walton had a degree in economics and he had strong operations skills combined with entrepreneurial spirit. People with those three characteristics generally aren't known for being people-oriented OR great communicators. However, his ability to ask questions and create meaningful conversation garnered him a reputation for being people-oriented. This is a powerful example that proves anyone can learn those skills and open the door to stronger relationships — both personally and professionally.

Final Thoughts on the Importance of Speaking Skills

Our ability to speak to others — one-on-one, in small groups, or in front of an audience — is critical to our success in life. We all have something important to contribute to the world that will most likely rely on our ability to use our voice.

- Butterflies are okay. They just need training to fly in formation. It's acceptable and natural to be nervous in front of a group.

- You can get practice by contributing and taking small roles in meetings, coordinating activities in the community, and talking to customers. You'll discover yourself getting more comfortable speaking in front of larger groups over time.

- Speakers learn more from their failures and mistakes in front of a live audience than they do from rehearsing in front of the bedroom mirror.

- The ability to speak is revered by people everywhere because so many people fear it. People are attracted to those who are skilled communicators.

- Gaining speaking experience will give you the courage to step out of the crowd, actively expose yourself to new experiences, and meet new people.

- Toastmasters (www.toastmasters.org) provides a supportive environment. The organization's mission is to improve speaking skills. There are clubs all over the world.

- Listening is the most powerful communication tool of all. It accounts for 70 percent of all communication.

- There is no substitute for two-way communication — live and in person. We can ask for clarification, read the speaker's facial expressions and body language, and hear their tone of voice.

CHAPTER 6
Why Don't People Listen?

Relationships are forged through conversations. They are broken every day over the smallest misunderstandings. The fabric of a great customer experience is woven from threads of clear communication. Study the successful people in your life. You'll notice right away that gifted communicators receive more opportunities in their career and community.

The most common communication error people make is believing that communication is about the speaker being heard. Clearly, we have messages we need to communicate. However, unless we understand the recipients of our message, there is a good chance they won't understand our message.

This chapter is for those who want to accomplish more with fewer words. Don't read this chapter if you'd never:

- Wondered why people don't listen to you
- Gotten a different outcome than you asked for
- Encountered someone who got angry with you for something you said when you don't understand what the problem was
- Experienced rejection from a prospect or client

As I began researching and teaching networking, I found myself answering an unexpected number of questions about basic communication. I had long believed that communication was one of the most important leadership skills. It didn't take me long to realize that the art of communication was as important to networking success. As my work on the topic developed, I realized that relationships don't develop past the prospect stage without understanding the nuances of communication.

This chapter is about the roadblocks to getting your point across and engaging others in conversation. Once you understand the factors that influence the way people use our messages, you can modify yours to accommodate the communication needs and preferences of your listeners — whether you are talking to one person or a crowd.

Types of Communicators

Let's start by understanding the way people absorb what they hear. People have different learning styles. Communication in the business world as well as in our personal lives depends on our ability to communicate based on individual learning styles. There are nearly 100 different learning-style models but many agree on three types of learning styles: visual, auditory, and kinesthetic. Understanding how to identify the learning style of your audience members will help you adapt your message to their needs. Knowing how people learn will help you deliver information in a way that the listener will comprehend it and retain it for later reference.

Visual Learners

The visual learner needs illustrations such as graphics, models, and video clips. Creating a visual image will help them understand. They enjoy the use of movement in your delivery.

About 30 percent of the population are visual learners.[1] They sit in your audience in the back where they can see clearly. This allows them to see how the other audience members are reacting to what you are saying.

When speaking, they use visually oriented words. They say things like "I *see* what you mean" and "I *envisioned* this being taller."

Auditory Learners

You'll find auditory learners are often gifted with numbers or technical skills. The auditory learner needs you to use word pictures and stories. They aren't as interested in the visuals and handouts; instead, they are interested in what you have to say about the topic. While they enjoy lectures, they like participating in discussion even more because it provides a variable listening experience. They enjoy pre-recorded messages such as books on CD.

1. Spence, Muneera U. "Graphic Design: Collaborative Processes = Understanding Self and Others." (lecture) Art 325: Collaborative Processes. Fairbanks Hall, Oregon State University, Corvallis, Oregon. April 13, 2006.

About 25 percent of the population are auditory learners.[1] They sit where they can hear the message best. Even though eye contact reflects trustworthiness and respect in our culture, it distracts auditory learners when they are listening or talking. Looking down or away removes some of the visual distraction and allows them to focus more clearly. When they are reading, they often find it helps their comprehension if they have music playing in the background.

When speaking, they say things like "I *hear* what you are saying" or "It *sounds* like this would be a good solution."

Kinesthetic Learners

The kinesthetic learners needs to be part of the experience. Business communication is often delivered in a visual or auditory mode which makes it difficult for kinesthetic communicators to comprehend. Hands-on communication increases their retention. In a learning environment, they benefit from participating in role plays or anything that enables them to be part of the experience.

About 45 percent of the population are kinesthetic learners.[1] In an audience, they sit in the front row where they won't miss a thing. They are likely to move around, fidget, or doodle on paper while listening to a presentation.

They say action-oriented things like "I *feel* like you need this," "We have to *move* on this opportunity," and "The solution seems *within reach*."

Understanding the Roadblocks to Communication

We encounter people on a daily basis who have had experiences that affect the way they perceive our message. Truthfully though, what you say can be translated a number of ways, and *their* perception is *their* reality. You need to predict potential misunderstandings as you prepare your message. If your listener did not understand you, it's your fault as much as it is theirs.

The greatest challenge is to find the right words and methods to convey your message. Several factors affect how others perceive the information you're delivering. Understanding those factors will help you ensure your audience (one person or a crowd) fully comprehends your message the way you intended. Paradigms, perceptions, mood, and filters are factors that can have the greatest impact on the listener's ability to understand your message.

Paradigms and Perceptions

The longer we're alive, the more paradigms and perceptions we gain about the world around us. When you are learning about the people who you must communicate to, you need to learn everything you can about the experiences they've had and how they view the world.

Norms vary from individual to individual based on a diverse set of factors. They are the typical or average experiences and behaviors that an individual has grown accustomed to.

Some people are more open to new ideas than others are. Age can affect willingness to embrace your information, and you may find that you need to deliver the same information in several different ways to meet the needs of different age groups.

A listener's belief system can impact your ability to deliver a message that is openly received. Someone may have had a bad experience with corporate restructuring and think that all corporate restructures mean that she will be laid off. Besides past experiences, religious beliefs are a major consideration. Once you understand someone's belief system, you may find that you need to choose different words to deliver your message.

The key to addressing all these issues is to create an open environment that fosters two-way communication so we can learn from each other. Most reasonable people appreciate it when you try to understand differences in cultures, norms, language, and religion. In some cases, they might just bring preferences to the communication table. For instance, you might find that your listener prefers to get just the facts without the lengthy explanations. Others in your audience might prefer extensive details. The more people you communicate to, the more challenging it is to cater to all of their needs.

Be willing to step out and make some mistakes in an effort to educate yourself and understand what is important to your audience. Come to them with an open heart and open mind and care lavishly. Ask them about their interests and concerns.

If we strive to follow the Golden Rule when it comes to communication, it means we would communicate to others as we'd like to be communicated to. However, it would be better to follow the Platinum Rule for communication which means we should communicate to others how they prefer to be communicated to.

Mood

Emotion affects how our listener receives our message. Some people are more emotional while others are low-key, non-emotional people. When possible, get to know your listener by engaging in everyday conversation so you'll understand their needs and preferences when the time comes to deliver critical information.

The mood that your supervisor is in can affect how he responds to your request. It affects how he'll feel as he reads your e-mail or listens to your voice mail. You have no control over how someone is feeling at the exact moment you are ready to communicate.

Timing is everything. There is rarely a bad time to deliver great news. However, if you are delivering a more serious or somber message in person to an individual, gauge their ability to handle the news first. Sometime we don't have that luxury, but it's always good to avoid something like discussing a team member's poor performance on the day he comes back to work after handling his father's funeral details. Feedback of any kind is not easily comprehended by someone who is in a stressed or saddened state.

Filters

It is difficult to size up someone's life experiences unless we know them well. Most of us don't think about the powerful effect that a person's life experiences bring to a conversation. Unless you are speaking with someone you know well, you won't realize they have a phrase or word that takes them back to a memory that will affect how they react to your message.

For example, Joan is a brilliant entrepreneur who is running a printing business. She is in her forties and divorced. She had been physically abused by two men and spent time in a previous career with construction workers who were generally "rough around the edges." The abusive relationships and the former career took place in the same window of time in her life. Today, men who are cocky or "cowboy-like" tick her off the minute she meets them. It is a post-traumatic stress disorder of sorts. No matter what words come from their mouth, their attitude transports her back to a time where she felt like she was a "nobody" because the abuse has robbed her of her perceived value. Old words still echo in her head.

She's fought hard to heal the wounds of abuse to feel like the valuable, smart woman that she is. She's hates that person she used to be — the more she felt insignificant, useless, and unworthy, the more people abused her. It took her years to find her way out of the vicious cycle of low self-esteem and abuse.

One of Joan's target markets is advertising agencies and design studios. Unfortunately, some of the most talented people in the design industry come off "cocky." When she encounters the decision maker with this persona, she abandons the relationship. Even if the owner isn't cocky, she'll encounter the occasional cocky artist, and the business relationship breaks down when she makes cutting, defensive remarks to the artist throughout their business transaction. While it is critical that she build solid business relationships with these companies who could use her as their exclusive printing supplier, she can't get a handle on her personal feelings.

Joan also has certain phrases that take her back to that painful time in her life. For instance, an insurance agent understands that life insurance is a joint decision made by both spouses in a marriage. One day, a well-meaning insurance agent was the guest speaker at a business women's dinner Joan attended. He said the simple phrase, "I would be flattered if you would take this home, think about it, and discuss it with your husband to see if it's right for your family." This agent was a mid-thirties solid Christian family man who is strongly involved in the community. Women who work alongside him would say he is the most supportive boss they've ever had, and he's a champion in their development in the insurance industry.

Joan had no other experience with him than as an audience member that day. But because he said, "… discuss it with your husband," she formed a negative attitude about him. Her knee-jerk reaction was to think, "I don't need a man to help me make a decision." Because of her past experience, she translated his comment to mean that he doesn't think she is worthy and capable of making her own decisions. In fact, when Joan encounters a discussion where his name comes up now, she says scathing things about him and urges people not to do business with him because he treats women like they belong at home barefoot and pregnant. That's not what he said or meant that day, but her perception is her reality.

A single comment took her back to a place where she was married, barefoot, pregnant, and bruised by her alcoholic husband, afraid for her life and the life of her other three children. That is how filters work — the spoken or written words are filtered through a lifetime of experiences as they are heard or read. I'm sure if he knew someone would react that way to that single phrase, he would have said that phrase differently.

This example is important because it's so prevalent in our society. One-third of American women have been abused — physically, sexually, emotionally, or mentally — by the time they reach 21. That's the documented abuse. Take a poll of the women you know well enough to ask, and you'll find another one-third qualify to be part of that statistic but didn't report it.

Abuse changes who people are and who they become. It also happens to men. Take for example the reports of Catholic priests who preyed on young boys in their parish. How do you think one victim of sexual abuse during his years as an altar boy felt at his father's funeral mass when the priest reminded him of the man who molested him?

Men as well as women bring those experiences with them into the workplace and into their interpersonal relationships. Sometimes the brain covers the trauma of the abuse, and the individual doesn't even remember the incident or who did it. However, a single phrase can remind them of the way they felt and spark reactions they weren't expecting and maybe don't even mean to convey.

Our workforce is made up of men and women. In the heat of a business transaction, not every person is prepared to say exactly the right thing at the right time in the right tone of voice for every listener. If a discussion goes badly and you examine it, you will likely find that the issue you are arguing about is not really the core issue at all.

Here's another example of how filters affect communication. George was a boisterous man six foot two and 275 pounds. He arrived at work early and read his Bible at his desk every morning. When he leaned back in his office chair, he folded his arms across his belly. He always greeted Darlene with a cheerful hello.

As time went by, George would make comments to Darlene that made her uncomfortable. She was new to the workforce, and thought reporting those comments would cast a bad light on her since George was such a senior employee. She endured and ignored his leering gazes and comments like, "How can someone wearing so many clothes be so sexy?" and "You really know how to brighten up an old man's day." There weren't many inappropriate comments, but each one was emblazoned in her mind.

Normally jovial, George also had a vicious temper, and it wouldn't take much to set him off some days. Darlene had to work on projects with him, and he would blow up occasionally. New to workplace problems, she would shrink back as he made loud disparaging remarks at her. Again, she would try to ignore the hurtful, bitter words, but they burned in her mind. The more she thought about the unforgettable comments, the more true they felt.

She left the company after two years and worked at three other companies over the coming years. Fifteen years after the job where she worked with the long-forgotten George, she accepted a new job. On her first day, she walked in and met the team. One of her teammates, David, sat in the next cubicle, and he liked to visit with his coworkers. Darlene could not figure out why he grated on her nerves. She thought his well-composed and logical business ideas and decisions were stupid. It annoyed her when she walked by his desk each morning and he said cheerfully, "Good Morning, Darlene!" She was most irritated by how he acted like a ten-year-old when faced with conflict as sometimes happens in the workplace.

One day during a business discussion, he said something that triggered a memory that offered clues to why she couldn't bear to be near this man even though he really hadn't done anything wrong. Darlene realized that David reminded her of George. When she walked in every morning, he was reading scripture from his Bible. When he stopped to talk, he leaned back in his office chair and folded his arms across his big belly. He even looked like George and laughed the same jovial laugh. That was the connection.

Once Darlene realized the connection, she began to consciously watch her feelings around him and overcome her urge to snap at him. After she worked with David for a few months, his father died. He opened up and told her that his father began beating him at age ten. Darlene, growing from her own experience, realized that she was working with a man during a normal office conflict situation, whose own filters transported him back to a place and time where he was abused. That realization continued to help her understand him better and heal from her own wounds.

She later learned that abuse can stunt emotional development. That could explain while he was handling conflict the way a ten-year-old boy would handle it.

Figure 1 (left). Timing is everything. The worst time to deliver tough feedback or news is when someone is in a bad mood.
Figure 2 (right). Does "Grandma" look like anyone you know? She has the approving smile meant to hide the fact that she doesn't understand what you are telling her.

Clues You Can See

Let's talk about some other clues you can probably see that will help you understand the listener better. When you are lucky enough to communicate with people face-to-face, you can read their facial expressions and body language. That can clue you in to how they might receive your message. This is why I'm a huge fan of face-to-face communication. You can immediately judge in many cases how the other person will react and if it's a good time to discuss the topic. The problem is that most people fear the reaction that someone will have when he hears what they have to say. Instead, we chicken out and put together an e-mail and press the send button. If we're feeling really brave, we leave a voice mail when we know they won't be there. It takes guts to get face-to-face with people. Technology has taken away the courage we develop when we use one-on-one communication.

In Figure 1, it does not take a rocket scientist to figure out this teenager isn't going to be open to or interested in anything you have to say. Does this look like anyone you work with, serve as a customer, or gave birth to? What she really needs is a hug, and this probably isn't a good time to talk about something she needs to change (such as her attitude). Because she's in a bad mood, your words may not mean the same thing to her when you say them. Worse yet, if she's reading your e-mail, she may be reading your message through an angry filter and could misunderstand your intent. If you are face-to-face, you can probably judge whether the time is right for your conversation. If it's not critical or related to her attitude, maybe your message can wait. Perhaps this would be a good time to talk about how things are going for her since she looks like she could use a friend.

Does Figure 2 look like anyone you know? This is "Grandma." She wants to please you and listens intently but doesn't understand a word you're saying. She doesn't want to hurt your feelings or reveal that she doesn't understand so she just smiles. If your assistant puts up a similar smoke screen, you may not get what you asked her for. If your potential client at a sales presentation looks like this, you aren't closing the sale. They might just love you to death, but they don't really understand the benefits of your product. A confused prospect doesn't buy.

In addressing this issue, avoid close-ended questions such as "Does that make sense?" or "How does that sound to you?" They can answer those questions in one affirmative word. Instead, ask some open-ended questions. The value of the open-ended question is that it is presented in such a way that she has to respond with a comment that is going to indicate her level of understanding.

If you are giving instructions to someone, have her explain what you've asked her to do. If it's a step-by-step process, offer to do it the first time together while you are by her side.

If you are in a sales presentation and you get the "smiling grandma" look, ask questions about her current way of handling the task your product or service addresses. Ask about problems she has with that process currently. That will provide clues about how well she understands the benefits of your product or service. Once you know what she understands, you will know what you need to tell her next. If she understands the value, it might be time to move to the closing part of the sales transaction.

The guy in Figure 3 looks like a large number of people in today's corporate workforce. As corporations throughout America implement programs to balance the demographics of their workforce, fifty-year-old white men are getting passed over in record numbers for promotions. If you are a thirty-five-year-old Asian female who is talking with a guy who has missed one too many promotions for younger, more diverse candidates in recent history, he might not be as open to your fresh, progressive ideas. He probably doesn't even realize he's become so openly jaded.

Figure 3. Different generations can encounter communication issues. Each brings different values and life experiences to the conversation. Overcome differences by leading meaningful conversations.

The best way to avoid the clash of the generations in the workplace or community is to engage in meaningful conversation. Asking people about their background and experiences helps you understand what life experiences they bring to the table. Often people have skill sets that they don't tell others about. When dealing with an older person, ask him what he would do if he were you. Ask for his opinions, but be sincere about implementing his ideas. When you do, let him know. When you don't, let him know why. He'll see that you at least gave his ideas careful consideration.

Reading Body Language is No Substitute for Meaningful Conversation

For many years, experts have translated body language. From furrowed brows and pursed lips to pen-tapping and tilted heads, they have created translations for them all. These translations have created excuses for people to draw conclusions instead of inspiring them to ask the right questions.

What if your listener is frowning with his head tilted down slightly, looking over his glasses. You can translate that to mean he is sending you signals of arrogance and haughtiness. However, he may also be frowning because he has heartburn from lunch and looking over his glasses because he's wearing reading glasses.

We've been told that crossed arms mean that people are closed to an idea or concept. People may cross their arms because the room is too cold or because they have indigestion. However, some people just like to cross their arms, and it means nothing. Some folks like to rest their arms over their stomach.

It is easier to read the body language of someone you know well. You learn through multiple contacts what each facial expression and body gesture means (if it has meaning at all). For sales people and professionals who meet people for the first time on a daily basis, they learn to recognize gestures because they dictate their next move. They can recognize whether someone needs more information or is ready to act.

If you are in question about what someone is thinking, ask him! Don't assume that because he is looking down, it means he is trying to hide something. As I mentioned earlier in this chapter, auditory learners are distracted by visual images and looking down can help them concentrate on the message they are hearing.

This doesn't mean you should say, "What is that look on your face?" If you are getting a facial expression or body language signal that you don't understand, ask questions to clarify what the listener is thinking. Questions such as, "What do you think about that?" and "Is there anything that I've left out?" will prompt them to respond verbally and open the gate for two-way communication.

Final Thoughts on Why People Don't Listen

It's challenging to find the right words and methods to convey what we mean. We seldom get lucky enough to work with, marry, or give birth to people who communicate the same way we do. We live in a fast-paced world of encrypted messages. The words we choose are important. If your listener doesn't understand what you are trying to tell them, it's as much your fault as it is theirs.

- There are three types of learning styles: visual, auditory, and kinesthetic. Knowing how people learn will help you deliver information in a way that the listener will comprehend and retain it for later reference.

- Create an open environment that fosters two-way communication so everyone can learn from each other. Most reasonable people appreciate it when you try to understand differences in cultures, norms, language, and religion.

- Be willing to step out and make some mistakes in an effort to educate yourself and understand what is important to your audience. Come to them with an open heart and open mind and care lavishly. Ask them about their interests and concerns.

- Some listeners prefer to get just the facts without a lengthy explanation. Others in your audience might prefer extensive details. The more people you communicate to, the more challenging it is to cater to all of their needs.

- Learn how to read you listener's nonverbal cues. When you are lucky enough to communicate with people face-to-face, you can read their facial expressions and body language. That can clue you in to how they might perceive your message so you can adapt it to their needs.

- Paradigms, perception, moods, distractions, and filters all create roadblocks to our communication.

CHAPTER 7
Communicate So People Will Hear You

Notice the way product manuals are written. All the warnings are located in the front. Some of the warnings seem ridiculous, particularly if the warning also appears somewhere else in the manual such as "Warning: Inserting your fingers into the fan while it is moving may result in amputation." Court cases have taught technical writers that product users don't always read the full manual.

The same thing happens to any communication piece. At any point in time, the reader can stop reading or the listener can stop listening. Even if readers return to finish reading the message, they might not receive the full message. To compensate, manufacturers put the important information in the front of the manual, on the box, in the instructions, and on stickers attached to the product.

The product manual is an example of a multi-dimensional approach to communication. By developing a communication strategy based on the needs of your target audience, you increase the odds of them reading and understanding your message. People have different learning styles and communication preferences. A multi-dimensional approach ensures that you utilize enough communication vehicles to meet the needs of everyone involved.

We all have an audience for our written and spoken messages. Whenever you communicate anything — from the cover letter on your résumé to the memo for your customers to the instructions for the dog sitter — you are responsible for delivering your message so that anyone in your audience can understand. You wouldn't expect an audience of people who speak only Japanese to follow instructions given in English, would you?

While that seems like an obvious example, we are faced with a multitude of communication variables that make it seem like you are speaking a different language. Our target audience could include people with literacy issues, knowledge and education differences, and distractions. You must deliver your message in such a way that everyone you are speaking to can receive and understand your message.

Using a Multi-Dimensional Approach to Communication

Suppose you are scheduling a fund-raising committee meeting and you need to send invitations. You have six people on your committee, and they all gave you their e-mail address and phone number:

Dan (age 52)   Bank executive
Angela (age 24) Stay-at-home mom with two small children
Dottie (age 64) Retired but active
Kelly (age 32)   Business owner with an active family
Carl (age 45)   Professional speaker who travels three days a week
John (age 34)   Programmer by day; musician by night

You need to send an invitation to the meeting. You choose e-mail because it's your preferred way to communicate. At the meeting the next week, only three people show up. When you e-mail them to find out where the others were at, they don't respond. You resort to calling them.

They didn't receive your message for a variety of reasons. Kelly doesn't check her e-mail all that often. Dan's message got hung up in his bank's spam blocker because it had multiple recipients on the message and spam-suspect words in the body of the message. Dottie has had a virus on her computer so she is afraid to open messages from people with e-mail addresses she doesn't recognize.

You live and learn when communicating with people. Next time, you'll know Dottie, Dan, and Kelly require a phone call. You might want to drop them a reminder postcard in the mail as well. You also learn that you can save a stamp by not mailing Carl a postcard because you learn by talking with him that he doesn't ever go through his mail.

Here's an example with some critical consequences. You work for a restaurant chain. Your company policy requires store management employees to make two bank deposits daily. However, your company is moving the night deposit drop to morning because of an increase of attacks on people making night deposit drops.

You hold an employee meeting and tell attendees that all deposits should be locked in the safe and delivered to the bank in the morning before the restaurant opens. Luke, a closing manager and single parent missed the meeting because of a sick child. Later that week, Luke is following the old policy because he didn't get the information on the policy change. He was robbed at gunpoint while making a night bank deposit and critically injured.

Because of the critical nature, this information should have been delivered using three or more communication vehicles. The employee meeting is a great way to deliver information because it can open the door for two-way communication. The company could have provided a sign to post at the time clock and also e-mailed the affected employees — the management team in this case. They could have sent a memo that must be signed by all managers as well.

Designing the Multi-Dimensional Communication Strategy

A communication strategy is very similar to a marketing strategy. You need to sell your information to a target audience, and deliver it in such a way that every member of that target market will embrace the message. In reality, that isn't 100 percent possible, but your goal should be to reach as many people as possible. Imagine how unsuccessful Pepsi or Nike would be if their marketing strategy included just one or two marketing vehicles.

The larger your audience is, the more communication vehicles you need. Important information also requires more vehicles to ensure that it is well-communicated. Using a variety of communication vehicles will increase the likelihood that everyone will receive and understand your message.

Know Your Audience

The first step in designing a multi-dimensional communication strategy is to determine the learning style and communication preferences of your audience.

Here are some questions you can ask:
- What is their learning style?
- How do they prefer to receive their information?
- What is the most convenient way to communicate for them?
- Who is least likely to read your message despite your best efforts? Why?

In many cases, you know exactly who you will communicate to. If it's your team, take the time to learn their preferences by simply asking the individuals. If you are dealing with a customer, communicating to them in the way they prefer is part of the overall customer experience. Here is my rule: I communicate to my customers in the manner they wish to communicate even if it's not my preferred method.

When it comes to dealing with larger audiences — perhaps an entire company or association — you will most likely deal with diverse learning styles and preferences. If you have the ability to conduct a survey, gather feedback from as many people as possible. Surveys generally have a low response rate, but the feedback that you gather can point you in the right direction on your audience's needs.

When I worked for Wal-Mart, I worked on the team that published the company's employee magazine. The main mission was to communicate to the employees (they call them associates) who worked in the United States. At that time, the company was expanding internationally, so we shipped copies of the magazine to the home offices of the international locations. Our audience in the United States largely worked in the retail locations and distribution centers around the country. Our publication was intended to be delivered to the break rooms so it was available for the associates to pick up or read on break.

We dealt with several issues. Some associates didn't frequent the break room. Others couldn't read the magazine because English wasn't their first language or they dealt with literacy issues. Some thought the magazine was just company propaganda (there are some of those people in every organization). For these reasons, we couldn't serve as the sole communication source for critical information. The magazine was a full-color, visually stimulating medium, but it only delivered the message to those who read it. Some people need to get their information in other ways.

Pick Multiple Ways to Communicate the Same Information

Information that is more important requires more communication vehicles. For instance, a top executive of a publicly traded company is announcing his retirement. The company will issue a press release to the news media. Another top executive will send out an e-mail to employees. The same letter will be faxed to offices without e-mail. A conference call will be held among top-level managers in the field locations to answer questions. Additionally, the announcement will be made at group meetings in cases where employees don't have access to other communication media.

A department fund-raiser has different needs because it affects a smaller number of people and is less critical. The committee may send out an e-mail, put up flyers in the break rooms and restrooms, and make an announcement at the weekly department meeting. That is probably sufficient to make the fund-raiser as successful as possible.

Changes to the company's health insurance benefits may only affect policyholders but the information may inspire non-policyholders to get on the program. The company should hold an informational meeting with visuals and handouts where employees can ask questions. They can supplement that information with an article in the company newsletter and reminders at department meetings. They could also mail information to the employees' homes (just like when we were in kindergarten). Some employees can't remember to take the information home to their spouse, and insurance coverage is often a family decision.

If you are looking for a job, your audience may be rather broad. You might send an e-mail with your friends so they can pass it along to their personal network of contacts. Of course, you would send it to human resources managers at the companies in the market where you want to work. You could post it on job websites such as Monster.com or on social networking websites such as LinkedIn and MySpace. Even though you are an individual with an individual need, you still benefit from a multi-dimensional communication strategy.

As shown in Figure 4, using more communication vehicles will provide a stronger message delivery. Almost any message is worthy of delivery to your audience using multiple communication vehicles.

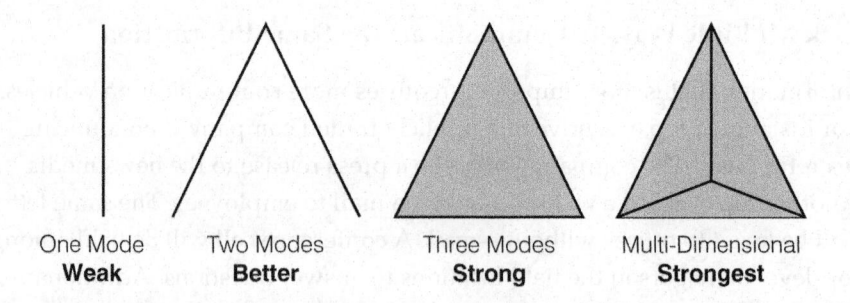

One Mode	Two Modes	Three Modes	Multi-Dimensional
Weak	**Better**	**Strong**	**Strongest**

Figure 4. More important messages require more modes of communication.
Compare building a communication strategy to building a structure. One stick won't stand alone. Two sticks won't provide a structure that will stand on its own. When you use enough sticks to create a stable structure, it will stand alone. A communication strategy must utilize enough elements to stand on its own too.

Pick the Right Information

Your audience has questions that you need to predict so you can provide answers. The last thing you want to do is leave out critical information in an expensive print communication piece. Today, many printable items are placed on an organization's website in the form of a downloadable PDF file. You can quickly make the update and download the new file to the website. With more people than ever connected to the Internet, thankfully communication is less dependent on print communication.

To avoid leaving out critical details, ask probing questions. If you are communicating a company policy change, consider asking questions like this to determine what your audience will need to know:

- Will your audience be curious about how this news will affect their jobs?
- How will it affect them personally?
- Who does the change affect?
- What do they want to know?
- What do they need to know to implement the change?
- What market or business conditions exist that are forcing the change?
- What are the benefits of the policy change?

If the message affects a large number of people, put together a focus group of a few people to test the communication with. When I worked for Wal-Mart's employee magazine, I had a review panel that read every article in every issue before it went to press. Among others, it included an attorney, a marketing manager, a grammar guru, a person who had an eagle eye for details (and errors), and one person who I knew to be critical and overly sensitive. When a reviewer questioned anything, our staff went back and considered making the suggested changes carefully.

Our staff members had a high-level of ownership in their work. However, we knew that if one small thing was noted by the overly sensitive reviewer, we should consider changing it. In a company that employs over a million people, one thing that offended one reviewer could easily offend hundreds of Wal-Mart employees sensitive to the same thing. Communication mistakes are easy to make but often uncomfortable and not so easy to fix. Putting the right controls and processes in place before you send the message out will reduce the chances for communication mistakes.

If you leave out crucial information, the grapevine will take care of it for you. It may not be accurate, but it's fast. It will take you much longer to re-communicate the correct information if you wait until the information travels the grapevine.

Types of Communication Vehicles

Let's start out by looking at all the types of communication vehicles we would normally use in our personal and professional lives.

E-Mail/Letters (Written Communication)

Remember the days when we wrote notes, dropped them in little envelopes, carefully wrote out the three-line address of our recipient along with our return address on the envelope, put a stamp on them, and walked them out to the mailbox? In just two to three days, the note would travel to our recipient. If they wrote back to us, we might receive their response in another two to three days.

HOW DID WE LIVE LIKE THAT? Like everything else in today's world, we want immediate gratification and that includes correspondence. We want it now. NOW!

Handwritten notes, e-mail, or text messages — it's all written communication. Of all the communication, written messages are most vulnerable to being misunderstood. That may seem ironic since having things in writing is the easiest way to protect yourself, right?

When we speak, we have many contributing factors in relaying the message to the listener — facial expressions, tone of voice, gestures. The problem with written communication is that we don't have all of tools available when our audience reads our message. All we have are flat, two-dimensional words left for the reader to insert their meaning. With text messaging, we only have PARTS of words.

Wouldn't it be cool if letters had those cues like a play to interpret what expressions go along with the words?

> **Joe:** [chuckling heartily and looking at him fondly] You're so funny, Dave!

Clearly, Joe is laughing at and with Dave. What if the cues were different?

> **Joe:** [rolling his eyes and groaning] You're so funny, Dave!

In the second example, Dave is probably translating that to mean, "What a loser you are, Dave!"

Sure, today we have emoticons, those little characters to add personality and flavor to our digital words like ;-) and ☺. Those are cute but most writers don't use them in business communication. They are still considered a novelty reserved for light, interpersonal written communication.

So where does that leave the millions of business readers who try to attach meaning to the words they read? The truth is that they are left to translate the words to their own meaning. Sometimes it's clear what the writer meant; sometimes it's not. Sometimes the reader is busy and doesn't read it correctly. Maybe they are in a bad mood because they had a crummy day. Maybe they don't like the writer and will read it with a jaded, surly attitude.

Dr. Albert Mehrabian conducted a study on the relevance of verbal and nonverbal communication (Chicago: Aldine-Atherton, 1972). He found that only about 7 percent of the emotional meaning of a face-to-face message is communicated through the actual words. About 38 percent is communicated by tone of voice. About 55 percent comes through nonverbal cues — gestures, posture, and facial expressions. The study also concluded that all three elements had to be congruent to be believable. If they were incongruent — like saying yes while shaking your head no — the listener was more likely to believe the body language. That shows exactly how

38%
Tone of Voice

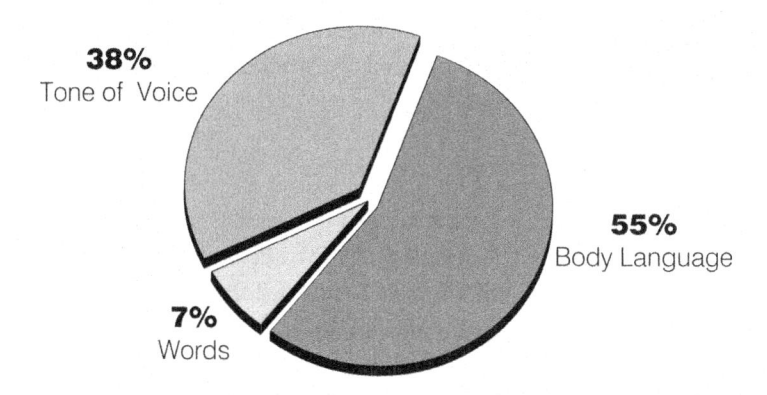

55%
Body Language

7%
Words

Figure 5. Dr. Albert Mehrabian found that there were three elements of face-to-face communication. Words only accounted for 7 percent of the emotional meaning. He also found the listener weighed tone of voice and body language more heavily than the words.

important it is for you to be totally convicted about what you are speaking about, because it will show if you aren't.

While Mehrabian's work is important research, there are some problems with the study that make it less relevant to business communication. Mark Sanborn, author of *The Fred Factor*, commented, "The problem with the study is that it used participants who were intimately familiar with each other such as friends and family members." Those are the kinds of people who know when you say one thing, you really mean something else. Those types of listeners would be familiar with what our normal communication clues such as facial expressions, body language, and familiar clichés mean. We don't have that level of familiarity with many of the people we encounter in our business life.

The second problem is that the research was based on face-to-face communication only. The study took place before we had today's communication technology which has reduced to need for face-to-face communication. Voice mail eliminates the facial expressions, gestures, and body language that we count on as we translate the messages we hear. With e-mail, text messages, and letters, all you have is words. The bottom line is that the words we choose are important.

Of course, there is nothing like face-to-face communication but the fact remains that we have turned into a society that utilizes e-mail to compensate for time and distance. There's no tone of voice, no facial expressions or gestures — just black letters hanging precariously on the white canvas hoping to be understood. For this reason, you better believe that words account for more than 7 percent of the today's communication.

Writing for the Busy Reader

Remember when "time" was considered the scarcest commodity? Today, "attention" is the scarcest commodity. Think about it: we sit at our desk, reading our e-mail as we talk on the phone, and the radio or television is playing in the background. Someone walks by your desk and whispers words to you so your caller doesn't hear them. We talk on our cell phones at lunch while we dine with a friend. We listen to books on compact disk in the car while we take our kids to school. We watch television in bed with our spouse while we both read. We are bombarded with stimuli from the time we wake up until the time we go to bed. We have become an over-stimulated society of people who pay attention to everything but comprehend only fragments. We've become a generation who turns the television on for noise because we can't stand the silence.

To ensure that your words make the impact you intend, always assume you are writing for the busy reader who is likely to glance through your message and move on to the next one.

Here are a few guidelines that will help you create easy-to-understand written messages. While this list addresses the needs of e-mail since that is the written communication medium of choice today, most tips adapt well to the formal written letter.

- State your main point in the beginning. Assume that your reader will read the first few lines more carefully than they will the rest. Start strong with the clear purpose of your message.
- Use their name. People love to hear their name. As they read your message, using their name signals them that you crafted this important message just for them.
- Use greetings such as "Good morning," "Hello," and "Great to hear from you." It softens your reader's mood to greet them warmly as if they were entering your home.
- Properly close. Use a proper signature, and wish them well with a closing like "Have a great day!" or "I can't wait to hear from you." Think of the close as a warm hug from an old friend who is leaving on a trip.

- **Use a concise, descriptive subject line.** The best thing about e-mail is that you can file it for later reference. Your subject line also sets the tone for the message.

- **Don't use the blind carbon copy (BCC) field for copying a secret person on your e-mail.** There have been rare instances reported of the person in the BCC field accidentally pressing Reply to All instead of Reply to Sender. The response e-mail from the person who was supposed to remain a secret instead copied everyone on his reply message. Accompanying it was a feeling of betrayal by the original recipient. If you must copy someone on an e-mail but can't include their name in the carbon copy (CC) field, forward the sent e-mail to them separately.

- **Understand the permanence of e-mail.** People can forward your message, use it in legal agreements, and request it in court documents. Everything you write makes an impression on you, and you can't take it back once you press the send button. If you are upset when you write it, hold it until the next day and re-read it to see if your message is overly emotional. If possible, ask someone to read it for you.

- **Regard the spellcheck function as your closest digital friend.** Some of your readers will make judgments about your professionalism when they see spelling and grammar errors. It just takes a minute to protect your image by spellchecking your message.

- **Use a grammar-checking utility when you can.** While most e-mail utilities don't include grammar check, it can save your image to take the extra time to use it. Spellcheck recognizes "their" and "there" to be correct spellings. However, only a grammar checker will catch the error in usage.

- **Respond to all e-mails within twenty-four to forty-eight hours.** This doesn't include "mass recipient" e-mails or spam. Many businesspeople consider follow-up to be representative of your business practices. If you can't provide them the answer they need immediately, respond to them and let them know when you can give them the answer. If e-mail seems to eat up a lot of your time, block thirty minutes once or twice a day to respond, read, and file your e-mail. Resist the urge to read and respond to everything as it arrives.

- **Use an out-of-office responder message if you are traveling and cannot respond to e-mail quickly.** Use caution if you work out of a home office because you could be notifying strangers that your home is unoccupied.

- Resist the urge to forward spam. Few people have time to read all the jokes, lengthy fictional stories meant to bring a tear to the eye, and the urban legend warnings that tell you to forward them to all your friends. Companies have strong employee policies about receiving and sending

The Value of Writing at the Eighth-Grade Reading Level

Business readers are overwhelmed. By writing for the eighth-grade reading level for all readers regardless of their level of education or business stature, you are providing them easy-to-understand content.

Your spelling and grammar checker in your word-processing program will generally include an option for measuring reading level. Using common words with fewer syllables means they don't have to stop and wonder what a word means. In addition, shorter sentences drastically increase reading comprehension. It takes time to learn to write this way, but it will help you be a better steward of your reader's time. They will be able to breeze through your message and understand it the way you meant it.

- **Present your information in chunks.** Using a bulleted list is a refreshing departure from sentence after sentences in a big, bulky, cumbersome-to-read paragraph.
- **Use short paragraphs.** When you must use a paragraph, keep it short. Your busy reader sometimes scans only the first sentence of every paragraph, so make it count.
- **Write in present-tense, active voice.** Your grammar checker will pick up passive-voice sentence structure and help you find ways to edit it out. Passive-voice sentence structure generally contains "be," "being," or "been." When you think of active voice, think action verb (as demonstrated in this bulleted list). Each bullet begins with an action verb like "Present," "Use," or "Act."
- **Write to the reader (the same manner this book is written in).** Directing your message to your readers engages them in the message. It is also a great way to trim unnecessary words out of your text.
- **Use parallel structure in your lists.** For example, every first sentence in this bulleted list is a complete sentence that starts with an action verb. Your bulleted list may be a series of items that are not complete sentences. Whichever you choose, be consistent throughout.

those messages. Spam blockers have been designed that keep us from receiving legitimate communications that we want. Never, ever send spam to your business contacts unless you don't need to do business with them anymore. ;-)

- **Send e-mail only during normal business hours.** Many people now have an office in their home. This means that you can answer your e-mail at 3:00 a.m. if you can't sleep. While this is a great way to use time that you could have used watching infomercials and music videos on cable television, it's unnerving to have someone respond back to your e-mail at that hour. They always want to know what you're doing up — maybe not the kind of business image you want to convey. If you must reply to e-mail overnight (any time between midnight and 6:00 a.m.), don't send those e-mails until after 6:00 a.m. You want to convey the image of a person who has a good handle on their time management and priorities.

Personal Data Assistant Etiquette

The personal data assistant (PDA) is one of those devices that connects us to all things happening. It not only holds our contacts and date book; we can get our e-mail and use the Internet.

Here are a few etiquette tips regarding your PDA.

- Put your PDA away during meetings to eliminate the urge to read that e-mail that just came across the screen.
- Wait to respond to e-mails until you can give them your undivided attention. It's easy to make silly typos on a PDA. It doesn't make any difference to the person receiving the short, cryptic, confusing e-mail just because it ends with "This message was sent to you using a Blackberry PDA" — it's still a short, cryptic, confusing e-mail.

Have Handwritten Notes Gone the Way of the Dinosaur?

How many cards do you mail these days? When you receive one, has it been pre-printed with a general message inside? How do you feel when you get one of those?

With all the technology we have at our fingertips that can save us time, there's still nothing nicer than the personal touch.

Send cards with hand-written notes when you can for something special — a nice thank-you message for instance. We are bombarded with a postal mailbox full of advertisements. It's refreshing to get something hand addressed with a personal message.

Obviously, it's more fun to use our computer technology to dress up our mass communications such as party invitations, holiday letters, and company or client newsletters. When you must send mass-produced communication pieces, add a quick handwritten note. Something as short as "Hope you can make it!" written on your preprinted party invitation will add your personal touch.

Telephone Communication

Most of us have a love-hate relationship with the phone. It is a powerful, live communication experience. Like e-mail, it can consume too much of your time and can lead to confusion in your communication message. Even though you can hear the voice inflection and the words and can ask immediately for clarification, you miss out on the facial expressions and body gestures that we count on to accurately translate a message.

Voice Mail

It seems sometimes like we play phone tag all day long. We live and work in a culture where we conduct business on the phone, meet one-on-one, and place our phone on voice mail to capture a few moments of concentration and peace. Voice mail is a necessary evil. We expect to get voice mail and have to wait for an answer to our question.

Here are a few tips to utilize voice mail effectively.

- Start the message with your name and phone number. If the listener didn't get it the first time, they just have to listen to the first part of your message again.
- Leave a detailed message so they may respond with a detailed message if they call back and get your voice mail.
- Make sure your voice mail greeting is brief but friendly and informative. Consider including your quick business tag line and website address so callers can get more information there. If you are traveling, include your message to include that information so callers understand there may be a greater delay in returning their call. Use caution if you work out of a home office where you may be informing strangers that your home is unoccupied.

- Just like a written message, begin your voice mail message with a friendly greeting, use his name, and end with a light ending such as "Have a great day!"
- Block time to check your voice mail and return calls regularly while you travel.
- Return calls within twenty-four to forty-eight hours even if you don't have all the information they requested. Your follow-up is a reflection of your general business practices.
- Avoid the urge to share your frustration that you have called someone and only got his voice mail. Your disdain will taint your recorded message, and it will cast a dark shadow on the relationship with the other person.
- If you call someone and get voice mail, LEAVE A MESSAGE. Unless they have Caller ID on their phone or can read your mind, they will have no idea you called.

Cell Phone

The cell phone has granted us the convenience of making and taking calls outside of our office but has given too many people the license to forget their manners. You may not be communicating verbally to those who are not part of your telephone conversation, but you are definitely sending a message to the people around you. Use these tips to project a professional image.

- It's okay not to answer your cell phone when it rings. Just because it is attached to your body doesn't mean that you can't let it roll to voice mail.
- Your callers don't expect you to interrupt your meal nor do they want to hear you eating your food in a loud restaurant. They might not feel comfortable with you discussing their business in a crowded area. Your callers would want you to enjoy your meal without interruption. You work hard, and you deserve a quiet meal.
- Never distract yourself while driving to answer a call. Let it go to voice mail. Talking on the phone drastically reduces your ability to react to all the crazy things that other drivers do. Your caller wants you to get to your destination safely.
- Silence your cell phone during meetings, seminars, networking events, and dinner. Unless you are expecting an urgent call, turn it off. We are naturally curious and distractible creatures. You will never be able to

focus on what is going on if you are checking your cell phone when it rings to see who is calling.

- If you are speaking to a group of people or conducting a meeting, make sure your phone is turned off. You are exhibiting your leadership skills, and your audience deserves your complete attention. If you accidentally leave it on and it rings, know how to silence it quickly. Never answer it during a presentation regardless of the circumstances.

- Never answer a phone call while you are meeting or dining out with someone. They took the time from their busy schedule; they deserve your undivided attention. In some cases, you may be waiting on an important phone call — warn your guest ahead of time, and only take the call if you recognize the number as that of the caller you are waiting on. Most people will understand an occasional urgent call.

- Avoid talking on the phone while you are exercising at the gym or walking in the neighborhood. You are usually breathing heavy during exercise, and it will sound as if you are having sex. That's not really the impression you want to leave with your caller, is it?

Office Phone

The office is no longer a traditional place we travel to, work beside others, and shut the door at the end of the day. Today, we have our offices in an office suite, a home office, our car, or our client's office. We can also set up our office at the local coffee shop where we hold client meetings. Your office can be any place you can use your laptop computer and your cell phone. Use these tips to maintain a professional presence on your office phone.

- Give your caller your complete attention. They can hear you type on your keyboard. Nothing says "I'm not interested in what you have to say" like reading e-mail or surfing the Internet while you talk on the phone. No matter how quiet you are, there is always the risk of getting an e-mail or hitting a website with audio files that activate automatically.

- Avoid using speakerphone for conducting calls and checking your voice mail. It is a distraction to your coworkers, and callers don't normally like to have their message broadcast throughout the office. Restrict its use to calls where several people must hear the caller. If possible, conduct the call in a conference room where you can close the door.

- Use conference-calling features as an alternative to speakerphone. The voice quality is much better, and the call is not broadcast throughout the office, disrupting coworkers.

- If you must participate in a scheduled conference call, be on time. Being late for a conference call is just like arriving late for any other meeting.

Videoconferencing

Videoconferencing technology has come a long way in the last several years. It is a great way to see the other person's expressions and show examples such as graphics and models. It provides a suitable way to engage in two-way communication, hear voice cues, and see facial expressions and body language. While it's still an expensive communication medium, it can save a company money. It is a great tool for interviewing job candidates because a company doesn't have to fly candidates in for interviews.

Here are some tips for making the most of videoconferencing technology:

- Try to position yourself within the camera's field of vision when speaking.
- Look at the video camera when you are talking, not the screen.
- Appoint one person at each remote site to operate the camera.
- Allow the on-screen site to finish speaking before answering. Multiple sites speaking at once can cause delays in the switching.
- Mute your microphones when not speaking. The microphones pick up side conversations and other room noises.
- Try to use complete sentences. Avoid one-word answers.
- Anticipate a slight delay in receiving the video from a site after a speaker begins. This is normal.

Background Noise

Background noise can leave a lot of questions for the person on the other end of the phone. We commonly talk on the phone while handling mindless activities as we enjoy the company of our caller. Ask yourself, "Will my caller recognize this background noise, and will they be offended by what I'm doing?" If you are taking a personal call, the caller won't be alarmed at recognizable noises such as loading the dishwasher or running water in the sink. They might not want to hear you clipping your fingernails.

If you are talking business, give the caller your undivided attention. While it's common to have a home office, you want your client to think he is the most important thing to you at that moment. Everything you do affects your professional image.

If you must type while you are talking on the phone, tell the caller what you are typing. For instance, if you are typing a few notes from your call or adding an entry on your calendar on your computer, tell her. This practice will reassure her that you are listening to her. If you wouldn't want her to know what you are doing while you are talking to her, you probably shouldn't be doing it.

Never talk on the phone in the restroom. Before cordless and mobile phones, the likelihood of talking to your caller in the restroom wasn't a real problem. Today, people work in one-man small offices or home offices with cordless phones. Our cell phones allow us to do business anywhere. The echo in the restroom is the first indicator you are in a restroom. Most people can recognize all the liquid sounds that happen in the restroom — you know the ones. The toilet flushing is a dead giveaway. Really, your caller would like you to have a few moments of peace to yourself and would gladly leave a voice mail.

I have a home office where I spend much of my day unless I'm in meetings at a client's office. It's the best room in the house — big sun-washed windows overlooking my front yard garden with lots of great office technology suitable for running my world headquarters. I love working at home, and one of my favorite things is spending time with my four-legged office mates.

Most of the day, they are quiet and well-behaved. You barely even know they are there. Then, 3:00 rolls around in the afternoon, and the school bus stops in front of the house. You'd think all the kids were running up to the house making faces at the dogs. It sounds like my office is in the animal shelter. During great weather, I take the laptop outside to work. It's wonderful, but you can hear every vehicle that drives by. Of course, the dogs have to alert me to people walking past the house and the FedEx delivery truck stopping next door. It doesn't bother me, but it sounds terrible to my callers on the other end of the phone.

If you work at home, avoid the barking dogs in the background. It's surprising in this day and time that some businesspeople still have outdated thinking that you aren't a serious businessperson if you work at home. It's the hottest thing in work-life balance for corporations to allow their valued employees to work at home, but some people are old fashioned. Make sure you sound like you are working from a corporate office at all times. Let the phone go to voice mail if there is commotion going on when it rings. Shut the shades on the windows if your dogs bark at predictable times each day. Send them outside or at least out of the office during those times.

The same thing goes with children. I never tried to work with a child at home full time. However, I keep wondering how old my teenage daughter will get before she overcomes the urge to tell me something while I'm on the phone talking with a client. Kids seem to have an uncontrollable impulse to have emergencies when we're on the phone. Create rules and quiet time at home that is yours to talk on the phone. You can always let your calls go to voice mail until you can return them in peace.

If you are running errands — like getting your oil changed at the supercenter — that might be a poor place to answer or make phone calls. The announcements over the personal address system will be a dead giveaway. Whatever you do, protect your professional image by maintaining a quiet space in which to talk on the phone where your client will feel like they have your undivided attention.

Face-to-Face Communication

Speaking face-to-face is like an old familiar friend. It is the way communication was meant to work. We can interact, get responses from people immediately, and gather additional meaning from their gestures, voice inflection, and facial expressions.

Here are a few ideas to make the most out of your face-to-face time.

- Make eye contact. Some people have a hard time maintaining it when they are talking, but definitely make eye contact when you are listening.
- Give the other person your undivided attention. People perceive that you are not interested in them if they see you looking around the room.
- Face the person you are speaking to.
- Understand that the most important aspect of communication is listening. Instead of formulating your reply to their comments, listen and then clarify that you understood what they had to say.
- Don't place too much emphasis on body language. We've been taught a lot of potentially misleading information about body language. If you are getting confusing signals because of incongruent body language, consider that a sign to ask some questions for clarification.

Networking

Networking is an activity that you might not usually consider as a communication medium. To many, it is considered a marketing activity. Networking is a great way to multiply your reach because you are speaking to people in hopes that they will tell others. With that in mind, you should consider the risks as well because people will tell others what you say if the information is intriguing enough.

While networking is an important marketing activity, its usefulness reaches far outside the business arena. Networking is a wonderful medium for looking for a new job, recruiting volunteers and sponsors for charity events, letting others know about upcoming events in the community, and making new friends.

Networking can be conducted in a variety of venues. You may attend formal networking events such as association meetings or chamber of commerce networking socials. Don't overlook the opportunity to network among your friends by visiting over dinner, e-mail, or community outings like youth baseball games.

Grapevine

The grapevine is one of the fastest communication methods. It is a close relative to gossiping. The more provocative and interesting the information is, the faster the information travels.

It is the medium most likely to be inaccurate. As the information changes hands, the story is altered as recipients try to translate and understand it in their own context.

Some organizations do a poor job of communicating information in a timely manner. Remember, if you don't communicate important information, the grapevine with take care of it for you.

Newsletters/E-Zine

You are probably familiar with the paper-based newsletter. The e-zine is the electronic version of the newsletter. The newsletter is useful for communicating to large groups of people. It usually includes visual elements like graphics, photos, and attractive text elements to charm you into reading each article. You can even include hyperlinks that can transport your readers to an Internet site along with video and audio files.

Here are tips to utilize this medium.

- Write for the busy reader. Follow the tips on pages 100 to 103, "Writing for the Busy Reader." Keep the articles short and concise. When you save 100 people time by investing a little extra time editing it into a concise message, you've saved your company or your customers money. There is also information at the end of the Chapter 11: Pit Bull Follow-Up.

- Make sure your message is applicable to as many recipients as possible. Your reader is tuned into WFII-FM — what's in it for me? They want to see news and photos about them and their department.

- Use your newsletter to share positive news and global information such as policy changes. Try to be upbeat although understandably some news is less cheery. Handle announcements such as the death of an employee or an increase in health insurance costs gracefully while including the appropriate information.

- Never use your newsletter as a "wall of shame" Don't use it for negative recognition such as listing people who have poor attendance or safety records. That information doesn't inspire performance improvement. It is best delivered one-on-one behind closed doors.

- Seek out important and relevant content. Share important information about your industry such as technology changes and news that impacts your customers. Use the newsletter to share company history and reinforce elements of your company culture such as an open-door policy and acts of extraordinary customer service.

- Make your newsletter graphically pleasing. It is part of your company image. Use appealing graphics, page layout, and fonts. Make your photos big, include captions that describe the photo, and list names.

Group Communication

Have you ever been in a meeting or presentation and thought your time could be better spent elsewhere? Group communication can be an effective medium for sharing information, creating a collaborative environment for brainstorming solutions, and making decisions. However, it can also be a place where hundreds or even thousands of dollars in productive time are lost in a single hour.

- Don't meet unless there is a valid reason to meet.
- Start and end meetings on time.

- Never chastise people who arrive late. The last thing you want to do is punish someone who is late because he had an emergency. If it is a consistent issue, deal with it privately.
- Ask attendees to submit agenda items, put together an agenda, send it out in advance, and stick to it during the meeting.
- Invite only the people who need to be there.
- Allow attendees to decline the meeting if they have nothing to contribute.
- If you have a standard weekly meeting for an hour, make sure you have sixty minutes worth of important information and activities. If not, shorten the meeting or consider canceling it.
- Utilize the stand-up meeting for communication and recognition purposes. They are shorter and people are often more attentive when they stand.
- Choose a meeting location that allows your group to be undisturbed while making sure they are not disruptive to others. If you work in an office of cubicles, take your meeting to a conference room so you will not disturb your surrounding cubicle neighbors. Besides, some information shared in a group meeting doesn't need to be overheard.
- Exercise caution when meeting in public places such as coffee shops, restaurants, and airplanes. Your conversation may include sensitive company information, and you never know who is sitting around you.
- For many meetings, you can utilize a round-table format. This format is conducive for getting participants fully engaged in the discussion.
- When you lead the meeting, pay attention to your position. Sitting at the head of the table reinforces your position as the meeting leader.
- Consider standing up as you lead the meeting. Standing is another way to position yourself as the leader. Particularly useful when you are facilitating discussion, location and positioning can regulate discussion with participants. Standing behind the overly vocal person can subdue them. Standing across from someone who is not vocal where you have direct eye contact will encourage them to interact more.

Final Thoughts on Communicating So People Will Hear You

You must deliver your message in such a way that everyone you are speaking to can receive and understand your message. By developing a communication strategy based on the needs of your target audience, you increase the odds of them reading and understanding your message. Communicators have different learning styles and communication preferences. A multi-dimensional approach ensures that you utilize enough communication vehicles to meet the needs of everyone involved.

- Today's communication technology has reduced face-to-face communication. Voice mail eliminates the facial expressions, gestures, and body language that we count on as we translate the messages we hear. With e-mail, text messages, and letters, all you have is words. This places a higher level of importance on the words we choose.

- At any point, readers can stop reading or listeners can stop listening. Make sure important information in most prominent in our message.

- To ensure that your words make the impact you intend, always assume you are writing for the busy reader who is likely to glance through your message and move on to the next one. When you write at the eighth-grade reading level for all readers regardless of their level of education or business stature, you are providing them easy-to-understand and quick-to-read content.

- Of all the communication vehicles available, written messages are most vulnerable to being misunderstood.

- The larger your audience is, the more communication vehicles you need. Important information also requires more vehicles to ensure it reaches every intended audience member. Using a variety of communication vehicles will increase the likelihood that everyone will receive and understand your message.

- If a listener doesn't understand what you are trying to communicate, it's as much your fault and as it is his. To increase your success, adapt your message to your listener's communication style.

- If you are dealing with a customer, communicating to them in the way they prefer is part of providing a great customer experience.

Transactions

Chapter 8   Creating Meaningful Customer Dialogue
Chapter 9   The Value of the F Word
Chapter 10   Be a Sales Consultant
Chapter 11   Pit Bull Follow-Up

Delivering an Unforgettable Customer Experience

What if you could spend less money and time on marketing and promotion? Where could you invest the money instead? Would you benefit by having extra time in your day to spend with the people in your life? What if everyone in your company understood the features and benefits of your company's offering AND the needs of every current and potential client?

You have a gold mine sitting in your current customer database in the form of information, additional sales, and connections to new clients. Your competitive edge lies in your ability to access it while delivering an unforgettable customer experience.

A U.S. Small Business Administration study found that customers stayed with companies where they felt valued. Another study found that a 5 percent reduction in customer attrition can result in a 25 percent to 125 percent increase in sales. Quality business relationships increase your profit through happier customers and employees.

The relationship is the currency in today's rapidly changing, competitive business climate. By building a series of meaningful transactions, you can create long-term business relationships that turn your clients into your marketing team and sales force. It's nice to have friends, but it's priceless to have fans who rave about you to their friends.

This section addresses the topic of delivering an unforgettable customer experience that enables us to forge a lifelong business relationship with our customers. We spend a lot of time and money getting customers in the door the first time. That investment comes in the form of advertising, sales commissions, and marketing support. It costs five times as much to get a new customer as it does to keep an existing customer. Successful businesses that invest in customer retention activities create customers for life and can reduce the amount of focus on their marketing effort.

The American Management Association says that only 65 percent of customers buy again where they bought before. Further, Ronald C. Goldstein, a professor at Georgetown University's McDonough School of Business says that 40 percent of customers leave firms because of poor service. Goldstein says that is why people switch brands and most never tell the company.

Creating loyal customers is a great way to market your business. A *Fortune* magazine survey revealed that a satisfied customer tells nine people. On the other hand, 85 percent of dissatisfied customers tell nine people, but 13 percent of dissatisfied customers tell twenty people.

Companies lose an average of 10 percent of their customers each year. Our customers switch businesses for many reasons. A U.S. Small Business Administration survey revealed why customers leave. Here's the shocker — only 9 percent of customers left a business because of price. Just 14 percent who left were dissatisfied with the product. Over 68 percent of customers left because they perceived that the business' staff didn't care. Ouch!

Paying attention to your customers is more than courtesy and common sense. It can ensure you keep your customers from leaving and taking their business to your competitors.

You know your industry. The next four chapters will give you the tools to help you dig deeper in your current relationships so you can utilize that expertise to improve your success and your bottom line.

CHAPTER 8
Creating Meaningful Customer Dialogue

One afternoon, my phone rang. It was a sales representative for a health insurance company. He obviously took the time to visit my website because he thought I employed a lot of people. Based on that criteria, he determined that I'm his target client. His company provides group insurance, and two or more people in an organization make a group. Without ever talking with me, he opened up his phone conversation based on the assumptions that I employ a bunch of people. I run a professional speaker bureau where I help organizations search out, negotiate with, and hire speakers for conferences and company meetings. The speaker is the product I carry, and I sell their services and programs to my clients. Even though speaker bureaus show all these speakers on their websites, the speakers aren't employees. In fact, I outsource everything and don't currently employ anyone. I thought I was never going to convince him that I didn't employ anyone. He acted like I was lying to him. If he had opened up his cold call with some meaningful conversation, I could have saved him some time.

In the Chapter 4: Leading Meaningful Conversations, you learned how to lead conversations when you are meeting someone new or just getting to know them better. In this chapter, we take it a step further and apply the same principles to building a deeper relationship with our prospective or existing clients. Relationships take time and frequent contact. That requires us to concentrate on learning about the other person and being engaged and interested. They aren't just business contacts — our goal should be to treat them as friends and business partners.

Interviewing customers is a crucial investment in building an unforgettable customer experience. It literally can define your business relationships. By asking a series of meaningful questions, you gather and understand customer wants, needs, expectations, and desires of their heart. People don't always know what they want when they hire you. If you ask the right questions, you can explore the possibilities of how your relationship could develop and evolve.

The beauty of creating meaningful customer dialogue is that you become a consultant instead of a service or product provider. Asking the right questions reduces the time you spend completing their job. It shows the customer how interested you are in them and identifies *other needs* they have beside their *perceived need*. It's really about getting the information you need to lead the relationship forward to something that is mutually beneficial.

Understanding Who Your Customer Is

We're in the business of serving customers. When you think of customers, you probably think of people who buy a product or service. That's true, but we serve many more customers than that. We have two types of customers:

- External customers may include people who benefit from our product or service, whether or not they buy it. They are people who are outside our organization. If you work for a company, they may be the people you serve outside your department. For a non-profit organization, they are the needy served by the organization. For a human resources manager, the customer could be a job applicant.

- Internal customers are sometimes the forgotten customers. They include people inside our department, family, or non-profit organizations such as:

    People we support
    Supervisors
    Peers and coworkers
    People who support us
    Donors
    Volunteers
    Our spouse, children, or even pets

Get to know your customers better. You probably support people within your company who aren't in your department. Schedule a meeting with them to find out what needs they have, and see if you are serving them adequately. Find out what changes they see in the business so you can be a partner in their success. When we look at the people we support inside our companies as customers instead of just being fellow employees, it changes the anatomy of the relationship. If your paycheck truly depended on how well *they think* you're supporting them, you bet you'd make sure you exceeded their expectations. I run a company, and my customers vote with future business on how well I'm taking care of their needs. When I lose a client, it's because I didn't assess and serve their needs properly.

Complete the customer identification exercise on the next page. A customer service transaction is an important component of a relationship. As you can see in the exercise, every customer transaction is a give-and-take relationship. For example, if your customer buys a product or service, you need repeat business and payment. If you serve your employees, you also need their loyalty and dedication.

Customer Service versus an Extraordinary Customer Experience

The key to a great customer experience is knowing what our customers — internal or external — expect. If you really want to know what your customers want, ask them. The biggest mistake in customer service program design is using criteria that we measure ourselves by based on how *WE* define great customer service. If you really want to deliver a great customer experience, focus on what *YOUR CUSTOMERS* want and need.

You've heard of the Golden Rule: Do unto others as you would have them do unto you. To deliver a great customer experience, you should follow the Platinum Rule: Do unto others as they want to be done unto! It's a humorous approach with a very serious undertone. *Customer service is what our customers think it is.*

Customers have wants and needs. Meet those and you have provided good customer service. However, customers have something else too — desires. They don't always speak the desires of their heart. If you can discover and deliver service that addresses the desires of their heart, you are on your way to creating an exceptional customer experience. Anyone is capable of delivering good customer service. Only a few can deliver an extraordinary customer experience.

Once we know what our customers expect from us, we can redefine how we deliver and measure our results. Once we align what we deliver with what our customers want, we all benefit. Customers reward exceptional customer service many ways, and they often vote with their dollars in the form of budget increases, future sales, and raises. There are different types of rewards

Identifying Your Customers

We all have customers. If you own a company, you have people who buy your products and services. If you work for a company, your customer may be your boss, peers you support in your job, or your employees who report to you. If you run a non-profit organization, your customers may be your donors, volunteers, or the people you help through your organization. If you are a parent or spouse, your customers are your family members and — silly as it sounds — pets if you have them.

Part A. Name three people you serve in your profession.

1. _____
2. _____
3. _____

Now think about your personal life. Name three people you serve.

1. _____
2. _____
3. _____

Part B. For each person, write down one need that you fill for him or her.

Professional

1. _____
2. _____
3. _____

Personal

1. _____
2. _____
3. _____

as well. An employee who strives to understand his customers' desires and serve them well may receive additional responsibility or promotions. Non-profits who understand what their donors desire can benefit too. They retain the donors they have but could get more donors because their existing donors told their friends how happy they were with the organization.

Part C. For each of those people you named in Part A, think of one thing you need from them.

Professional

1. _____
2. _____
3. _____

Personal

1. _____
2. _____
3. _____

Part D. Of all of those customers, which is your most important customer? Why is that person your most important customer?

_____
_____

Part E. Name some things for each person that they need that you aren't currently providing.

Professional

1. _____
2. _____
3. _____

Personal

1. _____
2. _____
3. _____

Customer service expectations for an administrative assistant might include arriving on time for work, producing timely reports, maintaining a pleasant attitude, and keeping a neat workspace. If the assistant also made sure his supervisor remembered important family birthdays and suggested gift ideas, he would be on his way to creating an extraordinary customer experience.

Focusing on the customer experience is about serving your customers' unspoken desires of their heart, but it also means addressing their needs and wants even before they have them. If the assistant built a solid business referral network for everything that he needed in his job (like office supply stores, copier companies, or shipping operations), he would make his job easier. However, if his business referral network served the needs of his supervisor as well (such as insurance agents, investment professionals, or home repair professionals) where he never had to spend time searching for those services, he would be on his way to delivering an extraordinary customer experience.

An Unforgettable Customer Experience Starts with Meaningful Dialogue

In Chapter 5: The Importance of Speaking Skills, I mentioned working on a training program that chronicled the twenty-three leadership principles that Sam Walton used to build and lead the Wal-Mart organization before his death in 1992. We interviewed fifty company leaders who had worked with him. They most commonly spoke of his ability to create meaningful dialogue to get ideas to correct problems and implement new ideas.

There was one fascinating phenomenon that we experienced with many of the people who had spent significant time with Sam Walton. The bulk of them were busy running the daily operations of the successful retailer. We wanted to be excellent stewards of the time they'd given us, so we got right down to business. With most of them, they started out by creating rapport and asking us questions — what we did, how long we had been with the company, did we have kids? Even Rob Walton, Wal-Mart Chairman of the Board and oldest son of Sam Walton, wouldn't go any further into the conversation until he got to know us better.

Here is the most valuable lesson in that experience: modeled behavior is easier to teach. Sam Walton probably didn't spend time telling all of those leaders that they should ask a series of questions to create rapport with people. Instead, he modeled it himself, and it was such an impactful lesson that they adopted the practice.

Meaningful Dialogue Starts with Meaningful Questions

Somewhere along the way, businesses came up with a great theory: people are more likely to do business with friendly businesses. It's a great theory, but it doesn't always translate to practice. It goes back to the Platinum Rule: treating others the way THEY want to be treated.

Many banks have a desk at the front where someone sits and greets the customers as they walk in. When I enter into my local video store, every employee in the building greets me. When you walk into many clothing shops, you'll often be greeted by a salesperson.

First of all, those gestures are nice and they do show customers that someone noticed they walked in. Greeting customers when they enter the building is also a great theft-prevention technique that places people on notice that someone is aware of them — thieves are less likely to steal merchandise or rob you if someone talked with them and made enough eye contact to identify them in a police line-up.

A company policy that requires every employee in the video store to greet customers when they enter does not genuinely create an atmosphere of friendliness. Customers know it's not a genuine response when the activity is automated or scripted. It shouldn't surprise you that customers think that aggressively friendly salespeople are stalking them so they get the commission before any other salesperson gets it. All these techniques are transparently insincere.

I know you've been in a store where the cashier asked you if you found everything okay. What happened when you said, "No, I didn't find everything I came in for." When I've said that, I got these responses:

- "I'm sorry to hear that."
- "That's too bad."
- "I can't do anything about it."

SO WHY DID THE CASHIER ASK IF I FOUND EVERYTHING OKAY? I can answer yes or no, and that can be the end of the conversation. We then spend fifteen minutes standing on opposite sides of the checkout station in awkward silence while the cashier scans my purchases. It's like when someone asks you how you are as a greeting — not because they care how you are. As the customer, I'm left wondering if the cashier will say anything to the manager about the items that were out of stock.

When people engage in a conversation with someone and they provide some feedback, how does that affect them when they believe no one ever does anything with it? They soon stop giving feedback because they assume no one cares.

Don't ask questions that are simply a greeting or filler. You'd be better off asking them where they went on vacation over the summer or what kind of pets they have. Ask questions that you can build a conversation with. MEANINGFUL DIALOGUE IS CREATED THROUGH A SERIES OF MEANINGFUL QUESTIONS.

Here's the most powerful secret to being genuinely known as a friendly company: engage in meaningful dialogue with your customers. The foundation of every great conversation is a series of open-ended questions — those that can't simply be answered with a one-word answer.

Closed-ended question:	Can I help you find anything? [No thanks, I'm just looking.]
Open-ended question:	What items have you been shopping for? Have you seen any great sales today?

When cashiers create meaningful dialogue, they are engaging the customer in the process and showing they are interested in them. It builds rapport, and customers are more likely to have a favorite cashier that they line up for every time they visit the store. If you are a salesperson, you want customers to look you up because they have a good relationship with you. They want to spend time with you because you care and make them feel valued. Business owners, sales professionals, trainers, human resources managers, corporate vice presidents, and non-profit volunteers all need to make meaningful conversation. The benefits will reap rewards that will benefit you personally, professionally, financially, and in many more ways.

Face Time and Revealing Questions

The first step in delivering an unforgettable customer experience is to create some face time with your customer. Remember, customers can be internal or external and include people we interact with in other departments or even family members. Don't attempt to create meaningful dialogue over e-mail. You can try it, but it loses its flexibility and impact.

With this approach, think of yourself as a consultant. My favorite question

> ## Questions That Create the Foundation For Meaningful Customer Dialogue
>
> Here is a list of questions you can ask that will reveal what your client really desires.
>
> - **"Tell me about your company."** Learn about the history and the products or services they provide.
> - **"What are your mission, vision, values, and goals?"** This reveals what they hold in high regard and what lies in their future.
> - **"What qualities do you hold dear?"** This gives you an idea of what is in their heart.
> - **"What is most important to you?"** Someone's values tell you a lot about how they spend their money — quality, price, or service?
> - **"What do you enjoy doing for fun?"** This question can be the gateway to discovering their passion. Do they love family time? Are they adventurous risk-takers?
> - **"What is your budget?"** This helps me determine realistic solutions. If they have a tiny budget that I couldn't possibly work within, it might be a short conversation. However, I could help them understand what a realistic budget might be, and point them to a viable solution.
> - **"What will you use the product, service, or information for?"** They may have a use in mind, but you can provide them related solutions and benefits that you could provide for a bit more money.
> - **"Is there anything I can do for you?"** When you are engaged in meaningful customer dialogue, you have to show that you aren't just there to sell them something or benefit yourself. The nature of the interview will reveal many of your customers' needs. However, vocalizing your willingness to help them reveals your genuine interest.
> - **"What colors do you like?"** This isn't always appropriate, but when it comes to purchases such as cars, clothing, and company branding materials such as logos and stationary, it points you in the direction you should go.

to ask my clients is, "What keeps you up at night?" That question can turn a ten-minute appointment into an hour's worth of information that can reveal how you need to proceed next with your client. You don't have to be a consultant to conduct your meaningful customer dialogue with a researcher/interviewer approach.

Here is an example of how this works. Say I'm a graphic designer meeting with a home improvement company owner for the first time who wants a new logo and some letterhead. Using this dialogue, I get ideas for images that his customer would be attracted to while embodying what he holds dear. By asking how the logo will be used, I find out that he'll want to put the logo on tape measures, yardsticks, and mugs soon. Right now, he just wants some stationary. The logo must be designed in such a way that it will look good in all those uses. He's a new business without a big budget. That tells me how many hours of my time he can afford to buy. He could get a more elaborate solution with a bigger budget, but my goal is to get him a suitable solution within the budget he has. A small budget means that he won't need fancy full-color printing. Something that he can produce in one or two colors is more suitable. When I know what his favorite colors are, I learn what colors would be suitable to suggest for the logo and stationary.

Here is where I really add value. With my supplier contacts, I can place an order for those tape measures and mugs so he can be ready for the upcoming local home builders association trade show (I win too because I'll make an additional commission on that sale). In the process of learning about his company, I learn that he could benefit from some networking groups, so I pass that information on to him. I also discover that he has a heart for serving needy families so I connect him with a volunteer opportunity with Rebuilding Together. The organization holds Rebuilding Days — annual events focused on repairing homes for people who own their home but can't afford necessary repairs. While he can't afford to be a cash sponsor yet, he finds he can volunteer his time and meet other people with the same passion.

See how that works? I get the information I need so that I can serve him better. In the process, I've demonstrated that I value his relationship and can be a beneficial resource to him as well. That is the value of meaningful customer dialogue to delivering an unforgettable customer experience.

Meaningful Customer Dialogue Paves the Way For Extraordinary Stories of Customer Service

Customer dialogue opens the doors to ways you can make a difference in your valued customers' lives. Kim Lancaster is a director of sales at a Courtyard by Marriott hotel in Bentonville, Arkansas. Her hotel is the "hotel of choice" for many of the regular Wal-Mart vendors who visit the retailer several times a year. The staff at Kim's hotel values their unique opportunity to develop relationships with their regular customers. Kim is active in the community and attends chamber of commerce events. She often comes across free passes to local events and knows about the amenities of the community. By simply creating some meaningful dialogue with her regular customers, Kim learns what they are interested in. She tucks away mental notes until she sees the traveler again.

When she checked in one frequent guest, she discovered he'd been diverted twice on his trip into the area and then nearly missed his connection to the Northwest Arkansas airport. Upon arrival, he was a frazzled mess. All he really wanted to do was work out, get a bite to eat, and then relax for the evening. She learned he worked out at a high-end gym at home. Knowing her hotel had a modest little exercise room with a couple of cardio machines, she offered him a free pass to a local gym she was saving for just such an occasion. The tense muscles in his face loosened, and he cracked a grin. She waved goodbye as he left the building for the gym after he unpacked and changed clothes. Kim thought it was fun to be able to turn the wiped-out look on his face into a look of gratitude by doing something that was easy for her.

Another regular guest had a heart attack while he was staying with them. When his wife arrived to this city she had only heard about through their conversations, they had map ready with directions to the hospital when she arrived and took care of getting her settled They even included directions to Wal-Mart just in case she forgot anything in her haste to pack and jump on a plane. They even put together a snack basket for her room expecting she'd be too preoccupied to stop for dinner. The hotel staff became her family away from home until her husband was well enough to accompany her home.

Recall that our customers are not just people who buy from our company. They include anyone who depends on us for something tangible or intangible. The staff at Kim's Courtyard by Marriott hotel is a family. When

Raise the Bar on Customer Service

Properly executed customer service will help you deliver an unforgettable customer experience. One of the best things about visiting Texas is the consistently high level of customer service. I didn't notice it or really appreciate it when I lived in the Dallas area, but I notice it now on my visits there.

Part of the contrast that I notice in Northwest Arkansas, my home since 1993, is largely due to our explosive growth and low unemployment rate. Our local companies can barely keep their companies staffed, let alone fill every position with the ideal employee.

"To me, there are different levels of customer service. Being great at customer service is about choosing to deliver great customer service AND being willing to serve others. Being intuitive at customer service requires listening to and engaging in another person's interests," says Northwest Arkansas businesswoman, Theresa Thompson.

Here are five methods to raise the bar on your customer service and differentiate your business from your competitors.

- **Measure and track customer service.** You can't improve anything if you don't measure your processes. These measurements can become benchmarks for taking your customer service to the next level. Before and during the sale or project, you can track processes like length of time to complete a customer's order; length of time a customer waits on hold; or number of return customers. However, customer satisfaction after the sale is difficult to track if you don't follow up. Call your customers within seven days of the sale or project completion to rate their level of customer satisfaction and thank them for their business. Ask them if they were happy with their purchase. Assure them you'd like to be their first choice next time. Find out if there is a service or product that you don't offer now that you should. Ask them to refer you the next time someone they know needs the same product or service. If you have a referral bonus program, this is an excellent time to mention it.

- **Understand what your customers consider phenomenal customer service.** Customers learn quickly what kind of customer service to expect. If they receive amazing customer service from you the first time, they will expect that same customer service experience every time they do business with you. "What you do is not nearly as important as doing what you do the same way, each and every time," comments Michael Gerber in *The E Myth Revisited: Why Most Small Businesses Don't Work and What to Do About It*. Remember, customer service is what *your customer* thinks it is, not what *you* think it is. Here is the customer service philosophy of Kerry Jensen of the Bentonville/Bella Vista Chamber of Commerce in Bentonville, Arkansas: "The answer is yes. How may I help you?" What would your customers think if you adopted that same philosophy?

- **Make doing business with you convenient for them.** Can you offer personalized services or take your product or service to your customers instead of having them come to your office? Mary Kay consultants have been doing this for years, but many other businesses can do it as well. Jan Lancaster, a mortgage loan originator had a busy customer whose only available opportunity to do her loan paperwork was while she was getting a manicure. Jan met her at the beauty salon and filled out the necessary paperwork. What is more inconvenient than packing up your computer to take it in for repair? Matt Worley of Matt the Computer Guy designed his business to make service calls at his customers' homes so they don't have to take their computer to a shop for repair. Can you provide such a personalized convenience with any of the components of your business?

- **Understand that creating customers for life is a critical promotional strategy.** "When you strip away all the executional detail, marketing serves two fundamental, critical business purposes: getting customers and keeping them," comment Kristin and Steven Ferguson, volunteers for SCORE (Counselors to America's Small Business). "Companies employ the basic marketing tools of advertising, sales promotion, personal selling, and public relations to get customers. But in the daily hubbub of focusing on customer acquisition, it is easy to lose sight of the business need to actively retain customers. Here is the basic truth: it's usually cheaper to keep the current customers we have than to find new customers. The promise of service, as in 'products and services,' is a big part of what companies offer as their business proposition. They employ marketing tools in various combinations to communicate that point — as a promise — when acquiring customers. The delivery of service, though, is how we keep them."

- **Develop your knowledge and problem-solving ability.** Kristen and Steven Ferguson add, "Companies keep customers by providing quality products, of course, coupled with impeccable service — by serving customers' needs and wants. But there's more to it! Service isn't just courtesy and helpfulness — it's also solving a problem. If there isn't a problem (no matter how small or trivial), there is no customer at the door. If we solve their problem, we've served them, and they will show their appreciation." It is as crucial for the entire staff to be knowledgeable and efficient as it is to be polite and prompt. It doesn't matter how nice they were, if they didn't provide what we needed in the manner we expected, they failed at customer service.

their receptionist, Kelsey, had a serious car accident that left her paralyzed from the waist down, they rallied around the young woman, raised money for her, and stayed close to her family to learn about her needs. Their regular guests even rallied around Kelsey. When they held a benefit chili supper at the hotel for her, guests would come down and drop $50 and $100 bills in the fish bowl and not even eat. Kelsey was part of their hotel home-away-from-home experience.

Krista, the hotel's general manager spent hours on the phone with Kelsey's medical providers and searching the Internet trying to assist the family in advocating on Kelsey's behalf. They welcomed her back when she was ready to return to work. Krista's example of servant-leadership no doubt made a powerful impression the hotel staff members that work for her.

For employees to create meaningful dialogue that leads to an unforgettable customer experience, they must watch it being modeled by leaders. They also require encouragement to feel fully empowered to take care of issues as they arise. Unfortunately, companies often honor their policies and procedures more than they honor their customers. Honoring both is necessary, but everyone needs to develop the ability and courage to act once they discover the needs of their customers. Action provides a fertile opportunity for people to make decisions that create a memorable difference in the lives of others.

Even when the response is not exactly perfect, supervisors must praise the little advances and help them understand how they can step a little further outside their comfort zone. Because Kim created meaningful dialogue with her customers, she discovered unique ways to created a customized and extraordinary customer experience.

Exceptional People Make It Possible To Overlook a Multitude of Flaws

One of my favorite hotels to stay at is Embassy Suites. I was in the Phoenix area one summer for a three-day seminar at that hotel. It was — like every other hotel in America at the time it seemed — under renovation. It was a dusty maze of detours with days punctuated by the sound of jack hammers.

The hotel offered a free shuttle service from the airport. Upon my arrival, the Embassy Suites' shuttle driver, Joe, greeted me at the airport. We had a nice visit on the trip to the hotel, and he recommended several restaurants. I hadn't eaten yet so Joe said he'd wait on me to get settled and then he'd take me to a Mexican restaurant where the food was cooked to order. I have food allergies and can't always eat at just any restaurant, but this one could customize my meal.

Joe took me and two others who were in town for the seminar to the restaurant and waited on us until we finished the meal (and by the way, it was one of the best meals I had on that trip). I discovered after he drove us back to the hotel after lunch that his shift was finished just after he had arrived at the restaurant. Impressed by his dedication to such great customer service, we all tipped him generously.

For the remainder of the time at that hotel, Joe was our generous host. Anything we needed, he had an solution for. He became a friend to us, and I even hugged him when it came time to leave. He made it easy to overlook the renovation mess at the hotel.

Hospitality Takes the Chill Off a Travel Experience

I took a much-needed pleasure trip to London, England with a couple of other ladies. It was a chilly March trip a week before spring break. We had five days to see a two-thousand-year-old city that really requires six weeks. The second day we arrived, we had to hail a taxi to get to our tour office. We normally would have considered that a splurge, but we didn't have time to navigate the underground railway.

Our taxi driver was Tony Egerton, a retired London police officer. He had retired to Texas. However, his wife's mother was ill, and he was back in London while they cared for her. He drove a taxi to support himself while they stayed in London. We talked about what we'd seen so far and what we planned to see. After a while, he asked if we'd like some suggestions. He gave us a brief history of the city and suggested that no trip to England would be complete without a trip to see the Crown Jewels at the Tower of London. He also recommended the pub with the best fish and chips and told us where to get the best Jack the Ripper tour — the only one conducted by Beefeaters (more about them in Chapter 16: Brands and Legacies: Not Such Different Creatures). He could even get us passes to the historic Ceremony of the Keys. There was a six-month waiting list for those!

Tony gave us his business card and said to call him if we needed a cab ride. We were also to call him if we wanted him to arrange the Ceremony of the

Yeoman Warder Richard Sands is just one of the legendary Beefeaters. This elite group of people is charged with protecting the Tower of London. They are also the point of contact for thousands of visitors who pass through the gates of one of London's most historic tourist attractions each week. They not only provide information and security, but also a heavy dose of customer service and hospitality. Shown with Richard and I are my fellow travelers Jana Wegner (left) and Melanie Mayner (center right).

Keys. Later that day, I called him to make the arrangements. He had his wife, Sheila, finalize the details. They not only arranged for passes to the Ceremony of the Keys, but we also got the chance to tour the Tower of London as the personal guests of Yeoman Warder Richard Sands. On that tour, we saw the Crown Jewels — the crowns of the royalty of England. The tower is rich in history. It was like a trip back in time hundreds of years in a historic setting completed by the Yeoman Warders' traditional clothing. Of course, it seemed a little comical when I saw two of them carrying a fifty-two-inch, LCD flat-panel high-definition television still in the box.

As Tony recommended, I came back that evening for the Ripping Yarns Jack the Ripper tour (www.jack-the-ripper-tours.com). Tony was right. It was fascinating and definitely mysterious to visit all the sites where women were murdered by Jack the Ripper. It still sends chills down my spine.

Upon my return that evening at 9:30 p.m. for the Ceremony of the Keys, I was greeted by Richard Sands and had the opportunity to interview him in the Yeoman Warders Club after the ceremony. He had worked all day at the

Tower of London, so I appreciated his genuine gesture of hospitality. It was an unforgettable chance to get an insider's view of the Yeoman Warders — the league of thirty-five known as the Beefeaters. Afterwards, the trip back to the hotel required an underground railway ride back. He escorted me back to the proper station — a much-appreciated gesture on a late night that included a Jack the Ripper tour.

It would have been easy to just limit my conversation to my travel partners, but I'm so glad that the Tony engaged us in some meaningful customer dialogue. It opened the door to one of the most memorable parts of the trip and helped me experience a side of London I wouldn't have seen otherwise.

Customers Reward a Great Customer Experience with Repeat Business

We have a Sam's Club in our town. It's a membership warehouse retailer that is a sister business to Wal-Mart, the discount retailer. Now that my family is grown, I don't need case quantities of anything, but it's fun to shop their high-quality meat selection and special buys on designer clothing and luxury-grade jewelry. They also have a gas station where members get a special discount on the gasoline.

The Sam's Club gas station is a fully automated self-service station. You can't pay cash — credit cards and Wal-Mart/Sam's Club gift cards only. They always have an attendant on duty because even the best automation malfunctions. Besides that, some people are hopelessly low-tech no matter how easy the gas pumps are to use.

The member discount is just a few cents, and it's normally out of my way so it would be easier to gas up somewhere else. However, I stop there because of Bill, one of the attendants who works at my Sam's Club gas station. I've pumped my own gas since I started driving, and I've never developed a personal relationship with a gas station attendant because they aren't required to interact with customers. The gas station attendants at Sam's Club aren't required to either.

Rain, snow, or shine, Bill considers it to be part of his job to greet the customers and talk with them. Even though he doesn't appear to know a stranger and could make conversation with anyone, he makes a point to get to know people and helps them as they pump their gas. I could buy my gasoline somewhere more convenient along my route, but I go out of my way to buy my gas on the days he works. I bet I'm not the only one either. I'd probably even pay a few cents more to do business with a person like Bill instead of just an automated gas pump.

It's not a glamorous job, and I'm sure he'd rather be fishing, working around the house, or enjoying retirement with his wife. However, what he's doing is a high calling. Because he spends his days creating meaningful dialogue with customers, he discovers opportunities to share a joke, help the low-tech customers get their car gassed up, and minister to the hurting. Customers come to the Sam's Club gas station because they need gasoline. The feeling he leaves people with is added value. I'd bet a tank of gas that people are more likely to return to the Sam's Club gas station just to see Bill. Because of him, we aren't just doing business with a company — we are doing business with a person.

Final Thoughts on Creating Meaningful Customer Dialogue

Lasting relationships take time and frequent contact. That requires us to concentrate on learning about the other person and being engaged and interested. People aren't just business contacts — our goal should be to treat them as friends and business partners.

If you really want to deliver a great customer experience, focus on what *your customers* want and need. You've heard of the Golden Rule: Do unto others as you would have them do unto you. To deliver a great customer experience, you should follow the Platinum Rule: Do unto others as they want to be done unto! It's a humorous approach with a very serious undertone. *Customer service is what our customers think it is.*

- Asking the right questions reduces the time you spend completing a customer's job. Additionally, it shows the customer how interested you are in them and identifies *other needs* they have beside their *perceived need*. It's really about getting the information you need to lead the relationship forward to something that is mutually beneficial.

- Customers reward exceptional customer service many ways, and they often vote with their dollars in the form of budget increases, future sales, and raises.

- A company policy that requires every employee in the building to greet customers when they enter does not genuinely create an atmosphere of friendliness. Customers know it's not a genuine response when the activity is automated or scripted.

- When you run a company, your customers vote with future business based on how well their needs were met. When someone loses clients, it's because he didn't assess and serve their needs properly.

- If paychecks were based on how well *customers think* they are cared for, more people would ensure they exceeded customers' expectations.

- Customer dialogue opens the doors to ways you can make a difference in your valued customers' lives.

- For employees to create meaningful customer dialogue, they must watch it being modeled by leaders. They also require encouragement to feel fully empowered to take care of issues as they arise.

CHAPTER 9
The Value of the F Word

It was the morning of the June fund-raiser our team had prepared for all year — the Cancer Road Challenge Poker Run and Motorcycle Show. It was the fifth year I had chaired the charity motorcycle event and the unthinkable happened — it rained. It wasn't just a little rain either. It came down in buckets from 7:45 a.m. and continued until 2:00 p.m. No lightning or wind — just the most rain I'd seen in years.

We had prepared for 500 bikes. It would be our biggest crowd ever, and we were ready. However, rain is the kiss of death for a motorcycle event regardless of how much bikers love the cause. Even though we had always heavily marketed to the genuine biker because they still show up when it rains, a huge number of motorcycle enthusiasts stay home on a rainy day.

We still had 125 bikes show up early for registration even though heavy rain was forecasted. In a poker run, participants ride the route and draw cards for points at stops along the route. We had a specified window of time for bikes to depart: they could leave any time between 7:30 and 10:00 a.m. A number of them got out before the rain started. The rest just hung around, bid on silent auction items, and ate breakfast waiting for the rain to stop. Some bikers are more experienced than others are and have logged many hours riding in the rain. Many bikers don't want to take the risk that wet pavement and reduced visibility poses, and I'm glad they chose to wait out the rain. Our participants' safety was important to us. As it neared 10:00 with the weather radar still showing more rain coming our way, it looked like I had to make some unprecedented decisions.

Even though the Cancer Road Challenge was a fund-raiser, we always treated it like a business. Likewise, we measured value as one of our competitive advantages. We weren't the only poker run that month or even that day. All the other poker runs raise money for great causes too. Bikers are incredibly generous, but they can only be in one place at a time. Bikers vote with their presence based on the cause but also based on the value for their activity dollar.

We delivered nine things in exchange for their poker run fee: breakfast, lunch, an event T-shirt, live music, free photographs of the participants and their motorcycles, vendor booths, a bike show, a great route in Northwest Arkansas (an area known for some of the best motorcycle routes in the country), and the chance to draw five cards for points towards a cash prize.

If the bikers couldn't get out on the route, how would they draw their cards for their points? A chance at the prize money was part of the value. How would they get that value? They could take the map and their T-shirt and ride the route some other day. They could still eat with us and enjoy the music and the vendors. They could even have their bikes photographed in the rain. They could do everything but participate in the chance at the money, and I felt that was a huge part of the value.

I had an idea. I discussed options with the key planning committee members — most of us had built this event together. I even discussed it with bikers who had been with us every year. We decided we would allow the remaining bikers to draw their cards at the event site without going out on the route. We announced it, and the crowd went wild. We were heroes.

Okay, we weren't exactly heroes in everyone's eyes. As the participants who braved the rain cruised back in with rain gear and wet poker run scoring sheets, they compared stories and talked about the number of hours they had logged on rainy rides. It was almost like they'd earned a badge of honor.

Some people were a little upset. Why weren't they given the option of not going out on the route? They considered riding the route to be part of the poker run. It wasn't fair that some people didn't have to go out in the rain to compete for the same prize money. Bikers hang out in groups, and they talk about all the places and events they've been to. If they love your event, they bring back all the friends they ride with the next year. The last thing you want is one angry biker telling all his biker buddies to boycott your event.

Fundamentally, we had made a good decision. However, bikers — like every other human being — often follow their heart and not fundamentals.

Also, like typical customers, they don't always tell you they are dissatisfied because they don't really like confrontation. They tell their friends, and then just don't come back again.

The Inevitable Confrontation

One angry biker decided he was going to give us a piece of his mind. He started out with the guy who was collecting the score cards — one of our founding committee members. Another planning committee member gave me a heads up that there was some commotion with one of the participants. With this event, we had participants who were willing to voice their opinions. We've always valued that — even when it was uncomfortable.

Over the years, I had logged a few of those difficult confrontational conversations. I handled them because I was in charge and felt that was part of my role as a servant-leader. I thought it was also a great chance to use a conflict resolution model that I taught in my communication programs — just to make sure it worked in all situations. You'll learn more about using the conflict resolution model when you read Chapter 15: Getting What You Want, Need, and Deserve.

This time, my angry biker was Mike, and he was dripping wet. He towered over me at six-foot-five and outweighed me by 100 pounds. This was not going to be fun. I introduced myself and I opened up our dialogue with, "Hey, I hear you're upset and I wanted to visit with you." Then, I stood there and listened as did his wife who stood by as well.

As you can imagine, I was getting some harsh words. I was also getting the F Word. However, it wasn't the F Word you might imagine, but we tend to treat this F Word with equal disdain. The F Word I was getting was FEEDBACK. Yes, he was angry, but he was willing to step up and tell me what was on his mind. If I was willing to engage in that difficult conversation, I had a chance to get his ideas about how he thought we should have handled it. Angry people generally have ideas about how they expect something to go. After sincerely listening to him, I had a chance to share the reasons for our decision.

Just giving him someone in charge to vent to diffused some of his anger. Once he had a chance to calm down, I explained our logic (something you can't do with an angry person). We were a committee of volunteers who had given hundreds of hours of our time planning this event, and no one was more disappointed than we were. We hadn't made a perfect decision, but we made the best one we could make given the circumstances.

I then did something I don't think he was expecting: I asked him what he would have done if he were me. A bit flustered, hungry, and soggy from the ride, he didn't have any ideas but he was calmer.

Mike and his wife went home, changed into some dry clothes, and returned to eat lunch with us. Afterwards, he came up to me with some great feedback — IDEAS on how to handle that situation in the future. Beautiful! I wrote them down, and I know we'll be implementing some of those in the future. He went from being an angry biker who could have killed our event by delivering bad press word-of-mouth — the fastest communication medium before the Internet — to someone who could be our biggest fan.

The Power of Being Nice

Dealing with Mike required me to stay calm and not let his anger provoke my anger. That is no small feat, and it takes practice and control. It's human nature to take the anger personally and defend ourselves. When we do that, the situation escalates and becomes more difficult to resolve.

Yeoman Warders at the Tower of London — or Beefeaters as they are widely known — are charged with maintaining security at the historic site. Because it is one of England's most prominent and famous tourist attractions, they encounter hundreds of guests each day. One of the requirements to be a Yeoman Warder is to have served at least twenty-two years in either the British Army or Royal Marines. They are no strangers to dealing with the public in sometimes stressful situations.

Long-time Yeoman Warder Richard Sands learned to not take anger and frustration personally. He said, "When people are being rude, they aren't really being rude to you — they being rude to the uniform. It's not you — it's the company." He also added that you should be nice to everyone because you don't always know who you are talking to. He added, "When you are nice to people, it changes everything."

Feedback Isn't the Enemy — It's the Answer

Why do we fear feedback? We fear it so much that we don't even want good feedback. Whenever we hear that someone has *feedback,* the hairs on the back of our neck stand up, and the pit of our stomach fills with dread.

Businesspeople are constantly seeking information. We devour business magazines and surf the Internet for information. We read the latest business books from the *New York Times* Best Seller List. We go to trade shows and conventions. We get personal coaches. We hire consultants — a practice that I appreciate because I am a consultant that helps organizations improve their strategy and business relationships. We are constantly searching everywhere for information on how to improve our personal and professional lives. We search everywhere except the most logical and inexpensive resource of all — our customer database.

Let's pause for just a moment and remember that you have customers regardless of where you are right now in your life. If you operate in a sales role or run a company, your customers are people who buy from you. If you work for someone, your manager is your customer. If you manage someone, that person is your customer. If you are a parent, your kids, spouse, pets, and other family members are your customers. If you work in a non-profit organization, the people that you serve as well as your volunteers and donors are your customers. We all serve someone, and those people will stay in our lives if we do a good job of providing a great customer experience.

Your customer database contains people who know your company in a way that no one else does. In fact, they probably know a good bit about buying your product or service because they evaluated your competitors before they decided to do business with you. They probably even know what you do best — your competitive advantage.

Our current customer database contains much of the information we need to take our companies to the next level — all we have to do is ask. Their ideas, opinions, and information hold the key to your future. You could read, experiment, and wonder for years, or you could just reach out to people who have already voted for you with their presence in your life. I guarantee they have feedback that could help you achieve your goals.

The Benefit of Asking the Right Questions

The payment terminal at the Wal-Mart checkout asks these questions:
- "Did your cashier greet you?"
- "Was your cashier friendly today?"
- "Was your store clean today?"

Why do they want to know and what will they do with that information? Will unfriendly cashiers be reprimanded? Will my store be cleaner next time I come in? Isn't there more to a good experience at the checkout than a cashier who makes eye contact and utters a word of acknowledgement?

Questions such as those that ask about the friendliness or cleanliness of the customer experience are subjective. They have a high rate of error because expectations may differ between the customer and the company and the cashier. Why doesn't a retailer ask something more useful and quantifiable like "How many items were out of stock today" and provide a selection of responses to choose. In a largely self-serve environment such as retail, finding everything in the store you want to buy is as profoundly valuable to a customer as being appropriately greeted by the cashier.

Questions That Will Provide Meaningful Feedback

Here are some questions to get you started. No matter what your role, these will open the dialogue. Once you ask one question to break the ice, you can dig deeper by asking related questions that draw more information out of your customer. The purpose is to initiate meaningful conversation that creates an environment for gathering feedback. Face-to-face feedback isn't easy to take, but it's even harder to give, so work hard to create a safe environment for your customer to provide it.

- **How well am I serving your needs now?** This is probably the hardest question to ask because it gets to the core of the good, bad, and ugly. All feedback is important. If I'm doing a good job, great. I want to know why the customer considers it great. If I'm not doing so great, I need to know why. It might be something I can change or I might just not be the right fit for their needs. We don't always know *what we don't know*. Customer service is what *the customer* thinks it is — not what *we* think it is. If we don't ask, we don't know what their expectations are.

- **Do you have any needs I'm not currently addressing?** If this is a business client, this could reveal a need that your company could also fill or give you ideas about a service your company doesn't currently even offer. Ask your spouse this question, and you'll learn what is on his or her heart. If you ask the donors for your non-profit organization, they might give you an idea for a donor benefit that is free for you to offer but would ensure they would continue to support you.

What if a retailer asked, "How do our prices compare to other retailers on what you bought today?" with selections that include Higher, Lower, or Comparable? Would it be useful to ask, "Why do you shop here?" and provide response choices that include Convenience, Price, and Both?

On automated response systems, the questions have to change periodically. When the questions never change, people assume that nothing is being done with the data that is collected. They soon stop giving feedback because they figure no one cares.

Getting great feedback you can use to improve has everything to do with asking the right questions in the right way. When you want meaningful feedback on subjective topics, you must ask them in person — not via some automated response system.

- **How often do you have that need?** This question will help you assess the potential for adding a new service that fills an unmet need. Maybe it's not a service you'll ever provide, but you can recommend where they can go to fill that need. Being a resource for trusted suppliers makes you invaluable to your existing customers. Your network of contacts is a highly regarded, value-added service.

- **What would you say my strengths are?** This can open your eyes. We tend to overlook the things people value most about us. Marcus Buckingham in his book, *Now, Discover Your Strengths,* says we need to focus our attention on what we do well instead of spending all our energy trying to improve what we don't do well. The feedback that you get could reveal your competitive advantage. No matter who you are, you are competing against someone or something. You need to make sure that you know your competitive advantages in all areas of your life — even your marriage. In this day of high divorce rates, if you aren't focused on being the best spouse you can be, you risk being replaced. Gosh, that's harsh but in this day and time, too many people seem to regard all relationships as disposable whether they are customers, employees, or spouses. Every relationship is sacred and most are worth saving. Knowing your strengths and developing those into powerhouse competitive advantages will make you a hot commodity.

If you need some rapport-building questions for the beginning of the conversation, check out Chapter 4: Leading Meaningful Conversations or Chapter 8: Creating Meaningful Customer Dialogue.

When it comes to building lifelong business relationships, getting face-to-face with your customer — internal or external — is priceless. Granted, it can be intimidating, and we don't always know what to ask. Asking the right questions is necessary to engage the customer in meaningful dialogue.

Final Thoughts on Gathering Meaningful Feedback

We tend to dread feedback — both giving and receiving — because it involves confrontation. However, not all feedback is negative. We can miss the good feedback when we don't create a way to gather it and embrace all feedback with an attitude of openness.

- Typical customers don't always tell you they are dissatisfied because they don't like confrontation. Instead, they tell their friends about their experience and then just don't come back again.
- Being willing to engage in difficult conversations with unhappy customers offers the chance to get their ideas about how they thought we should have handled a situation. Angry people generally have ideas on how they expect something to go.
- It takes practice and control to stay calm with an angry person. It's human nature to take the anger personally and defend ourselves. When we do that, the situation escalates and becomes more difficult to resolve.
- Even in the face of adversity, being nice can change everything. Besides that, you don't always know who you are talking to.
- Getting great feedback you can use to improve has everything to do with asking the right questions in the right way. When you want meaningful feedback on subjective topics, you must ask questions in person — not via some automated response system.
- Your customer database contains people who know your company in a way no one else does. In fact, they probably know a good bit about buying your product or service because they have evaluated your competitors before they decided to do business with you. They probably even know what you do best — your competitive advantage.

CHAPTER 10
Be a Sales Consultant

Every time I spend my money, I want the same thing — value. For many of the buying transactions I make, that means that I expect the company I'm buying from to provide advice and product knowledge as well as the right product, responsive service, and a fair price. Truly though, if a company is providing me information that I don't have to research on my own, I'm not as price-sensitive. However, I still expect the right product and responsive service. When I get all those things, I experience buyers' euphoria! Maybe if I got all those needs met with every purchase transaction, buyer's euphoria would get a little old. I think I'd still like to try it just to see. Who knows? I might turn into a great customer experience junkie. How bad could that be?

Here is my biggest pet peeve in the whole world when I make a purchase: sales people who simply fill out a sales order based on what I think I want. It infuriates me to figure out later that I was making a bad purchasing decision when the salesperson could have helped me explore different products that better suited my needs. Let's face it; customers aren't always right when they are making a purchase. If customers are faced later with buyer's regret — the sinking feeling that they should have bought something different and it's too late — do you think they will purchase from the same loser salesperson who let them make a wrong decision the last time?

Here is my second biggest pet peeve: salespeople who try to sell me products I don't need or won't use. Frankly, if they asked the right questions, they would know if I actually need additional bells and whistles — at least they would know WHICH bells and whistles I could use. It becomes obvious when salespeople are more motivated by the additional sales commission instead of doing what is right for their customer.

We're All in Sales

Our everyday lives are full of sales transactions. Not all of them require selling a product or service to an official customer. In our careers, most of us had to convince an employer to hire us and later promote us. When you propose an improvement for a new company process or policy, you have to sell the idea to someone.

However, we don't just sell in our professional lives. Perhaps you had to encourage your grandma to give you just one more cookie when you were six years old. What about when a mom has to talk her baby into eating the spinach goop in a glass jar? Think about the young man who has to convince his one perfect love that she should spend the rest of her life with him. Whether you operate in a sales role where you bear the official title of salesperson, operate your own business, or simply live life — *you are in sales.*

The shocker is that people who end up in business ownership often discover they don't want to be a salesperson. They simply throw open their doors for business and expect customers — lots of them — to flock to their doorstep. For that to happen, prospects who have a need must be educated about the business' offering and then convinced to buy.

If entrepreneurs discovered that they didn't want to be salespeople before they invested their life savings in a business, they could change their plans before it was too late. Life is too short to spend it doing something you loathe. If you hate sales, don't ever go into business for yourself. You'll be miserable or you'll starve.

I'm not so naïve to assume that you either love sales or you hate it. You can really, really dislike it but learn to tolerate it and succeed. Generally, this involves incorporating a process that includes knowing and believing in your product or service. To be successful in sales, the first person you have to sell on the product is yourself.

Buyers Want a Consultant — Not a Salesperson

The Internet has become a major shopping mall. I'm convinced that it's popular because we can get all the information we need to compare products without ever dealing with a salesperson. If salespeople looked at their role as a consultant, more people would choose a human transaction.

Shopping on the Internet isn't that easy or fast, and you don't know if you'll be ripped off. Just ask me about my miserable transaction with online camera retailer Fotoconnection.com. They pulled a "bait and switch" and then didn't send me the same products they promised (and some of what they sent didn't work). They refused to take my order back without a restocking fee and then they made it really difficult to get any of my money back after I returned the merchandise. For months, I dealt with my credit card company and the Better Business Bureau of New York. According to the multitude of stories on the feedback websites, Fotoconnection.com has cheated hundreds of other unsuspecting people too, but somehow they still get to operate. We trust people to operate fairly but when we can't touch what we're buying, there is risk involved. I would much rather purchase something I can hold in my hands before I plunk down my hard-earned cash.

When I remodeled my bathroom, I visited a couple of local lighting stores. I could walk around the store and look at their selection or look at their catalogs. I also had questions about the options for the small room and wanted to know about the energy-efficient options such as compact fluorescent and LED lighting. The first company I went to had lighting experts, but they were too busy to answer my questions and help me order the lighting I wanted (they did finally contact me six weeks later to see if they could help me). The second company I went to didn't really know very much about the new energy-efficient lighting, but they were ready to help me select my purchases from the traditional product lines they carried.

I ended up ordering traditional incandescent lighting for my remodel from the second store. Sadly, the second store failed to tell me that my lighting was backordered until I called a month later. They had held up my bathroom project long enough. I cancelled the order and ordered something different from an online retailer and received it five days later. I tried to do business with a local company, but both local companies I worked with failed to provide acceptable customer service. When all you offer in today's world is product selection, you compete with companies around the globe. Regardless of whether you serve customers locally or around the world, expertise and customer service will provide a competitive advantage.

Buyers want a salesperson who gets to know them and their needs. When you get into premium products, that interaction becomes even more important because the prospect likely has a million other important decisions to make. They seek out sales consultants who will advise them on the right product for their needs. Provide them with an excellent buying experience, and they will tell others — and shoppers of premium products tend to hang out with other people like themselves.

Does this mean that the budget shopper doesn't expect a consultant too? If you read *The Millionaire Next Door* by Thomas Stanley, you learned that most people don't become millionaires from overspending and living lavish lifestyles. Never assume that someone who is looking for a bargain does not have great purchasing power or influence. Even if they are truly a budget shopper because they don't have a lot of money, the chances are good that they will have more purchasing power someday. Treat them like they were spending a million dollars now, and they will remember you when they are ready to purchase again.

Choose to Be a Sales Consultant

Whether you choose to be in a sales role for a company or you discover you have no choice but to sell because you run your own company — you can choose to be a sales consultant. Look at the sales process as a consulting opportunity, and you will view sales differently. Some of the tasks will still be less pleasant, but you will truly begin to see your role as one of helping others as you build your customer base. Here is the beautiful thing — your customers will see you as someone who can help people like them and refer them to you.

What If All Employees Learned to Sell?

Tim Cornelius is a Texas attorney and college professor. He's also an entrepreneur and lifelong learner in a big way. He reads a book a day, and he spends the time he's not working coming up with new ideas — at least that's how it seems to me when I visit with him. On top of that, he's an engaging, curious person. If we could bottle those characteristics and sell them, we'd make America the number-one entrepreneurial force in the world. For now, we just have settle for him inspiring one classroom of students at a time.

When I sat down with him to discuss a potential collaboration, he started talking about the lost art of suggestive selling. In the online world, we might call it "up selling." You've seen it if you shopped an online bookstore. "Readers who bought this book also bought this other book." One click on a hyperlink and you're launched to the description of the suggested book. It's impulse marketing at its best.

Three Steps to Being a Great Sales Consultant

Even the most novice of salespeople can follow these three steps to sales consulting success.

1. **Know your product and who best benefits from it.** Salespeople make a living based on completed sales transactions. Ability to identify prospects and convert them into customers is how sales consultants earn their money. Product knowledge provides a salesperson a competitive edge. By knowing their product intimately, they can research what type of buyer it benefits most. Proactive sales consultants seek out leads for future customers by telling others what kind of buyer they are looking for. Let's face it, lots of people need the products we sell, but not everyone is willing or able to buy. Educate yourself on your target buyer. Most important, be willing to tell a customer when your product isn't right for him. Buyer's regret makes for a terrible reputation for both the salesperson and the company.

2. **Ask questions and listen for meaning and understanding.** Ask me, "Can I help you?" and I'll say, "No, thanks. I'm just looking." Ask me, "What are you shopping for today?" and I have to respond with an explanation. The first option was a close-ended question where I can respond with "yes" or "no." Ordinary salespeople use the first type of question because they are happy to lurk in the merchandise shadows waiting to pounce on a customer seeking a place to pay for their purchase. Sales consultants use the second type — the open-ended question — because it generates conversation. That conversation gives the sales consultant the information she needs to help the customer make a buying decision that best fits his needs. It also tells her which related products the customer needs to know about.

3. **Follow up after the sale.** Smart salespeople know happy customers are the most inexpensive source of marketing. They also know that it is easier to create a return customer than to find a new customer. Sales consultants stay in touch after the transaction so they maintain top-of-mind awareness. If you don't make contact with customers at least once each quarter, they aren't your customers anymore. Make contact periodically even if you just send them a postcard. eBay, the online auction company, sends my husband a customer anniversary card. He has no idea what date he first became an eBay customer (or eBay junkie), but the card helps eBay maintain top-of-mind awareness.

In the last few years, we've witnessed the disappearance of the sales clerk from the big-box retailers. In the retail world, it's about making a store easy to shop with all the merchandise replenished at just the perfect time and pushing huge amounts of merchandise out the front door — hopefully through the checkout lines. Shoppers like the self-service format and about all a human is needed for is to unload the trucks, put the merchandise on the shelf, and ring up the purchases. Some of that is even automated these days. There are only a handful of people in the store who are taught real product knowledge. Department managers only communicate with the people who work in their department. The rest of their time is spent walking around gazing at their handheld inventory devices and making sure the department is stocked.

Tim posed the question, "What if we taught big-box retail employees simple sales techniques?" At first, it seemed alien. On most of my shopping trips, if I need an employee's help, I have to hunt them down like small woodlands creatures and trap them in a corner. The last encounter I had with a sales clerk who actually engaged with me was when I was picking out a new laptop computer. He asked me if I had the typical additional accessories — jump drive, laptop bag, etc. When it came time to offer me the obligatory sales pitch about extended warranties, he didn't just ask me and move on after I quickly answered "no." He told me about how he had benefited from his when he dropped his laptop recently. I think extended warranties are a rip-off, but he almost had me convinced to buy one. When we were done, he mentioned that he sold more warranties than anyone else in his store. While he wasn't paid a commission for the extended warranty sales, his sales numbers were tracked, and he was recognized for his accomplishments.

So back to Tim's question, "What if we taught big-box retail employees simple sales techniques?" Tim told me about watching his uncle sell when he owned a grocery store. His uncle would spend hours out on the sales floor engaging with customers and calling their attention to merchandise like the fresh produce. He remembered his uncle stopping a woman and telling her about how wonderful those fresh peas were at dinner last night. He thought her family would enjoy them. Sure enough, she took some home that day.

What if every sales floor employee was taught sales techniques? They are just taught to fill orders. What if they were encouraged to give advice or talk about complementary products? What if they knew the features and benefits of every product in their department? I'd be happy sometimes if they just knew what the products were used for. If every employee spoke to customers during their shift and could convince just ten customers to buy a ten-dollar companion product for things they were already buying, what kind of difference would that make to the company's bottom line? Ten dollars is nothing if you work in the electronics department. I thought Tim's question was a compelling one.

Final Thoughts on Being a Sales Consultant

Customers expect value from their buying transactions. That equates to getting the right product, responsive service, and a fair price. However, customers aren't always right. When they make the wrong purchase choice, they experience buyer's regret — the sinking feeling that they should have bought something different. A skilled sales consultant will use her product knowledge and expertise to help a customer make the right choice that best serves his needs and desires. Buyers want a salesperson who gets to know them and their needs.

Our everyday lives are full of sales transactions. Not all of them require selling a product or service to an official customer. We sell ourselves to a potential employer in a job interview. We have to convince our family members to do things they don't want to do. Whether you operate in a sales role where you bear the official title of salesperson, operate your own business, or simply live life — *you are in sales.*

- You can really, really dislike sales but learn to tolerate it and succeed. Generally, this involves incorporating a process that includes knowing and believing in your product or service. To be successful in sales, the first person you have to sell on the product is yourself.

- If salespeople looked at their role as consulting, more people would choose a human transaction.

- Provide customers with an excellent buying experience, and they will tell others — and shoppers of premium products tend to hang out with other people like themselves.

- When all you offer in today's world is product selection, you compete with companies around the globe. Regardless of whether you serve customers locally or around the world, expertise and customer service will provide a competitive advantage.

- Teach sales techniques to every employee. If all sales floor employees spoke to customers during their shift and could convince just ten customers to buy a ten-dollar companion product for things they were already buying, it would that make a big difference to your company's bottom line.

CHAPTER 11
Pit Bull Follow-Up

Keeping a personal touch in an electronic, number-driven world is no easy feat. A key part of creating a great customer experience lies in the ability to implement a consistent strategy for keeping in touch with the people in our lives. Our society has created opportunities where we don't have to leave the house for our jobs and social interaction. I have more technology in my home office today than I did at my first job out of college, and I worked for a technology company! The Internet allows us to work anytime with anyone around the globe. We can utilize space on social networking sites to reveal the details of our lives without ever making personal contact with anyone. Our lives are busy, and we are bombarded with hundreds of marketing messages each day and more information than we can possibly comprehend.

This chapter is devoted to ways to keep in touch so you take advantage of the new acquaintances that come your way. Follow-up is really the art of making contact in frequent and meaningful ways so you can build lifelong relationships. These deeper relationships enable us to build trust and familiarity by modeling values and character. People are more likely to refer people they know and trust.

Keep in Touch with Customers

If you don't contact your customers at least once every ninety days, they aren't really your customers anymore. The old saying that "absence makes the heart grow fonder" doesn't apply to your customer base. Many things can happen over the months — mostly new relationships. We live in a relationship-driven economy. You can get suitable products, customer service, and prices anywhere in most cases. However, the folks you most want to do business with don't have time to sort through all the choices. Furthermore, they want someone who is going to make them feel valued and special. Nothing does that like a well-maintained relationship.

This doesn't apply just to customers. Imagine if you only contacted your friends when you needed something. How popular and genuine would you be? Would you have those friends long? All relationships need frequent attention. A consistent follow-up plan is the key to maintaining top-of-mind awareness with all the people in our life. We want to make sure that people remember us when that next sales or career opportunity comes along. According to the U.S. Department of Labor, only 5 percent of people obtain jobs through the open job market compared to 48 percent who attain their positions through referrals.

Keeping in contact with your customers gives you the chance to show how much you care about them. Just because they used your company once does not mean they will remember you when they have the need again later. It gives you the opportunity to educate your clients on new products or industry information. A phone call, e-mail, or simple direct mail piece is easy and inexpensive. Most important, it provides real value in helping you maintain that all-important top-of-mind awareness.

Find Places to Make Frequent Contact

Most of us have an opportunity to join organizations that have frequent meetings. This is a great place to network for new contacts. Networking is a great way to develop prospects and market your business. Most powerful of all, though, is the way that networking enables you to build relationships, learn about others through meaningful conversation, and help people by providing nice, warm, gift-wrapped leads. It's interesting that people who call me ready to do business on January 2 are people I made contact with during the previous October, November, and December. I had maintained top-of-mind awareness because I stayed in the networking game all year.

As I sat at the first official networking event of the year, I couldn't believe the number of people who said they resolved to do more networking. They realized that it was important to their business, and they were going to start that day. My expertise is networking, but I was still surprised. They spoke of it as seriously as they would if they were about to try to stop smoking after years of bitter attempts to quit. The networking group had spiked in size similar to the way the fitness center attendance increases in January.

Depending on your current professional situation or objective, the networking location of choice will vary. If you work for a large company, you may have social or professional organizations within your company such as women's affinity groups. You may choose to join a professional association that serves your industry. You might even choose to volunteer your time on a board that meets frequently so you can network with people who are interested in the same thing but come from different walks of life. If you are networking for sales contacts, you might choose to join a professional association that serves the needs and interests of the same type of customer who falls within your target market. Whatever you choose, just pick an activity that gives you regular opportunities to see the same people so you can build deeper relationships. If the group is healthy and dynamic, there will always be new people joining as well. This provides the best of both worlds — old relationships and new.

Frequent contact is key to maintaining relationships. Even among people who I hold in high regard, I'm surprised at how frequently we need to maintain contact because we experience changes in our lives and businesses. I sometimes forget to tell my oldest friends about new services or products in my business just because I thought they already knew. Make time to stay in contact and learn about changes in the lives of the people you know.

Find Reasons to Make Contact

As you become more skilled at networking, you will create the need to follow up. Finding creative reasons to follow up will allow you to maintain top-of-mind awareness without feeling like a pest. It doesn't take long to make a quick phone call, leave a friendly voice mail, or send an e-mail. Alternate between at least two means of communication (e-mail and voice mail for instance) because some people prefer one or the other. Just do something besides ask, "So are you ready to purchase from me yet?"

Here are some typical follow-up scenarios that many of us can use regardless of what stage we are in professionally.

Leads for Potential Clients. What is your plan for following up when someone gives you a lead for a potential client? If you don't have one, you should. Follow-up is a key indicator of extraordinary customer service, and you must posses a sense of urgency. If someone gives you a lead, follow up within twenty-four to forty-eight hours. As soon as you contact the lead, follow up with the person who gave you the lead to give her an update.

If you are giving a lead to someone and you don't hear anything, follow up on that lead. Even though you aren't responsible for babysitting leads you give, your reputation as a reliable source of contacts could be on the line.

After Meeting Someone New. You have many opportunities to meet new people, and the activity of daily life can cloud their memory. Giving new acquaintances a call, sending them an e-mail, or dropping them a handwritten note are perfect ways to help them remember who you are. It also gives you another chance to remind them about your business and who a good potential client is. If you talk with them over the phone or in person, ask them what kinds of leads they need. Make sure you asked enough questions to build your knowledge about that new contact so you can find many creative reasons to follow up later.

After a Trade Show or Convention. If your business depends on trade show or convention exposure, you understand how demanding it is. Booths, entry fees, and travel are major expenses alone. But then there is the number of working days devoted to getting ready, traveling to and from the event, and the long days devoted to on-site presence. Return on investment is critical.

You can create both passive and active exposure for your organization. The booth itself is passive exposure. Just because someone talked with you or picked up your brochure doesn't mean he will remember you in a few days. You need to make contact later, and that means collecting contact information.

People aren't dying to be on another contact list, so you have to offer incentives. One common technique is to register attendees for a drawing. It should be a high-demand material item — not a free appraisal of their financial situation. That's a tired old technique in the financial services industry, and people know it's a lead generator for sales calls. They also know that there isn't just one prize — everyone gets the prize. An item that is scarce has more perceived value.

You'll probably be surprised that 90 percent of leads generated at a trade show are never followed up on. After investing all the time and expense and gathering all those names, few people bother to do something with them to create top-of-mind awareness. Send a letter to everyone who visited your booth and registered. You can also announce the winner of your drawing while you include your business card and some information on your company. If possible, make phone calls to thank them personally because it's easier to gather additional information to prequalify them if you can have a two-way conversation. You made the investment in the event; now invest an equal amount of time following up. It could determine whether you attain return on investment or not.

After a Sales Presentation or a Job Interview. The follow-up thank you note never goes out of style. In the case of a sales presentation or job interview, you were probably one in a sea of people who were interviewed. Today's competitive economy offers many quality options. Good follow-up

---

Follow Up on Leads You Receive

When the day comes that your new networking buddy sends you a lead, follow up quickly — wait no more than forty-eight hours. Get a name, phone number, and e-mail address. Stop in or call the lead and follow that up with an e-mail. Next, follow up with the person who gave you the lead and tell her how the visit went. Most of all, provide excellent service to your new customer. Good news travels fast, but bad new travels at light speed. If you spoil the first lead that you receive, it will probably be your last. Do a great job, and you will become the referral of choice for your product or service.

My role model for sense of urgency in follow-up is Kerry Jensen with the Bentonville/Bella Vista Chamber of Commerce in Bentonville, Arkansas. He contacts the lead immediately and then follows up with the person who gave him the lead to let her know he made contact. One time, I e-mailed him a lead, and he e-mailed back within thirty minutes to let me know that he had an appointment with the person that afternoon. Wow!

Why is follow-up so important? It reflects the kind of customer service that you will provide your prospective client. If someone has poor follow-up, they might not win the new client because someone else reached the prospect already.

Once you make new acquaintances, contact them. Don't follow up with them because you want to sell them something although they may be a potential client. Follow up to build a relationship of trust and familiarity. The more times you visit with people, the more they will learn about your business and understand what kind of person you are. People are more likely to refer a friend to someone they know and trust.

It takes many contacts before you convert a typical prospect to a customer. Prospects may not have a need right now, and they may forget about you by the time they do. The world is a crazy, busy place. Don't give your prospect the chance to forget about you.

is an indicator of the kind of customer service and attention you will provide. It could be the deciding factor.

Updates on a Project. While you are working on your client's job, it is important to keep them updated on the progress. A good rule of thumb is to provide periodic updates as soon as you start billing hours to their account. A few years ago, I was selling a house as I had done many times. If you've ever been through the process, you know it's not terribly logical, and roadblocks pop up along the way. Realtors tend to be gifted sales professionals who sometimes don't possess great organizational skills. They also tend not to provide all the necessary communication that buyers and sellers desire.

On this particular sale, the selling agent turned the process over to her assistant, Anne, once the initial contract was accepted. Anne's job was to escort the sale through the finance and closing process. Over the next few weeks, I almost grew tired of hearing from Anne. She called me every other day even if there wasn't a problem — just to keep me updated on the progress. When problems did arise, she called me immediately and often had suggestions for handling them. I had sold the property as a "for sale by owner" transaction. Even though Anne was representing the buyer, I felt comfortable with the proceedings every step of the way. This level of communication in the real estate industry is extraordinary.

Post-Business Transaction. Make a point to follow up with your customers after you finish their job. This is a great opportunity to find out how they liked your product or service, learn how you can improve, ask for referrals, and thank them for their business. Errors in the business transaction happen to us all from time to time, and this is a great way to repair a customer service or product problem that you might not have discovered any other way.

Following up allows you to ensure that your company delivered a great customer experience. Make it even more memorable — follow up personally. Customers are impressed when someone takes the time to call. This is as important for internal customers as it is for external customers. You never know who you will have an opportunity to work for or with in the future.

Be Unique When Periodically Checking In With Potential Clients. Levinson, Frishman, and Lublin in their book, *Guerrilla Publicity*, comment, "Keep in touch. Periodically call, e-mail, and send information to remind your contacts that you're still alive, kicking, and available to them as a resource. Since everyone sends holiday cards, distinguish yourself by sending something they don't expect such as funny postcards on odd, little-known occasions." My favorite resource is www.holidays.net. Check out their list of fun and wacky holidays. My favorite is National Dog Day on August 26. One year, I sent my article "Marketing Lessons from My Dog Jazmin" (see Chapter 3: Tips and Techniques to Get the Most from Networking for the full article) to my contact database and got great response.

If the greeting card idea seems stale, consider sending them articles that they would find interesting. Lots of people send articles to people that quote or feature them. If you want to be truly memorable, get to know people well enough to know what they are interested in, and send them articles about those topics. They'll be impressed that you cared enough to understand their interests. Whatever you do, never send e-mail spam. It has grown into an Internet nuisance as we struggle to stay on top of business-critical e-mail communications. Besides, forwarded mass e-mails that are not relevant to the person's specific interests are impersonal.

Memorable follow-up is personally delivered. Customers are impressed when people take the time to follow up in person. Techniques can include calling to wish people happy birthday and sending out postcards with new services you offer with a quick, hand-written note. People often appreciate when you take the time to invite them to local networking functions that they may not know about. And, of course, the nice warm gift-wrapped lead is still an admired favorite.

My friend, Eric Elander, is a locksmith. We became friends because of his frequent follow-up just to say hello. I'm also his customer because of his frequent follow-up. There wasn't a phone call that he didn't start out by saying, "Hey, this is your favorite locksmith." Maybe it was the power of suggestion, but he ended up being my favorite locksmith.

Making Mass E-Mail Contact Meaningful

I'm an information junkie, so I sign up for a lot of e-zines (pronounced e-zeenz) — e-mail newsletters. I love learning new things, and e-zines provide the information I need to keep up with the changes in the industries I work with. I also sign up for e-zines from companies that I'm considering doing business with in the future — just so I don't forget they are a resource.

The e-zine is a popular marketing vehicle for many companies. It's incredibly inexpensive, and you can create and send it the same day. For people who have a great idea and want to act on it NOW before the idea burns up in the atmosphere (a common problem that plagues visionary people), it's a perfect solution. Follow-up is critical in forging lifelong business relationships, and an e-zine is a great follow-up tool.

I never mind getting an e-mail from a company that I might do business with in the future — as long as it has value. A quick way to inspire me to hit the delete key the minute I get an e-zine is to send me an advertisement with no meaningful content — especially if the message is unsolicited. In fact, after I receive three or four "empty content" messages in a row from the same company, I'm inspired to unsubscribe from the list completely.

Nobody needs another e-zine or e-mail advertisement. It is a great way — and sometimes the only way — to reach some potential customers. However, we are dealing with a "what's due now" culture and reading someone's e-mail advertisement isn't a high priority. In fact, too much e-mail in my inbox stresses me out. It feels like a never-ending to-do list. That's never a good thing when your e-mail contributes to your target client's stress.

If you want people to engage with your company, your message to your prospect or customer — regardless of the medium — must be meaningful. I work with people who plan meetings and conferences to help them find the right professional speakers, trainers, and consultants, so I'm on many speakers' e-zine lists. Most of them understand the concept well. They write an article on their topic of expertise and e-mail it to their permission database (people who have subscribed and given them permission to send them a mass e-mail). In the e-zine, they probably mention something about a new book or seminar they have coming up. Since I run a speaker bureau, I hang on to those because I can send them to my potential clients (people who plan meetings) because it demonstrates the speakers are more than just pretty faces with motivational messages — they are experts who can deliver important concepts and ideas to audiences in an entertaining way.

Here is the formula for a valuable e-zine: 75 percent meaningful content and 25 percent marketing message. This translates to a content-rich article that dominates 75 percent of the space — a topic your prospect or customer is interested in. It might be related to your company's product or service — such as an accountant sending out articles on wealth management issues or tax law changes. It might just be a more general article that would interest your target client such as the forecast for peak fall color in your area (assuming your target market is in one particular region of the country).

The purpose is to provide something that benefits them before you hit the "here's something you can buy from me" message also known as the "call to action." That's basically the same information/marketing breakdown you'd see in a print magazine. The magazine business isn't about providing information — it's about providing a marketing medium to a target client so they can sell advertising. The magazines draw the target client by providing meaningful information. Your e-zine or e-mail contact can have the same objective only on a smaller scale.

Engaging Your Target Market

We live in the information age. If you want your e-mail contact to be meaningful, you really must add value with every e-mail you send to total strangers. Even if everyone on your list is your fan or valued customer already, you still need to add information value.

People want to learn something that will improve their lives or fuel their interest in a particular topic. They want to receive information that is interesting to them. If you can customize your e-mail message to particular groups, do it! For instance, if your target client is real estate agents, send them information that is interesting to people in their industry. Become a conduit for the information that interests them so they don't have to search for it on their own. You add value when you save your target client time.

Value Is More Than Just Good Content

Other key ingredients include entertainment (such as humorous stories), organized, concise content (because people are more likely to read it), and graphically pleasing layout (tasteful and easy to read). Readers like information but they like to get it in a visual, quick-to-read, and entertaining format. Think of it as cheese sauce for your broccoli.

Great Examples of Meaningful E-Mail Contact

To engage our prospects and customers on the Internet, we can invite them to our website via e-mail. While there is something magnetic about a hyperlink in an e-mail, we still have to entice our audience to click it to cross over to our web site. I'm not a recreational Internet surfer, but I can be lured by the right invitation.

I'm on the Gap and Old Navy advertising e-mail list because their ads help me keep up with fashion trends. They don't send me articles, but they show images of how to put the clothes together. I'm really busy and can't remember the last time I bought a fashion magazine. When I shop, I need to make exactly the right purchase in a short amount of time. While I may not shop Old Navy each time, they maintain top-of-mind awareness while providing me information I value. They first attract my attention with a highly graphic, visually interesting e-mail. When I click on some element that interests me, it drives me to their website where I stay a minimum of fifteen minutes — even though I promise myself each time that I'm just going to delete the message without reading it.

I get some e-zines from photographers and graphic designers. I love it when they include things about their lives or portfolio images. I'm a photographer and do a good deal of my own creative work so I enjoy looking at their work. I also outsource some of my creative services for client projects. I'm asked for referrals often, so it gives me a chance to give my clients options that best fit their needs. It's good to have a variety of options because one size does not fit all clients.

I saw a brilliant ad one day on Weather.com. It was this sidebar ad for Acura. Now, I never click on those flashing ads but this one caught my eye. One image said, "Could a car company save a life?" and then the next image showed a picture of a big yellow Labrador retriever and so on — five images in all. I like dogs and I was curious so I clicked on the ad. I landed on the Acura website where it had a ten-minute video segment about an organization that trains special-needs dogs. I watched the entire thing and even got teary-eyed because the dog had saved someone's life. I don't even know the connection between Acura and this organization other than the woman they interviewed drove an Acura and the dog rode in it. The important thing is that I ended up on their website and once I got there, I traveled around the website.

Is E-Mail Contact Becoming an Endangered Species?

The public's rejection of e-mail marketing happened gradually over the last several years. It started with the endless stream of spam from uninvited sources and then everyone thought forwarding jokes and funny stories to all their friends was the greatest thing ever. Then more and more companies attempted to reach us via e-mail with content as meaningless as the online pharmaceutical e-mails. Then companies and Internet service providers designed a slew of spam blockers that blocked the messages we wanted to get but still couldn't filter out the e-mails from third-world countries inviting us to help them cash checks for their heirs. ARRGGHHH!

All this has caused e-mail to be less effective. We can't even keep up with the business-critical e-mails anymore — if we even receive them! People are spending less time on the weekends and evenings sending e-mail because they are bombarded with meaningless e-mail comingled with their business-critical e-mail all day. They are turning their Blackberries and Treos off at night because they can't take the e-mail overload. There is such a thing as too much information.

Meaningful Content Can Cause Your E-Mail to Rise to the Top of the Inbox

I depend on e-mail. I have a number of clients who prefer to use e-mail for the bulk of their communication. I have several different databases that I communicate to for different things — events, information, etc. I understand the power of the medium, but I've also watched the decline in its effectiveness. Witnessing this phenomenon take place has inspired me to make changes in how I communicate to my potential clients.

We must revamp what we communicate so every e-mail has meaningful content that interests our target clients. For our e-mail contact to have peak impact, we have to develop a reputation for sending messages that speak to the interests of our clients. They will place a priority on reading our messages when they trust us to provide customer-centered communication.

Business relationships are really where the power resides in this high-tech, low-touch world. People are starting to realize that we can do business easier around the world than in our own town. However, we are beginning to miss human interaction and friendships that lay the foundation upon which relationships are built. And in business, repeated contact using a variety of methods is where lifelong customers come from. And lifelong relationships translate to more clients, bigger paydays, and sweeter success. I want that and I know you do too.

Final Thoughts on Pit Bull Follow-Up

Follow-up is the art of making contact in frequent and meaningful ways so you can build lifelong relationships. It's not just a tool for working with new acquaintances who aren't your customers yet. Keeping in contact with all the people in your life gives you the chance to show how much you care about them. Customers want to feel valued and special. Nothing does that like a well-maintained relationship.

A consistent follow-up plan helps maintain top-of-mind awareness with all the people in our life. People are more likely to do business with or refer people they know well. We want to make sure that people remember us when that next sales or career opportunity comes along. It's surprising how we can neglect to update our oldest colleagues and customers about the changes in our personal and professional lives. Schedule time to check in with the people your already know to make sure those existing relationships stay current and healthy.

- If you don't contact your customers at least once every three months, they aren't really your customers anymore. The old saying that "absence makes the heart grow fonder" doesn't apply to your customer base. Many things can happen over the months — especially new relationships with your competitors.

- It doesn't take long to make a quick phone call, leave a friendly voice mail, or send an e-mail. Alternate between at least two means of communication (e-mail and voice mail, for instance) because some people prefer one or the other. Just do something besides ask, "So are you ready to purchase from me yet?"

- If someone gives you a lead, follow up within twenty-four to forty-eight hours. As soon as you contact the lead, follow up with the person who gave you the lead to update them.

- Errors in business transactions happen to us all from time to time. A quick phone call is a great way to repair a customer service or product problem that you might not have discovered any other way.

- Almost everyone wants to learn something that will improve their life or fuel their interest in a particular topic.

Brand Equity

Chapter 12 The Hard Skills Necessary for Becoming a Person of Influence

Chapter 13 The Unspoken Rules for Becoming a Person of Influence

Chapter 14 The Secret to Being Attractive

Chapter 15 Getting What You Want, Need, and Deserve

Chapter 16 Brands and Legacies: Not Such Different Creatures

Building a Lasting Brand That Grows in Value and Leaves a Legacy

Without a doubt, you are potentially your best promotional tool. That's right — in brilliant living color — YOU! The definition of a brand has evolved as the study of marketing has developed. Twenty years ago, when we thought of a brand, we thought of a name or logo like the Ralph Lauren polo horse, the Izod alligator, or the Nike swoosh symbol. It was something that you trademarked, and the brand carried a certain level of prestige depending on the marketing message that was associated with it. It was considered a valuable asset — something you could sell with your company. The process of connecting the attributes to the name or logo was known as branding.

Today, you hear more about branding than every before. Online dictionary *Wikipedia* says, "A great brand is one you want to live your life by, one you trust and hang on to while everything around you is changing, one that articulates the type of person you are or want to be, one that enables you to do what you couldn't otherwise achieve." You probably know it as your professional image or your reputation. It captures the essence of the stuff legacies, legends, and the lines in your face are made of.

What makes branding fascinating is that it is an intentional act of determining who you are and making it clear what you stand for. The more clear you are, the more powerful your brand. We all come into the world with a name; and we all end up with a Social Security number; but only a select few are willing to work hard enough to define and earn a powerful personal brand.

Think about your tombstone. The dash between your date of birth and date of departure from this life is where you choose to make the most of the time you've been given. Those choices are the building blocks for your brand.

We all have a brand whether we define it or not. Some brands are well known and others are simply a secret to just a few people. The more we understand about the power of a personal brand, the more important it seems to intentionally define it. I don't know about you, but I want total control of how people remember me.

What do you think of when you think of Donald Trump or President Clinton? What about Mother Teresa? When people think of my friend Angela Robinson who owns *The Job Guide*, a regional job advertising tabloid, I'm sure they think of the little packs of Juicy Fruit gum that she leaves when she calls on her clients. If they've ever had a conversation with her, I'm sure they think of her hopeful, cheerful spirit and her warm, engaging smile.

When people make a purchasing or hiring decision or a choice to donate to a charity, they tend to vote with their heart. All logical things considered, the intangibles such as the feeling something gives us still matters.

Branding a person is a thousand times easier than branding a logo or a name. A logo or a name can't interact with you, and they only give people a perceived feeling of significance. You, on the other hand, can engage with people and make them feel any way you choose. The feeling you leave people with determines the quality of your brand. You have a choice in how you define your personal brand, and this final section is about doing just that.

CHAPTER 12
The Hard Skills Necessary for Becoming A Person of Influence

Tragically, we've become a society of people who think our titles define us and that someone else is in charge of determining how much value we have to our organization and society as a whole. While there is an ounce of truth in that, my earnest desire is to help everyone understand that they can harness the true dynamics of power simply by making a series of planned and intentional choices — choices that define an influential and extraordinary life.

You have almost total control of your personal brand. What would you like your brand to stand for? When you are gone from your organization, what will the people you worked with remember or miss about you? When you breathe that final breath, what will that dash on your tombstone consist of — what legacy will you leave?

The first three sections of this book contained important steps and information that will aid you in your life success through networking, communicating, or taking care of your customers. In this chapter, I cover three key items that are necessary to earn you the right to become a person of influence: expertise, experience, and goal setting. These are areas that you can control and guide. They will create the foundation for the influential brand you were meant to own.

Your Experience and Expertise

The experiences we have and the expertise we gain shape our personal brand. They earn us the right to take a place in life as a person of influence. We don't always get to choose our experiences, but we can choose how we react to them and what we learn from them.

We can control the development of our expertise. We all possess natural gifts and talents, and we can use those to select what skills we develop over our lifetime. Invest enough time in those skills, and they will define your expertise.

The Value of Expertise

Our customers (internal and external) depend on us to have up-to-date information. The level of your expertise can differentiate you from competitors. If you are not a student of your field, you will become extinct. The information is at your fingertips. Subscribe to trade journals, online newsletters, and business publications. Professional associations publish articles and provide teleseminars you can download to listen to when it's convenient for you. Your library has books and audio and video programs. We live in the information age, and it's not hard to find fuel for our expertise; it's just hard to find time to take advantage of it.

Invest thirty minutes a day in your field of expertise. My goal is to spend sixty minutes a day relaxing or exercising because those are my stress relievers. That is a great opportunity to listen to an audio program on CD (or download it to my MP3 player) while I work out or relax. It's a great time to read a book or magazine article related to my field. Capitalize on those times when you are doing chores around the house or sitting in the doctor's office to catch up on the latest information. Your clients — current and future — are counting on it.

If your expertise will give you a competitive edge, you need a goal too. Carl Potter, CSP (Certified Safety Professional) is known as a guru in the field of safety. He makes his living as a professional speaker and consultant in the safety industry. I book professional speakers and had a chance to present a list of speakers for consideration to a safety conference committee. When they saw the list and his name was on it, every member of the conference planning committee said, "We HAVE to hire Carl." Carl has earned the right to speak to that industry because he spent years working for a utility company. However, his additional research for the multitude of books and articles he has written has "showcased" his expertise. His articles appear in

Expertise Inventory

Make a list of the items that might characterize you as an expert. Don't limit your topic to something professional. You might have an undergraduate or graduate degree in a particular topic or years of experience in a particular field. On the other hand, you might have run a successful business for twenty years and that qualifies you to be a small business expert. You might be an expert in getting your family of nine out the door on time every morning without forgetting anything AND manage to get them all around the dinner table together five nights a week. Don't leave any stone unturned when considering what your expertise is because you never know when you'll be called on to use that expertise. Write it all down.

Expertise to Develop

List the areas you'd like to develop expertise in. Also list what it will take for you to gain expertise in each area. This will give you a starter list for your goal worksheet later in this section. For example, you might want to become an expert in viral marketing. To gain expertise in that area, you might read thirty minutes each day and attend a conference on the topic. To get some hands-on experience, consider using what you learn with a small project at your company or a local non-profit organization. Perhaps your particular area of expertise requires getting a college degree or certification in that topic. It belongs on this list too!

What are some areas you'd like to develop expertise in?

___

What do you need to do to develop expertise in that area?

___

trade journals throughout the industry, and he speaks at professional association conferences as his schedule permits. He's the guru on safety.

Carl's advice to other speakers on their way up is to set a goal to be the guru. You could give "book report" speeches where you recite someone else's research and ideas or you could deliver training for a company that someone else developed — but why? You'll never reach your earning potential delivering someone else's material. Invest the time in your expertise. Get the education, advanced study, credentials, or certifications you need. It's too important to your brand image to let another day go by.

Using the Expertise Inventory and Expertise to Develop exercises on pages 169 and 170 will help you evaluate and plan your expertise portfolio. While you may never have thought of yourself as an expert in anything, this might serve as a wake-up call that you might be missing out on a competitive advantage if you aren't an expert in something.

Using Experiences to Define Your Brand

We can choose to wander through life as victims of chance, or we can look at the experiences we have as growth vehicles and signs of our true calling. We've all made choices that took us down a bumpy road. Sometimes we think we are making the right choice, but it turns out to be incredibly wrong — or seems to be wrong at the time, right? The crazy thing about life is that sometimes God lines us up for some experiences that will develop us for that next step.

Perhaps you were raised in a single-parent family. As a result of that experience and your parent's courage, tenacity, and resourcefulness, you learned how to help other single parents raise their families. You may end up as a volunteer or in a career where your heart for single parents gives them a greater chance to succeed.

Someone who feels as if she missed some opportunities because of her race, gender, or disability may share her wisdom from the experience as she mentors others like her. She may work hard to make sure that doesn't happen in the company she works in. It might also make her hardened to those who expect to get help advancing in their career but don't want to work as hard as she did to earn it.

An accident or disease can change the anticipated outcome of life. Those who are resilient enough to adapt and overcome the challenges positively impact their future. Resilience is a skill that permeates every aspect our lives. Resilient people are more able to handle the inevitable change that happens in their professional life. Resiliency helps emergency services personnel overcome the tragic instances that are part of their job. It also helps married people adapt when a spouse passes away.

Your experience can strengthen your character and resilience, but it can also be a selling point. I book professional speakers, and there is an unspoken qualification that meeting planners don't realize they want: a speaker who has earned the right to speak to their group. Speakers think that the right topic, degree, or expertise is enough. However, a savvy meeting planner knows that when his attendees approve of a speaker, the meeting is a success. Audiences can be fickle. The better a meeting planner (and the speaker bureau) matches the needs and preferences of the audience, the better the meeting planner looks at the end of the speech. Demographics and life experience are important things to look at in the booking process.

This isn't just true with speakers. In every place where people work together in teams, finding the right fit is crucial to team success. Life experiences shape who people become. Someone who is older might be more compassionate and professional than someone who is just entering the workforce because they have years of experience dealing with difficult or challenging situations. Some charities prefer to hire staff members who have experienced the same challenges that the charity's clients face because they want the staff to be empathetic.

Our experiences often shape the values that drive us and the stories that we have to tell. The stories from our life are one of the best ways to teach others and create a legacy. Regardless of what your experiences are, they can be a powerful part of your personal brand. Be grateful for the experiences — good and bad — and the associated learning because they could be preparing you for the next big step in your life.

Use the Experience Inventory exercise on the next page to make a list of all the experiences you've had in your life. The only list many of us ever write is the professional experience summary for our résumé, but there is so much more to do with such a list. You might need that list to convince yourself that you should be doing something you aren't doing now. For example, if you have enough experience as part of a married couple, you might qualify to lead a class at your church for couples who are engaged to

Experience Inventory

List your experiences here. Take nothing for granted. If you've been a parent or spouse, put it here. If you've been a student, managed people, or herded children, write it down. If you were abused as a child or spent time as a homeless person, include it in the list. These experiences might provide proof to yourself and others that you've earned the right to do certain things.

Experiences You Want to Have

Some people look at this as the list of things they want to do before they die. Be serious but have some fun with the list too. Maybe you want to be a company president or raise $1 million for your favorite charity. Maybe you'd like to be a lottery winner or visit all seven Wonders of the World. Perhaps you'd like to become a college graduate and you never even graduated from high school. Remember, anything is possible.

What are some experiences you'd like to have?

_____
_____
_____
_____
_____
_____
_____
_____
_____

What do you need to do to have those experiences?

_____
_____
_____
_____
_____
_____
_____
_____
_____
_____
_____
_____

be married. That could inspire you to write a book for newly married couples or even create a business that offers marriage retreats. Making a list of your experiences can open your eyes to an area of your life where you could achieve more success because of experience you had overlooked.

After you do that, use the exercise on page 174 to list all the experiences you want to have. For example, my list includes seeing all the cathedrals in the world and selling 100,000 copies of this book (thank you for helping me in my desire to experience that). This list can become a great foundation for your goal worksheet later in this chapter.

Set Kick-Butt Goals

Ask anyone you know who produces great results, and you will find a common thread in the fabric of their success — the ability to set and meet goals. As I've seen in my life with amazing frequency, goals are miracles simply waiting to happen. Here are key elements to use in your goal-setting strategy. Once you review them, fill out the goal worksheet at the end of the chapter.

Define Your Purpose

When the goal-setting process begins by spending time reflecting on why we are here on earth, we achieve greater success through our goals. Once you know why you're here, you should write goals that support that.

What if you don't really know why you are here? You can relax because you are among many others who feel the same way. Your purpose when you are forty years old is often much clearer than when you are thirty years old. As you mature, time and your perspective will reveal your true purpose. For some stages in life, it's easier because our purpose is defined by our culture — such as being an active and engaged parent. How you use your life's activities to support that purpose is up to you.

Success is a casualty of professional or personal goals that don't line up. For example, a father may believe that his purpose is to be a parent who actively participates in his children's school activities. Both personal and professional goals must support that purpose. If his professional goals include advancing in a career that requires extensive travel, he'll find it difficult to achieve all his goals.

Here is my purpose statement:

> My purpose is to encourage and equip others to improve their own lives by becoming effective individuals; be God's vehicle and recognize His will in my life; love my friends and family; and express my gratitude for my challenges and lessons as well as my blessings and opportunities. I will accomplish this by pursuing things that match my gifts, values, and interests; upholding a solid moral/ethical reputation; listening to my heart and feeding my soul; basing decisions on principles rather than emotion; and building deeper relationships.

Even though my purpose statement is long, yours may be simpler and shorter. I set goals for years without a purpose statement and most of the time, I hit the right mark with my goals. However, the purpose statement has given me something to gauge each of my goals by so I have a greater chance of investing my time in the right goals to support my purpose here on earth.

Understand Your Values and Personal Mission

Make a list of those things that are important to you and are necessary for maintaining a solid reputation. Then use those to write a mission statement that describes what you feel called to do with the precious time you've been given on earth. Goal-setters can get caught up in their long-term goals but fail to take advantage of today. Every single day is a gift, and we must focus on those things that line up with our personal values and mission.

Ray Pelletier, the late professional speaker and master consultant, recommended writing a mission statement for every task you take on — right down to individual business calls. He wrote down his goal for each task so that he met his objective.

Write Goals for Both Personal and Professional Areas of Your Life

Professional goals may include job promotion or change, training, or productivity. If you own a business, you'll want to look at marketing, productivity, growth, or product-development goals. Personal goals may include fitness, family, education, and financial goals. Many people fail in life because they don't set goals that relate to their family life. Who you are in your personal life is vitally important, because it creates the foundation for who you are as a professional. One of the most important legacies we leave is how we live our personal lives.

I like to see people set goals for their community service life. Hopefully, you got a chance to experience "service learning" — the process of learning through volunteer work as part of your education — when you were in high school or college. If not, it's encouraging that it's never too late to take advantage of the lessons learned while volunteering in the community. I didn't learn about the value of volunteering until I was in my thirties, and I wish I'd done it sooner. I'm totally addicted to it now, and I have so many great opportunities that the only problem is deciding which one to take on.

The biggest benefits you'll receive from service learning are meeting lots of new people (expanding your network) and getting tons of great experience for your résumé. You can use it to strengthen skills you already have or volunteer for tasks you've never done before so you'll develop new skills. The goal-setting process is the perfect time to take a long look at your skills and talents and choose volunteer experiences that will bolster your expertise. My network is two or three times the size it was before I started volunteering, and the best experience on my résumé is my volunteer work. Both the relationships and the experience have opened doors for me that I never dreamed I'd be able to walk through.

You may not have a lot of free time, but everyone can carve out some time to help with one charity. If you are a parent of school-aged children, you can help out at your children's school in a variety of short-term volunteer assignments. A short-term assignment might be a one-time event such as planning a fund-raiser. A longer-term assignment might be serving as president of the parent-teacher organization. If you have enough time, drive, and interest, you might want to serve on the school board. If you are active in your church, you may want to serve in a short-term role such as greeter or volunteer more time to teach a Bible study or Sunday school class. Many people like to join civic clubs such as Kiwanis, Rotary, Lions, or Optimists because the club participates in a few charity causes, and all the club's members work on their events. Your company may allow you the time and opportunity to serve on the board of directors of a local non-profit organization. The options are endless.

While you want to focus on the destination (or "begin with the end in mind" as Stephen Covey suggests in *Seven Habits of Highly Effective People*), goals are really more about attaining the right tools and preparing for the journey. It's more difficult to make a trip to somewhere you've never been without a map or transportation.

Use the Right Words and Incorporate Action Verbs — Lots of Them

Include components that ensure success. Use the SMART model for structuring your goals (specific, measurable, achievable, realistic, and time-bound to a deadline). Tony Robbins, motivational speaker and business coach, says we need to have an RPM Plan: Know the RESULT you want, know your PURPOSE, and compose a MASSIVE ACTION plan.

Writing your goals with a specific, positive, active voice will help you implement change in your life faster. Hhhmmm ... perhaps everything we say should be said with a specific, positive, active voice and maybe every day would be a more powerful, purpose-driven experience. That's just something to think about.

Here are some examples of typical goals. See the difference between using a negative voice and using a specific, positive, active voice.

> Negative: Stop eating food that is bad for me.
> Positive: Eat fruit and yogurt instead of chips and candy.
>
> Negative: Don't watch television or play video games after supper.
> Positive: Go for a thirty-minute walk after supper.

Most goals rely on creating new habits to replace old habits. It requires an average of twenty-one days to form a habit, and the secret lies in the commitment to invest the time. However, choosing the right language will help you reframe your habits in your mind. Writing your goals in a way that reflects the new habits you need to form will increase your success.

Find an Accountability Partner

You probably have a long list of people who would gladly stand in line to hold you accountable. Sharing your goals with other people means that they can ask you about your progress occasionally so they can encourage you. You also feel like you let them down if you haven't made progress when they check in with you.

If you really want to kick this up a notch, get into a mastermind group. It is a group of people who serve as your accountability partners as well as your personal board of directors. It is often made up of people with varying expertise in different businesses — a good thing because they bring different ideas and perspective to the table without worrying about anyone stealing their market competitiveness. However, you may find some mastermind groups that meet only by phone who are in the same type of business such as realtors who are working only in their local or regional market. They can use ideas that they learn from realtors in other parts of the country.

Write a Variety of Goals and Keep the Number of Goals Realistic

Write some long-term goals (three to five years), mid-range goals (one to three years), and short-term goals (one year or less). Break this year's goals down by quarters. Often, your short-term goals are steps to achieving your long-term goals. Try to limit yourself to three to five goals in each category. Having too many goals dilutes your focus.

I've spent decades being goal-focused and invested months of time designing my goals for the upcoming year. After one personally challenging year, I experienced something that had never happened before — I had made progress on my goals, but I had completed very few of them. I thought maybe they were the wrong goals but upon careful evaluation, I realized they were good goals but God had just made other plans for my life that year. I decided to keep the entire set and vowed to work on them another year. The only two goals I added were simply to experience joy and brag on the people in my life. I made good progress on my goals the next year, and I did indeed experience lots of joy and bragged on the people in my life.

One thing that I've discovered is that some goals belong on your list every year. The outcome doesn't have to be more or less than the previous year to be successful. Sometimes that's a sign that you've found your "sweet spot" — that place where your life is in perfect rhythm in that area. I leave those items on my list of goals just to make sure I keep my focus balanced.

Push Beyond What You Believe Is Achievable

I spent two years as the president of our local chapter of the American Society for Training and Development (ASTD). When I asked the officers to set goals, some set "safe" goals. Those are the kind of goals that you'd probably achieve if you just showed up for life. Those are goals people have learned to turn in for their performance evaluations at work because their annual raises depend on how well they meet their goals. No matter how low they are, if they meet them, they are still successful.

Safe goals are one of the most dangerous things you can do to your future Here is the funny think about goals: if you have a goal of any size, you'll only shoot for that goal. If it is a low goal and you reach it, you've met your goal but it really wasn't that spectacular. If you set a high goal, you also stand a chance of reaching it. If you create an environment that provides a safety net for failure when people don't quite reach that "stretch" goal, you offer people the chance to work in a high-performance environment.

Be willing to fail. You don't meet goals that you don't set. If you set a goal at 200 percent of what you believe is achievable, are you a failure if you only make 120 percent of the achievable goal? Of course not — you're extraordinary! Besides, achievable goals are for sissies and you are definitely not a sissy.

When I received "safe" goals from some of the ASTD chapter officers, I went back and multiplied them by two. I didn't want to meet safe goals — I wanted the officers to see the magic of setting fearless goals in an environment where it was safe to fail. Did we meet every 200-percent goal? Of course not, but we far exceeded every one of their original safe goals.

Keep Your Goals Out In Front of You

Post your list of goals on your closet door or in another location that you visit at least once a day. I post mine in my bathroom and review them each morning when I brush my teeth. I keep a set at my desk so I can review them there too. I have my best success when I choose the most important ones and ask myself, "What am I doing today to achieve that goal?"

Mark LeBlanc, professional speaker, business consultant, and author of *Small Business Success* requires his clients to ask themselves in the morning, "What am I doing today to meet my goal?" At the end of the day, they must also ask, "What did I do today to meet my goal?" I've been through his Achiever's Circle program (www.markleblanc.com), and it was one of the best investments in my business that I could have made. It provided me the opportunity to clarify my focus.

If you are responsible for a company or organization, make sure you keep those goals in front of the whole organization. One of the most common reasons goals are not achieved is that they are put in a nice notebook and filed away on a shelf and seldom reviewed.

If your goals are worth writing, they are important to your organization's success. Put them on big signs on the wall near the areas where all employees walk such as the break room. Print the goals on bookmarks and given them to employees for their day planners. Quiz employees at team meetings about the goals. Monitor the progress toward the goals and report the progress to the team. Better yet, ask each team to report on their progress toward the goals. This will keep individuals engaged in their progress, and they will know their peers will hold them accountable.

Final Thoughts on the Hard Skills Necessary for Becoming a Person of Influence

You are on your way to becoming a person of influence and your best days are ahead. There is some chance that you are feeling a bit intimidated and un-empowered about harnessing the power of your experience and expertise. If you are, please start by writing some easy goals. After twenty years, I look back fondly at my first written goals that included earning my bachelor's degree as a working parent. I look at how that one important goal set the stage for the future goals I would never have even dreamed were possible at the time.

I hope you took inventory of the experiences and expertise you had in all areas of your life. That list will guide you in many areas of your life. Don't take anything for granted because you never know when something like "volunteered at my daughter's school" can translate to "organized a fund-raising team with twenty parents that raised $12,000 with a net profit of $11,750" or "conducted a feasibility study and wrote a business plan for running a school bookstore to fund the gifted-and-talented program." Something like that looks really sharp on a résumé.

Most of all, I hope you believe that anything is possible if you just plan for the possibilities.

- Our customers (internal and external) depend on us to have up-to-date information. Your level of expertise can differentiate you from others. Those who are not a student of their field will become extinct.
- Your experience can strengthen your character and resilience, but it can also be a selling point. In every place where people work together, finding the right fit is crucial to team success. Life experiences shape who people become. Our experiences often shape the values that drive us and the stories that we have to tell. The stories from our life are one of the best ways to teach others and create a legacy.
- Goals are miracles simply waiting to happen. If something is important, create a plan for making it happen.
- Your personal goals must complement your professional goals. Success is a casualty of professional or personal goals that don't line up.

Goal Worksheet

Reflect on these questions, and write your responses. These will provide you a strong foundation to build your goals on.

Purpose Statement

What is the reason you are here on earth? What do you think you are supposed to accomplish while you are here?

_____
_____
_____
_____
_____
_____
_____

Financial Goals

What are three key areas you need to address to improve your financial standing?

_____
_____

What is one habit you need to create or break that will make you more successful in this area of your life?

_____

What are some tasks to do every paycheck, month, or quarter that will improve those three key areas?

_____
_____
_____

Fitness/Health/Diet

What are three key areas you need to address to improve your fitness level or health?

_____
_____
_____

What is one habit you need to create or break that will make you more successful in this area of your life?

_____

What are some tasks to do every day, week, or month to improve those three key areas?

_____
_____
_____

Family/Spiritual/Emotional/Mental

What are three key areas you need to address to improve your family, or spiritual, emotional, or mental well-being?

_____
_____
_____

What is one habit you need to create or break that will make you more successful in this area of your my life?

_____

What are some tasks to do every day, week, or month to improve those three key areas?

_____
_____
_____
_____

Community Mission Statements

What community service roles do you fill? Create a mission statement for every organization you serve. Your mission statement will include your role, the tasks you want to accomplish, and your plan for accomplishing them.

Volunteer Role/Organization #1

_____
_____
_____
_____
_____
_____

Volunteer Role/Organization #2

_____
_____
_____
_____
_____
_____

Volunteer Role/Organization #3

_____
_____
_____
_____
_____
_____

Professional

What are three key areas you need to address to improve your business practices or your professional future?

_____

_____

_____

_____

What is one habit you need to create or break that will make you more successful in business?

_____

What is one skill you need to learn that will make you more successful in business?

_____

What is one professional service or type of employee you need to hire to be more successful?

_____

Want to Download Your Goal Worksheet?

To download a copy of this worksheet in a Microsoft Word format, go to www.soarhigher.com/networkingtools.htm.

CHAPTER 13
The Unspoken Rules For Becoming a Person of Influence

We hold people of influence in high regard, but we don't always know why. It's like there's some secret code or maybe they are just born influential — like a Kennedy. It's really not magic though — it's just the product of a series of experiences, choices, and goals that positions them there. However, those three tools that positioned them originally can't guarantee they'll flourish there. They are simply the keys to the executive suite that open the door. What they do once they get there determines their true success and the quality and longevity of their personal brand. The staying power of a person of influence depends heavily on his or her ability to acquire and sustain a very distinct set of characteristics.

Anyone can become a person of influence. You don't need a title, and you don't need to wait for someone to anoint you with leadership oil. Whenever you refer a fellow employee to a realtor who does an outstanding job helping him find the perfect home, you are a person of influence. Your friend is scared to death of dentists but absolutely must go because she's in pain. When you tell her about your dentist who makes her feel relaxed and safe, you are a person of influence. When you pass your cousin's résumé along to your human resources manager and the company offers her a job, you are a person of influence.

This chapter is about the characteristics of a person of influence. I can't think of anything more important to your brand than embracing these characteristics as part of your personal truth. Becoming a person of influence is a matter of mastering a set of qualities that involve your personal contact with others, calling, grace, humility, consistency, dependability, values, courage, character, sense of urgency, servant-leadership, ability to help others discover their personal genius, and interest in serving something bigger than yourself. Master these and you own the executive suite as well as almost any other thing you desire.

Willingness to Maintain Personal Contact with Your Customers

One of the first big lessons I learned as a business owner was the power of presence. No one should work for themselves if they can't stand to sell their company, their product, or themselves. Unfortunately, many business owners live for the day when they can hire a salesperson and enough staff so they can get out of the public eye. While they are paying someone else to take care of the less-comfortable part of running a business, they are giving up something that is highly valued by their customers — personal exposure.

Potential clients as well as existing clients get really excited when they get to do business with the business owner or a high-ranking leader in the company. While making personal contact at networking events and delivering your products to your customer may take valuable time, customers feel honored when a business owner does that. Something as simple as a follow-up card or phone call makes a huge difference to a customer. No matter how big your business grows, your professional image can always be a defining element of your branding strategy.

Personal exposure builds trust in your company. When your company is large, it offers a human element. People don't do business with companies — they do business with people. When Dave Thomas, restaurateur and founder of Wendy's restaurants, was still alive, he was the face of Wendy's that you saw on the commercials. We liked the food at Wendy's, but we felt like we were doing business with Dave.

Michael Shassere owned a sign and banner company called Logoworks in Rogers, Arkansas. After a successful career working for a consumer package goods company, he bought this small business and expanded it. He ran the business, but he realized that he was the best person to sell for the company. He hired salespeople and invested in their training, but they could never accomplish what he could.

Since he had payroll to make every two weeks, he was probably a bit more

Professional Image and Interpersonal Skills Make a Big Impression on Customers

Here are a few quick tips for those business owners who want to make the best splash with their customers through their image and interpersonal skills:

- **Strive to create customers for life.** Be customer-focused in everything you do. Treating them the way YOU want to be treated (Golden Rule) AND the way THEY want to be treated (Platinum Rule) will make a substantial investment in a lifelong business relationship.

- **Put your professional biography on your website or in your business proposals.** Write your bio so that it shows what you can do for your customer. People care what you know, but they care more about what you can do for them.

- **Be genuinely interested in other people, and become an active listener.** Ask questions to help you understand and clarify their needs. Customers don't care how much you know until they know how much you care. You don't have to be a people-person to become people-oriented. If you skipped Chapter 4: Leading Meaningful Conversations, go back and read it. It's an important investment in your success.

- **Display impeccable manners.** Always extend a ready, firm handshake and show courtesy though the language you choose with words such as please, thank you, sir, and ma'am. All people at all ages appreciate great manners.

- **Pay special attention to your phone etiquette as it is often the primary contact you'll have with some customers.** In a time when everyone packs a phone everywhere they go, you phone manners are on display to people you aren't even talking to.

- **Wear your company logo and display it everywhere possible.** If you drive a vehicle with your company logo, make sure you drive with courtesy too.

- **Handle your stress with grace.** How you address the daily challenges defines you as a person of influence to everyone you come into contact with. When we're the brand, we are always on display to our current customers as well as our potential customers.

motivated than a typical salesperson. However, part of his sales power was that he was the man in charge, and he valued his customers enough to make personal contact. Other business leaders know how busy people like them are, so they appreciate the gesture. When you are serviced by a staff member who treats you like every other customer, you feel like you are just doing business with a company. However, when people did business directly with Michael, they were doing business with a person.

Personal contact builds trust in you and your company because customers realize they are dealing directly with the decision maker. People like to do business with people they know. People who ask for a referral from a trusted peer are less likely to base their buying decision on price. Even if they do and prices are close, they will choose the company with the track record and people they know.

Be willing to become the brand for your company. The more you connect your personal brand and your company's image, the more success you'll achieve.

Knowing and Living Your Calling

In our day-to-day life, we get so tied up with the urgent things and simple survival. It's easy to lose focus on what is important. We all have a purpose for our time here. The challenge is in figuring it out and then knowing when an old purpose transitions into a new purpose.

Resolving to manage those priorities and challenges means giving up some fun but not the satisfying meaningful pursuits. I miss things like quilting and watching television, but when I realized those things wouldn't leave a useful legacy — okay maybe the quilt would be useful if I actually finished it — I willingly let them go. Instead, I devote my leisure time to volunteer work and writing because that's what I feel called to do.

For some people, their life's calling means spending thirty years with a company putting in a hard day's work every day. Their legacy is modeling loyalty and work ethic to other employees for all that time. And don't forget their efforts that served the company's customers.

Sometimes the activities required to be able to pursue the more meaningful pursuits aren't really all that fun. For instance, I have a back injury and if I don't weight train on a regular basis, the pain prevents me from being as effective as I could be in living my calling.

But here's the beautiful part — when I'm living my purpose and calling, I'm on fire. Every sense is heightened, I'm alert, and my thoughts are clear and positive. I believe I can accomplish anything. Even though there are frustrations along the way and the work can be exhausting, I find the ability to overcome the challenges and keep going. Call it "living in your sweet spot" or whatever, there is nothing like it.

Carrying Yourself with Grace and Humility

When you are living your calling and purpose, it's easy to bask in the successes that naturally come. Celebrate them but don't bask long enough to get sunburned. When you are a graceful winner, the world will celebrate with you. When pridefulness rears its ugly head, it seems to steal the sunshine. Life doesn't promise sunshine all the time, but the cloudy days are more frequent when I've let my pride get the best of me.

On the other hand, when I remember that all my experiences happen because God allowed them and give Him the credit, the sunny days are more plentiful. Even in tough times, be thankful for the challenges and consider them learning experiences. Similarly, it's easy for a manager to take responsibility for the great work of her team, but a true leader gives credit to the entire team where credit is due.

Remember, you may need a title to be a manager, but you don't need a title to lead and become a person of influence.

Acting Consistently and Dependably

One of the top expectations people have of us is that we act in a consistent, predictable manner and that we do what we say we are going to do. Of course, that applies to being consistent, predictable, and dependable in a good way — not being consistently bad. People count on us for honesty and dependability. Our children depend on us to tell them the truth and help them form good routines and define boundaries.

Much of the efficiency we are able to gain is due to knowing expectations and forming habits. Humans are creatures of habit and knowing what to expect brings us great comfort. Imagine if your supervisor told you that you didn't need to create a weekly progress report and then downgraded your performance review because you didn't turn in weekly progress reports. You would probably be surprised because he had an expectation that was different from what he told you.

Defining Your Values and Living by Them Courageously

What do you stand for? In the United States, we are fortunate to live in a country where we free to worship because there are so many countries where their people risk dying for their faith. We can start a business without roadblocks and restrictions that are prevalent in other countries. No one tells us how many children we can have, and our women are allowed to wear what they please (within reasonable boundaries, of course). It shouldn't surprise you that a shocking number of people take these simple freedoms for granted.

It is easy to stand by your values when they are the same as everyone else's values. However, your beliefs and values are not always the same as those around you. What if you suddenly decided that your company was doing something unethical? Your gut feeling is that you should report it, right? What if your son needs a liver transplant, and you badly need the company's insurance coverage? You can't stay at the company after you report it because the guilty individuals will make your life miserable. To make matters worse, jobs in your community are tough to find. What would you do in those circumstances? Could doing the right thing cost your child his life or destroy your financial security?

Most of us probably won't face decisions with such serious consequences. It's a true test of character to stand by your values in challenging times. Most people cringe at the thought of challenging something that goes against their values. Why are people who do wrong things also people who will get in your face and make you feel like a villain when you challenge their actions?

I've been fortunate to work for ethical employers and have rarely had to deal with times that challenged my values and character. I wish I could say the same thing about some of the people I've encountered in my volunteer work. I've had to confront a teacher who cheated on a school silent auction (the same teacher didn't pay for her pizza at the fund-raiser either). I've had sponsors suggest sponsorship trades for products that were far more their product's value. I've had to deal with the awkward discussion about why we couldn't accept a painting of a naked man for a silent auction where children would be present. While these weren't life-threatening challenges of my values, they were awkward confrontations. In all cases, the party on the other end of the conflict thought they were doing no wrong.

Situations like these hone your ability to act quickly. In some situations, I doubted my value system and didn't follow my heart. Instead of handling the situation immediately, I waited until I got more information and other opinions. Waiting made the confrontation more difficult and the situation more complicated to correct. Through those experiences, I've learned to trust my instincts and defend my values in tough times as well as easy times.

Being courageous was difficult at first. I wasn't taught how to handle opposition, and that took practice. Also, many of my values were imprinted on me from my family, and I didn't really understand why those were the right values. If I had understood more about the background, it might have prepared me for making a black-and-white decision. Instead, I found that simply knowing something is wrong alone didn't prepare me to defend it when the time came. As I matured and developed my own values based on my own life experiences and what I learned from others, I found that I "owned" my values. Ownership made it easier to stand by them in a way that allowed me to courageously risk it all.

What if one of your values is living your faith in your professional life as well as your personal life? The United States was based on religious values and oddly, as the government removes faith from the schools and from our government, there is a rising interest in bringing faith into the workplace.

When you profess your faith to your clients and business associates, they look at you and your business differently. For some reason, people think that if you are a Christian, you must be perfect.

It's incredibly risky to display the ichthys — know as the Christian "fish" symbol used for centuries — in your marketing and advertising materials. It gives people a right to hold you to a different standard. People will expect you to run your business with high quality, ethics, truth, and the Golden Rule. If you stick the symbol on your car, people expect you to drive with utmost courtesy. Placing your faith out for the public to see is like putting your life out there for people to judge. Those who may not know how to live their faith often think that Christians are perfect — or at least think they are perfect. True Christians use that symbol as a reminder to themselves or to profess their faith.

Although I'm a Christian, I choose not to display the fish on my business marketing materials or my car. I believe if you have to tell someone you're a Christian, maybe you aren't doing a good enough job incorporating your faith and your values into your actions. I'm sure that just made the hair stand up on some necks. You actions will always speak louder than your words (or your symbols).

My friend told me about a collision she was in with a minivan that had a fish emblem on the back. The other driver had pulled out in front of her, and my friend couldn't stop in time. The woman who was driving the minivan jumped out and didn't tell the police officer an accurate story. My friend tells it like it is, and she called the woman on her untrue story. The woman exclaimed, "I would never lie. I'm a Christian." Not only did the woman lie, she used her faith to sway the police officer to believe her story. My friend was angry with the woman and anybody else with a fish emblem on their vehicle for a long time.

Christians can make mistakes, cut people off in traffic accidentally (and sometimes on purpose), and do wrong things just like everyone else. For someone who doesn't necessarily buy in to "the whole faith movement," those things can push that person away. A simple symbol could make a person who is struggling in their faith feel less worthy and resentful of the "holier than thou" people in their world. And besides, a fish symbol on their business card does not guarantee that they are a good business to deal with — it says nothing about their qualifications, time in business, or customer service. Bad businesses who display the fish symbol give Christians a bad name.

It's much more powerful to use our actions to demonstrate our faith and values to the world. When we make a mistake, we have a chance to demonstrate how Christians handle and overcome their mistakes and solve problems. When we are fair and honest, it sends a powerful message. Treating our customers the way God would want us to and using practices that Jesus might have used gives us a chance to glorify God in a way that a symbol can't. Your actions and your words are the things that reputations and brands are made of. The beautiful thing about living your life by faith is that it gives you the courage to stand by your values and your character in challenging times as well as good times.

WorkMatters (www.workmatters.org) is an organization devoted to the movement of bridging the gap between faith and work. WorkMatters president David Roth quoted trucking giant J.B. Hunt one time at a WorkMatters breakfast event. J.B. Hunt invested an hour every morning reading the Bible and praying. David recalled, "He was talking about his quiet time in the morning and he said, 'I'm just amazed at how God gives me ideas about business deals I'm working on when I sit in my favorite chair and read the Bible and pray.'" J.B.'s values were instrumental in his success, and he inspired many people to live and work differently through his example.

Speak and Live with Truth and Honor

No matter how private we think we are, our lives, choices, and values are on display for the world. We don't realize that people are watching and learning from our actions every day. Others can see things about us that we don't realize they see. Sometimes they are misjudging, but they see who we are with amazing clarity. That's why it is critical that we be congruent — being the same person in our personal life as we are in our professional life.

Congruence is a key factor in being viewed as someone who is sincere, honest, and transparent. It can be as simple as saying what you mean (and feel), and meaning (and feeling) what you say. You don't have to share everything you think about everything, but people need to feel they know the real you to trust you. For this reason, people who are living unethically in any part of their life will never be considered ethical in their professional life. Business author John Maxwell says, "There are no business ethics; there are only ethics."

Here is how this plays out in real life. Motivational speaker and business consultant Michael Fortino was at the top of his game. His company was the Center for Lifestyle Management, and his website touted him as an author and speaker whose clients included Exxon, the Air Force, and AT&T. He was a well-paid and in-demand speaker who helped organizations and their staff overcome obstacles.

He was on the road in November 2005 traveling to a speaking engagement for a non-profit organization's board retreat. He began having computer problems the day he left. Once he landed at his destination, he took his computer to the local Best Buy store for help. They ran a diagnostic scan to look for problems like viruses and spyware. In the process, they also found over 1,000 pornographic images — many were sexually explicit pictures involving children.

He didn't make it to his speaking engagement the next day. The store technicians called local police, and he was arrested. Over the next year,

Michael Fortino watched the intimate details of his life laid out for his family, trial participants, and the public to see. Not only did he possess pornography, he had been making his own movies involving underage girls. His opulent life which included a wife, an executive home in Pennsylvania, and a successful consulting practice had suddenly tarnished.

Michael's experience wasn't caused by one bad choice that just about anyone could have made. It involved a long series of bad judgments, addiction, and lies. His behavior had transformed from a series of bad choices to an unethical lifestyle. Michael was tried in federal court and originally received a 135-month prison sentence with a $10,000 fine and twenty years of supervised probation upon his release. He had gotten a light sentence because he had helped with the prosecution of another child porn case in California. However, there is more to the story.

The mother of his infant daughter in Arkansas called prosecutors to ask about the outcome of the sentence. They were surprised to learn she was disappointed the sentence was so lenient — something odd considering that she allegedly wrote a two-page letter asking for leniency that was presented in Michael's defense. It prompted an investigation of the evidence in the case. The letter she allegedly wrote had her name misspelled and contained the wrong birth date of Michael's daughter. When she was called to testify, she told the court that he told her he had broken up with his longtime girlfriend, he'd never been married, and he lived on a yacht on Lake Erie. He, in fact, lived with his wife and family in Pittsburgh, Pennsylvania.

It wasn't all a lie. There was, in fact, a boat where he had videotaped three girls changing clothes who were 11, 13, and 16 years old — caught with a hidden camera in its changing room. There were two other forged letters fabricated for this case. One was allegedly written by the father of one of the girls who stated he forgave Michael for videotaping his young daughter while she was changing into a bathing suit. He also seriously undervalued his net worth in the financial information he provided to the probation office. Michael failed to mention his mini-yacht, his 9,000-square-foot home, several bank accounts, or the number of real estate properties he owned. A local newspaper reporter wrote, "The judge remarked at one point that he didn't think there was anybody Fortino hadn't lied to and that there is 'a serious problem with Mr. Fortino's ability to provide the truth.' ... 'I regard what has happened here to be extremely serious,' [Judge] Hendren said."

When it was said and done, Michael Fortino's attorney quit, and the judge increased the sentence to the maximum twenty years and the maximum $250,000 fine. An Internet blogger said, "Imagine my family's surprise and dismay when we discovered earlier this year that we were living next to a sex offender. Although I wouldn't wish eleven years in federal prison on anybody, I find it hard to feel too much sympathy for a guy who had us over for sundaes (with our two young daughters) and actively deceived us. When I realized what he was about and deduced he was probably trying to groom us for an opportunity to check out our daughters, it was pretty much a no-brainer to establish a clear and impermeable boundary between us and him. Ultimately, he should have known better and not given in to his deviant sexual impulses. I guess he's probably realizing that now."

I couldn't have said it better myself. A pretty boy like Michael Fortino will likely be very popular in prison. When he does see the light of day as a free man, he won't be able to have unsupervised contact with children or access to the Internet and must register as a sex offender.

In my work with professional speakers, I'm astounded by what a high calling the profession is and what a privilege it is to address an audience. Just being invited to ascend the platform automatically positions a speaker as a leader. Speakers have the chance to share their experiences and ideas. They earn the ability to change the lives of more people though their work than they realize. Just changing the outlook of a single audience member could empower that individual to inspire a generation.

When an organization hires a speaker, the organization is buying a program or message and the speaker's platform presence. However, the speaker's professionalism and character are the value-added services they provide. When a speaker is the same ethical, honest, and caring person on the platform and off, it reinforces the validity of the message. It proves the power of the platform exists and makes a case for the responsibility of the speaker to live the message they teach on the platform. When a speaker like Michael Fortino lets his personal indiscretions and addictions overcome his ability to manage his life, he squanders his future potential and discourages the thousands of people who were formerly inspired by his messages.

A client once told me why his company no longer purchased training classes from a particular training company. He had gone to a training class a little early and noticed the trainer was sitting at the bar preparing for his class. The trainer downed two vodka martinis before he went in to teach a program on confident communication. That particular company was in bankruptcy at the time of our conversation, and they were paying some of the lowest trainer fees in the industry. If the trainers wanted to make a good income, they had to sell huge amounts of supplemental training materials to the attendees from the product sales table in the back of the classroom. Attendees paid affordable class fees in exchange for the right for these trainers to give product pitches during the programs.

These were trainers who traveled from city to city delivering training programs. They risked their lives as they gave their all to the training class in one city and then jumped into a car fatigued to drive to the next city where they were scheduled to deliver training the next day. Many of the best trainers left the company to find jobs where the working conditions were better (and safer). The trainers that were left were those like the communication trainer who needed a couple of stiff drinks in order to hide the fact that he couldn't speak with truth and honor. The only person he was fooling was himself.

The more public our lives become, the more transparent we are whether we like it or not. Whether it's our personal or professional image, living the congruent life we'd be proud of showing off to our grandmother or to God is crucial to becoming a person of influence. Our personal truth will always define us. Choose to live a life of ethics and integrity.

Making Decisions with a Sense of Urgency

People of influence understand that they must seize the moment. If you don't reach out and snag the brass ring, someone else will. My husband is great at deciding what he wants and making the purchase immediately. I, on the other hand, have to weigh all the options and then decide whether we should spend the money. My motto is, "Just because you can doesn't mean you should." One of us had to be practical and frugal or we would never have a dime saved for retirement.

Indecision is the greatest enemy to the ability to act with a high sense of urgency. One of my huge challenges is not being confident enough in my judgment to trust my first decision. It was holding me back in all areas of my life. I would face a decision — it could be as simple as choosing a new countertop for my bathroom remodel — and I would know what the choice should be when I first started. Then, the madness would set in. I would carefully evaluate the multitude of other choices and then I would waffle and play the "what if" game. I was terrified that I would have buyer's regret! When it was said and done, I would finally wind up with the first choice I made. I could have saved a ton of time by trusting my first instinct.

My husband and I wanted a Corvette for years. We knew we would own one someday. When we shopped for the last car, we drove every sports car available. It came down to a Corvette and a BMW Z3 convertible. Both were comparably priced but I couldn't wipe the smile off my face when I drove the Corvette. However, being the practical mom I am, I consulted the *Consumer Reports Auto Buying Guide*. It didn't rate the Corvette as high as it did the Z3. That made my decision. I went the practical route — I chose the white Z3 with the tan convertible top as my daily driver because *Consumer Reports* liked it better.

Although the BMW was safe and reliable, I realize that you don't buy that kind of a car when you are worried about being practical, reliable, and safe. You buy a sports car because it makes your heart race. I loved the BMW for five years, but I never got that feeling I had when I testdrove a Corvette.

The day came when my husband thought we should look at Corvettes again. I had determined that we should buy one that was two or three years old, and I wasn't sure if I could be so decadent to get a convertible. It cost a lot more than the hard top, and the Corvette didn't have the roll bars like the Z3 — in case we flipped the car. I was being "practical mom" again. If you know anything about rollover accidents, they rarely happen to a car with such a low center of gravity. Never mind that I only drive about ten miles a day and rarely get on the interstate.

One cool spring evening on our way to dinner, we drove by this luxury pre-owned dealership. It was a small unassuming place, but they always parked their "eye candy" by the street, and I always lovingly gazed at all the choices — I really love beautiful cars. I have always loved American muscle cars, and this dealership always kept a fresh selection of Corvettes on hand.

There it sat twinkling in the late-day sunshine — our dream car. It was an eight-month-old Corvette with everything on it except miles. It sat in someone's garage and only had 1,300 miles on it. It was black with a tan convertible top and interior. It did everything for you except turn itself on and steer. We bought it a few days later, and I would sneak out to the garage just to look at it. It was stunning, and I still can't believe that I get to drive it. In the driver's seat, I couldn't wipe the smile off my face. Wow! Was this what it felt like to be spoiled? I was absolutely giddy!

Nevertheless, I had this nagging feeling that we had bought something too decadent. I felt so rushed by my husband in the car decision. I wanted to make sure we were making a good solid decision, and I had done all the research. He was afraid that someone would snap it up, and we'd miss the chance to own this car. I was worried that we were making a bad snap decision that we'd pay for later. The practical side of me said, "That black car is going to be so much hotter in the summer than the white Z3 was." "This paint is going to show swirls in time. How long will the paint look this beautiful?" "This black car looks dirty so much faster than the white Z3 did. I don't have time to wash a car more often than I do now!"

Not thirty days later, I drove by the same dealership, and I saw something that took my breath away — it was a nearly new white Corvette with a tan convertible top. I thought, "I knew I acted too soon. If I just had just waited, I could have gotten the white car and then the paint wouldn't show dirt and those subtle little scratches that happen over time. It would have been much cooler in the summer too!" I mentioned it to my husband, and he gave me the look — you know the one. It's the confused look that just proves that he doesn't understand what I'm talking about. He LOVES the black Corvette because it's stunning today and he's always wanted one. He doesn't care what it will look like in ten years. Hmmph! Impractical man.

Silly me intentionally drove by the dealership several times over the next few days and questioned my judgment even though it was clearly too late. I studied the white Corvette and noticed the sunlight didn't dance joyously on the white car like it did on the black one. The chrome wheels didn't glimmer against the white car as much. The headlights didn't look quite as sleek on the white one either. And the Corvette logo didn't pop off the white car like it did on the black one. Even though the white one would feel the same when I was going zero to sixty in four seconds, and it would tuck down into the corners like the black one, the white one didn't look as powerful. I finally came to my senses and determined that I had developed buyer's remorse because I didn't make a "practical mom" choice. I reminded myself that YOU DON'T BUY A CORVETTE BECAUSE IT'S PRACTICAL. YOU BUY IT BECAUSE IT IS YOUR DREAM CAR, IT LEAVES YOU BREATHLESS, AND IT MAKES YOU FEEL LIKE A ROCK

STAR. Practical decision or not, I have to live with it now. I bet I know how to make the best of it. ;-)

One of my greatest personal struggles has been to reprogram myself to realize that it's not the end of the world if I make a less-than-stellar decision. We learn far more from our mistakes than our successes. Most of us are fortunately equipped with the skills to overcome a faulty decision as long as we don't start with the biggest one we could make. Overcoming mistakes teaches us coping skills and resiliency. When we don't practice making quick decisions during less-risky times, we aren't prepared to act when we face adversity in unfamiliar territory.

History's greatest leaders learned to trust their instincts and act even when they didn't have all the information they needed to make a sure decision. Their ability to make decisions, show a sense of urgency, and act fearlessly defined their personal brand. They weren't born with it, but they bravely took bigger and riskier chances that defined them as people of influence. Tomorrow's courageous leadership starts with a willingness to take smaller risks today.

Acting on Requests with a Sense of Urgency

We are presented with requests every day. We start the day out with our to-do list and then the requests get stacked on top as the day goes on. Our supervisors count on us to be available to handle whatever tasks they hand us. Our family members have needs — even our pets have requests for us. Most of these requests are options, and the requestor knows it. However, addressing those items with the sense of urgency they deserve will define you in their eyes.

My to-do list is long and contains the exact number of items I can handle in a single day if I get no interruptions, everything goes as planned, and no one requests anything else at the spur of the moment. I am an efficiency machine when it comes to planning my day.

Like everyone else who serves anyone and lives in this flawed world, I am met with interruptions, delays, and urgent requests. I do whatever any other normal person would do — step up, help others, and move my to-do list around. Besides, what person on their deathbed got really excited about finishing everything on their to-do lists?

The people in our lives — supervisors, coworkers, customers, friends, and family members — need our help sometimes, and we need theirs too. I look at handling requests with a sense of urgency two ways:

- I'm demonstrating that I am an interested and helpful partner in their success.
- I'm putting favors in a bank that I may need to call on later in the form of pay raises, promotions, or simply assistance.

Sometimes we don't know what we need, but we just know we need help. We ask and hopefully someone says, "Yes, I can help you!" Occasionally someone steps in and solves a problem in such a wonderful and unexpected way that you tell others.

My husband and I like to eat at Rib Crib, a Tulsa-based barbeque restaurant (www.ribcrib.com). The food is always very good quality, and the service is fast and pleasant. One evening, I ordered a catfish dinner and my husband ordered a pork sandwich. When I cut into my catfish, I realized it wasn't fully cooked. The server very apologetically corrected the problem with the fish while I ate my onion rings and fried okra. The cook was new, and he had simply pushed the wrong timer button. It was an easy mistake to make.

All I really wanted was some cooked fish which they provided cheerfully and quickly. But then, they did something I didn't expect. The server said he was giving me my meal for free. It wasn't required, and it really surprised me.

On another visit there, our server had taken our order, and brought us our appetizer. We noticed our food was taking a little longer than usual, but we were still snacking on our appetizer. Finally, our food arrived and our meal was cooked perfectly. Our server asked us if we needed anything else and then she said, "The kitchen took too long to get your meal, so I'm going to give you the hamburger for free." I assured her it wasn't necessary, but she insisted it was the right thing to do.

The server was in my line of sight for our entire visit. I saw her talking with cook, and I never saw her talk with the manager on duty. She knew her job, knew how long it should take to prepare a meal, and felt empowered enough to take care of the problem in a way she felt comfortable with. You bet she got a great tip, and we have been back many times. If those two trips hadn't ended on such a positive note, I'm not so sure we'd still frequent Rib Crib like we do. I know there are restaurants we don't go to anymore because they made a mistake in quality or service that they didn't even acknowledge. Customers vote with their dollars. They don't spend their money where their needs aren't satisfied with a sense of urgency.

I worked at a Long John Silver's Seafood Restaurant while I was in school. I knew my job well, and I went through the motions serving food to customers. However, I really didn't understand what SERVING the customers meant nor did I understand that I had complete control over their experience at our little fast-food restaurant simply by doing something unexpected.

One manager, Steve Wheelock, did things differently than all the other managers I worked with over the five years I spent with the company. Most managers would dish up the food on the plates because they were usually faster than the other employees. They could monitor preparation and portion control during rush times better that way too. During a busy evening, Steve would ask a proficient employee to dish up the food while he took orders or assisted customers as they came through the line. Then he would go out to the dining room and talk with customers. It gave him a chance to thank them for coming in while he checked the cleanliness of the dining room. He would even clean tables if the other employees were busy.

If Steve thought customers had to wait too long for an order, he would offer them a piece of pie. They didn't always take him up on the offer, but I guarantee that I saw them come back again. If he had unhappy customers he couldn't satisfy — and we all have customers that seem more difficult than others in perfect situations — he would ask them what they would like for him to do. He would do his best to satisfy their requests. I saw him refund the cost of a meal more than once. Those customers who we had honestly done wrong came back again and again. Those customers who were just trying to cheat us out of some free food never seemed to return. For Steve, it wasn't the principle of being right or wrong. He believed that the small amount of profit lost was a big investment in a lifelong customer relationship. Because he acted on the problems proactively, personally, and with a sense of urgency, he was able to save a potentially lost customer relationship.

My former insurance agent could have used a lesson from Steve. From 1986 through 2008, I had not even offered another insurance company a chance to bid on my home and auto insurance. It was the same company that had covered my parents for many years before that. I had been a customer paying for my own insurance since I started driving in 1981. We were great customers, and we had few claims. My agent since my relocation to

Ten Ways to Change Your World by Changing Your Point of View

Life is funny. It's just one learning experience after another, isn't it? People who haven't had one in awhile might need a different point of view. Here are ten ways to change your world by simply changing your perspective.

- **Watch for everyday blessings and miracles.** Wouldn't it be cool if everything came carefully labeled "miracle" or "blessing?" Sometimes the simple things in life such as a cool summer breeze on a hot day when you need to work outside is a simple blessing. Perhaps that narrow miss at a busy intersection was really a miracle. Approach everything that happens as if it were a miracle just to be on the safe side. Possess an attitude of gratitude.

- **Understand your purpose.** Why is it you are here on earth? If you've ever been at a place where nothing seems to be going your way, perhaps you were doing something that didn't line up with your purpose. Once you discover your purpose and then embark on the journey of following it, things fall into place more easily. Ready to find your calling? Start by reading *Purpose Driven Life* by Rick Warren.

- **Set goals and create a plan for your life.** For every person who ever sat around overlooking the obvious while waiting for God to tell them in plain terms what their next step is, here's a news flash — you don't get what you don't ask for. Thoughtfully committing time and energy to goal setting will create a blueprint for guiding your life. When you review those goals daily and submit them to prayer, they become miracles simply waiting to happen. Never be afraid to tackle the seemingly impossible through your goals. Just make sure that all your goals support your purpose for your life. If they don't, it will compromise your ability to achieve them.

- **Get a mentor.** While a mentor's job is to be objective and give you honest feedback, they also see the positive about you. It is a risky thing to give a person feedback, and tough feedback requires an extreme act of bravery. If your mentor gives you feedback, listen objectively, thank him or her, and give it careful consideration. The purpose of mentoring isn't to create a person who becomes a replica of the mentor. Mentoring creates a foundation for reaching our potential by understanding who we were meant to be and gaining insight from the experiences of others.

- **Banish victim mentality.** Even the most pessimistic of us would admit that we run from the victims around us who drag all their baggage behind them. Everyone has tragedy and adversity in varying degrees. Have you ever noticed though that the people who have the greatest reason to succumb to victim mentality are using the experience to grow and expand? Everyone is allowed a certain amount of time to grieve or grumble. After that, it's time to ask themselves what they learned and begin to move on.

- **Eliminate "me-centered language" from your life.** When we get down, we are often afflicted with a case of "me-centeredness" — "Why is this happening to me? What am I going to do? People just don't understand what I'm going through." When people who are too focused on themselves, they often look up to find themselves alone. People just don't want to hang around with those who constantly talk about themselves. Meaningful conversation is two-way communication that enriches the life of the other person. When you find yourself talking too long, turn the conversation around.

- **Focus on things you are passionate about.** What is it that you wake up thinking about? What is your calling? For every single thing that is out of our control, there are a multitude of other things that are within our control that deserve our full attention. Time and energy spent with those things yield dividends that make a difference in ways that you may not immediately see. Sometimes, our days are made up with a series of bland and yucky tasks that require a different perspective. For instance, a new mom's day may be filled with endless housework, dirty laundry, and smelly diapers. Those tasks may seem unfulfilling. However, she's been trusted with an important responsibility — the task of raising an individual who can make a difference in the world. Nothing worth doing is without hard work and sacrifice. Perhaps the purpose of passion is to motivate us through the challenging times.

- **Encourage others.** Something beautiful happens when we lift the spirits of other people — their glow of gratitude lifts us up too. I discovered that it is meaningful to compliment someone on her outfit or hair. However, to pay the most profound and sincere compliments, you must create meaningful conversation to learn more about others. That is not always an easy task. People who need compliments the most are sometimes the people most difficult to engage in conversation. The outcome is worth the effort though. On a side note, I've learned the task of looking for the good in others makes it difficult to find the time to feel sorry for myself.

- **Pray for others.** One of the most powerful benefits of networking and creating meaningful conversation for me is the insight I get into the needs and interests of others. I consider it a high calling to pray for the needs of others. Even when we are most helpless in a situation, we can still pray. Prayer is really the most powerful and important thing we can do, but sometimes we can help in other ways too. Sometimes it's just not God's will, but I get really charged when I see prayers answered. There's nothing like a miracle to restore my faith in the human race.

Arkansas in 1992 was formerly a district manager but was really easing into a slower workday. Mostly, his assistants handled any requests and needs his clients had.

If I came in on a day he was in the office, he'd sometimes peek his head out of his office and speak to me briefly. If I had an insurance question about my coverage, he would answer my questions with as little engagement as possible. I didn't understand what I was buying, and he never offered to explain it. He was the insurance expert, and I thought he was making sure we were covered for whatever we needed. I really trusted him.

One day, that relationship changed with the agent and the company. My husband's father passed away, and he rented a twenty-foot-long box truck to transport his father's belongings back to our house 1,300 miles away. It was late one night and my husband, Tom, ran over one of the bollards that protect the gas pumps at a convenience store. He was fatigued and didn't think to take a photo of the damaged bollard with his cell phone's camera. He felt the truck rock a little, but the truck didn't have any damage. In fact, he wasn't sure he even ran over it, but he suspected he had. He went inside to give his insurance information to the clerk who didn't know what to do. She was unaware it had even happened. Four days later, the manager of the store called Tom to work out the details.

When we called our insurance company to report it, our agent's assistant immediately forwarded us to their claims-handling service that they outsource to another company. We passed along the contact information to the store manager. The claims handler called the manager and immediately informed him that our insurance policy wouldn't cover his damage. Imagine how it felt when we heard that information first from the store manager. In fact, the claims handler didn't call us and tell us at all. You bet we called him when we found out though.

When we called and got no answer, we called our agent to let him know what was happening. He was out of the office (of course), but his assistant said she'd give him the message. We called the claims company back and went to the claims supervisor. She explained that we weren't covered, and there wasn't anything she could do. She was very sorry that the claims handler has not told us first (or at all in this case).

I used a nationally known company because I felt like I was better protected. I suddenly felt very vulnerable. This store was 1,100 miles away.

We didn't know if this manager was going to deal with us honestly or add a bunch of extra items on the estimate. We didn't know what any of the necessary repairs cost. We didn't even know if Tom had really hit the bollard. There was no sign of even a scrape on the rental truck.

Knowing that a claims handling company should be familiar with fair costs and handling things like this, I asked if they would send a claims adjuster out to the store and take a photo of the damage. I wanted them to look over the estimate to evaluate whether we were getting a fair estimate. The supervisor said she couldn't do that because Tom wasn't covered while he was driving a big box truck. She told us that it just didn't make smart business sense to provide service to customers for things they weren't covered for. They had their bottom line to think of. I thought that was a shocking statement considering all the profit I had put on their bottom line in twenty-two years.

Once she was done with her dissertation on why she couldn't help us, I finally got a chance to ask another question: "You handle claims all the time. Do you think that you could have just explained why we weren't covered and then spent the time to offer us suggestions on how we could manage the repair process ourselves just because it's the right thing to do for a customer?" There was dead silence for a few seconds, and then she said, "Well, you didn't ask for that." Of course, how silly of me to need something I didn't ask for.

After my lackluster conversation with the claims service supervisor, I called my agent's assistant back to update her on what they told me. I asked her if she could find an agent to take a digital photo of the damage for us and e-mail it to us. She contacted an agent whose office was close to the convenience store and made the request — twice. In eight weeks, the digital photo never arrived. So much for benefiting from using a nationally known insurance company.

Our own agent never even called us to discuss the issue or apologize for the unprofessional handling by the claims company. Our agent's assistant was very understanding, and she followed up with us several times. However, the damage was done, and we took our business somewhere else. We found ourselves questioning what our insurance did cover and realized the trust had been broken. We could no longer feel good doing business with this company.

We had failed to buy the optional insurance when we rented the truck because we thought our insurance company would cover us no matter what we were driving. Thankfully, it was only a $2,000 repair and the convenience store manager was honest. Not checking with our insurance company first was our mistake. Not buying the optional insurance when we rented the truck and running over a bollard at the convenience store were also our mistakes. Continuing to trust this insurance company was another mistake that we weren't willing to make.

A few extra minutes on the phone giving some advice to some reasonable and honest people when they are in crisis is a small investment in a customer relationship. Providing a little extra customer service over and above the routine for some long-term customers would have taken them very little time. Notifying us first that our insurance didn't cover this accident was a common customer courtesy that we could have overlooked once we reported it to the claims supervisor. Her lack of charisma and our agent's lack of interest in our crisis showed me they also lacked sense of urgency and didn't deserve our business.

When you handle requests — those spoken and unspoken — with a sense of urgency, people take note. They look at you different. When you are a person who steps forward and makes things happen because they simply need to be done, you earn the respect you deserve. You position yourself as a person of influence.

Adopting an Attitude of Servant-Leadership

Robert Greenleaf, a leadership development expert, introduced the term "servant-leadership" in his essay, "The Servant as Leader" in 1970. It simply suggests that the servant-leader is one who is a servant first. Servant-leadership emphasizes collaboration, trust, empathy, and the ethical use of power. The benefit to the organization and those who work in it is individual development. It increases the focus on individual involvement while improving teamwork. It creates an environment where information is shared openly, visions are embraced, lessons are learned, and all members of the team participate and lend their creativity.

If you have a team you manage now, this is a perfect time to evaluate your leadership style. When you make decisions, do you consider the impact on the team of individuals who work with you? Do you ask them for their opinions on decisions? Do you engage your team in activities that cultivate innovation? Do you create a safe environment for your staff to give you feedback about your ideas and management style? If you don't already, make an effort to practice an attitude of servant-leadership. The impact on your team's attitude, productivity, and buy-in will provide all the evidence you need to make servant-leadership a practice for life.

You might not be in charge of a team right now. You can practice servant-leadership with your peers, family, or volunteer activities. Looking at every responsibility as an opportunity to serve will position you in the minds and hearts of others as a leader. You will be identified as someone who others would like to support or work for. It could open doors for you that you never imagined. Over a period of time, adopting a servant-leadership style will transform you into the kind of leader that people would walk through fire for. When high-potential people choose role models as well as managers, they look for people who embody the spirit of servant-leadership — even when they don't realize that is what they are looking for.

Helping People Discover Their Personal Genius

A person of influence takes an interest in others. That may manifest itself in the form of volunteering for a cause or a charity. It may mean helping others see their gifts and talents. Early in my career, I worked for a manager named Bob Duncan at Texas Instruments. I was just three years out of college, and I still viewed my career as just a job. I had previously worked in a department that didn't invest in professional development for their employees outside the company's tuition reimbursement program. I didn't know companies sent employees to training seminars, and I didn't yet understand the value of professional associations.

When I transferred to Bob's technical publishing department, he suggested I go to a SIGGRAPH conference that was happening in Dallas where I lived and worked. I thought, "Sure, since I'm getting paid for all the hours, I'm there." When he suggested that I get involved with a local association that focused on electronic publishing (a brand-new field at the time), I said I'd be glad to if they let me off early on Friday in exchange for the evening hours I invested and they reimbursed me for my meeting fee and mileage. He agreed. When he suggested I join the Lone Star Chapter of the Society for Technical Communication, I obliged as long as they met the other conditions and he paid for my membership. He heartily agreed. I would even read industry publications as long as I could read them on the clock and they paid for the subscriptions. I was an hourly employee and that was the law after all. Of course, he agreed.

Now if some young punk kid gave me all those conditions today if I suggested they get involved with professional associations, I'd think they weren't very serious about their future with my company. However, I cross paths all the time with people who are thirty-five years old or more who tell me they won't attend a professional association meeting because their company won't pay for it. They are often the same people who whine about how they are passed over for jobs and how their job is dead-end and lackluster. They usually don't have a supervisor who saw something in them and their potential enough to push the issue to become a partner in their professional development.

Bob Duncan could have just looked over this young punk kid who suffered from self-entitlement, "you owe me something" mentality. Thank God he didn't because his suggestion to get involved in those conferences and associations opened my eyes to the career that my job could be if I became an active participant in my professional development. Attending those meetings pushed me out of my comfort zone, and I met people who were passionate about the field of publishing. I learned how other companies were using technology in their publishing departments. I met people who were freelancing. I started taking the trade publications home to read in the evening. I just had an associate's degree at the time, and it clarified what studies I might want to pursue for a bachelor's degree. I was learning important things that I was bringing back to my company — it was totally worth the company's investment in me.

Bob was excited to hear about what I was learning, and he was beginning to depend on me for buying decisions and recommendations based on what I was learning about our industry. All the while, it was broadening my perspective on myself, my industry, and my future. Wow! Because of Bob's interest in my professional development, he helped me discover my personal genius and inspired me to set a cornerstone that secured my future. That was in 1988, and I attribute his encouragement to get involved with professional associations as a key factor in my success today.

Today, I do the same thing for others and encourage them to invest in themselves even if their employer won't pay for it. Professional associations are a great place for getting continuing education in your current field or for checking out a field you'd like to get into.

Possessing a Genuine Interest in Serving Something Bigger Than Yourself

I spent four-and-a-half years with Wal-Mart's employee magazine. Each month, we received 250 pieces of mail from associates — what Wal-Mart calls their employees. Our mailbox was full of stories from the field, poetry about life in a Wal-Mart store, and letters from customers wanting to show appreciation for an act of kindness or extreme customer service. Some of the stories were hysterical — associates shrink-wrapping their store manager to a pole in the entry with a bucket begging charity donations from sympathetic customers; employees getting married in Action Alley; and fun merchandise promotion tactics. Some were about heroic acts of bravery like truck drivers pulling accident victims from burning vehicles or a Sam's Club associate saving a choking baby. We laughed and cried as we opened and filed the mail. The greatest regret that we had was that we couldn't recognize every wonderful deed and story because we had a limited number of pages in our magazine.

One story that burns in my memory years later involves a night maintenance associate in a Wal-Mart Supercenter. At break one night, he was listening to a fellow associate share her concerns about her husband's grave medical condition. He was suffering from a rare kidney disease and needed a kidney transplant. His illness had left the family in dire financial straights. Even if they could raise the money for the transplant, he was an incredibly difficult match, and he may not live long enough to find a donor.

Clearly sympathetic to her situation, the maintenance associate asked his worried coworker many questions and listened as she poured her heart out. The chance to share her worries with a caring soul probably lightened her emotional burden that evening. I bet it helped her finish her shift a little easier. That was a small gift that cost the night maintenance associate nothing but his time, but it made a big difference.

However, there is more to the story. During their conversation, he realized that his kidney might be a match for her husband. Without saying a word, he had the necessary tests run and found his kidney was likely a good healthy match. In a selfless act that carried with it uncertain risks, he told his fellow associate what he discovered and offered his kidney to her

Change Your World by Changing Your Environment

Let's face it, sometimes the world doesn't beam with hope and optimism. However, we have the ultimate choice — the power to choose how we feel about or view our experiences. If we want to live a positive life as a person of influence, we have to be the kind of person who others want to be around. No one wants to hang out with people who whine and complain. People flock to those who are positive and optimistic — the kind of people who never look up and wonder why they are alone because they are always surrounded by people. Relationships are something we cultivate and earn. The first step is being someone people are compelled to be around. Here are eight ways to change your world by starting with your environment.

- **Turn off the news.** Bad news and controversial stories create strong network ratings. Consequently, the news networks strive to meet the demand. When we talk with people, we talk about current events. People who watch sports talk about sports. People who watch politics talk about politics. Current events drive what we talk about in casual conversation at the water cooler. So what happens when great human tragedies happen such as a devastating hurricane, terrorist attack, tsunami, or coal-mining accident? Reporters sometimes get the investigation details wrong, make incorrect assumptions, and write articles that just waste our time and positive energy. Once you've gathered the details, move on to something more positive.

- **Stop looking for hidden agendas and conspiracies.** For those who work in a highly bureaucratic or corporate environment, this may sound too "Pollyanna." It sometimes seems the pessimists of the world are determined to expose every negative aspect of the world as if they are saving the rest of us. There is a certain amount of things that we can affect. Focus your energy on that which you can change and accept the fact that you are simply not called to affect those things you can't.

- **Create a quiet moment to think and listen as often as possible.** With a million little urgent details that nab our attention everyday, we deny ourselves the moments of reflection that balance us. Can't get away to a perfect environment? Capture moments in a quiet car during your commute or just behind the closed bathroom stall door. It's not the environment so much as what you do with those moments that count. They can create peace that restores and rejuvenates you.

- **Surround yourself with positive people.** Think about people you love to be around. I wouldn't characterize myself as a people-person, and I can be pretty satisfied with sitting alone. However, I'm fascinated with complex people who have rich life experiences that they are willing to share — not because they are victims but because they have overcome challenges in their life. Listening and learning from them broadens our perspective and prepares us for what may lie ahead in our own lives.

- **Listen to positive messages and music.** Angry messages and violent rhythms of intense music can shape how we feel. We don't always realize how violent themes in movies and television shows affect us. Observe how you feel when exposed to negative messages versus how you feel when exposed to happy messages, images, and themes. Listen to uplifting music. Read books with motivational messages. Check out your library's collection of motivational videos. The self-help or professional development section features books on topics with techniques and ideas to address whatever challenges you face.

- **Run from mean people.** Sometimes we marry, work for, or give birth to people who treat us badly. It's one thing for someone to be in a bad mood and say something that they will need to apologize for later. However, no one has a right to say and do mean things. If you are exposed to mean people, it will begin to chip away at your spirit and self-esteem. You have to stop it or rid yourself of it. When confronting meanness, the first step is to tell that person how she makes you feel. She may not realize it or perhaps you are misunderstanding her intent. If the mean behavior continues, ask her to stop. Let her know if doesn't, she may lose you. Life is too short to spend it with mean people. They not only hurt themselves; they drag you down with them.

- **Eat a healthy diet.** When you feel good, you look good. When you look good, you radiate positive energy. Who wouldn't want that? There's so much information out there, and we run from one diet methodology to another instead of listening to our body. Many problems that people have today have less to do with what they need to put in their bodies (medicines, herbs, vitamins, etc.) and more to do with what they are currently putting into them (chemicals, food additives, foods we can't tolerate, etc.) Symptoms like depression, fatigue, gastrointestinal distress, and weight problems are your body's way of crying for help.

- **Actively care for your physical health.** Physical activity releases endorphins that lift your spirit. This translates to an activity that is as good for your head as it is for your body. Of course, if your body looks better because you exercise, you will have greater self-esteem. Working out is a chore for me but I devote several hours to it each week, not counting the drive to the gym. I hurt my back about twenty years ago but it rarely causes me pain because I exercise and weight train regularly. My business requires me to stand on my feet for long hours and lift heavy things at times. I care enough for my customers and my calling that I work out regularly so I can serve them more effectively.

husband. Speechless and tearful, she hugged him and thanked him. After the final necessary tests and preparations were made, he donated one of his kidneys to the ailing man in a life-saving operation.

One man not only listened for understanding and asked the necessary questions, he took it to the next level. He took the information he had gathered, overcame concerns for his own well-being, and performed a single selfless act that saved another human life. He served something bigger than himself.

It not only matters what you say, but what you do. To quote Helen Walton, the first lady of Wal-Mart and wife of founder Sam Walton: "In life, it matters not what we gather but what we scatter." Through a simple act of taking a genuine interest in others and creating meaningful conversation, you have the power to change lives if you take it further and act! Your actions will always speak louder than words.

Becoming Extraordinary through Passion and Vision

I was talking with a manager about his team one morning. He mapped out the individual team member's promotion potential on a grid based on performance and potential. As we evaluated the individuals, we identified the people who had demonstrated they were promising management candidates based on their performance and potential. We identified three others who were capable if he invested more in them through mentoring and professional development.

As we looked at the three who fell into the area for low potential and low performance, we evaluated why we thought they lacked promise. They had indeed not performed to the best of their abilities. However, we realized that they lacked a passion for the profession. Almost as prominently, we realized they lacked a vision for what their role with the team could be. In fact, while they occasionally had some opinions, they generally preferred that he tell them what to do and didn't do anything unless they were told.

Think about people you know who are going places in their life — either personally or professionally. They love what they are doing, and they are fascinated by it. They are driven by learning more about it. They wake up at 3:00 a.m. thinking about what drives them. They hit the floor running in the morning because they can't wait to get to it.

What drives you and sets your soul on fire? You've probably heard the Dale

Carnegie quote, "Act enthusiastic and you'll be enthusiastic!" That's really a bit artificial, but when you are truly passionate about something, it's like enthusiasm on steroids. Passion isn't always loud because it comes from somewhere deep in your soul — a smoldering intensity without the volume.

There's life, and then there's life on passion. Life is the tan Ford Festiva — a basic, dependable car that will get you where you want to go economically. A red Ferrari sports car, on the other hand, is life on passion — fast, rich, and sleek. Tan beach sandals are a good example of an ordinary life too. They are comfy, easy to wear and — yawn — ordinary. However, a pair of red stiletto shoes are exciting, sexy, and beautiful and they make women stand taller. They reflect a life pumped up on passion. There is a time and place for both. But when you are genuinely passionate, your passion will spread like wildfire, and it will inspire vision.

One lady I knew worked for a company with a corporate culture that didn't resonate with her. In her department, the actions of the managers weren't congruent with the company's culture. In short, they didn't practice what they preach. It also didn't align with her personal beliefs. She ended up leaving the company because she felt she lived a lie. She likened it to being caught in a cult like The People's Temple led by Jim Jones. The cult met its abrupt end in 1978 when the followers agreed to commit suicide by drinking a grape beverage laced with cyanide and a number of sedatives including liquid Valium, Penegram, and chloral hydrate. She explained, "I just never drank the Kool-Aid." She just couldn't be part of the experience anymore so she escaped. She worked in a passionless job she had no vision for.

The same thing can happen in our personal lives too. An extraordinary life is a series of intentional choices. You probably know people who live passionless lives. You know the ones. They whine, "You don't understand, I can't help my life is ordinary. I don't have any control over most of the things in my life. I have to do this because of my kids, my wife, my parents, etc." Some people prefer an ordinary existence because it's safe and they know what to expect. Even if they have been sitting in a room full of horse manure for years (figuratively speaking, of course), they are not likely to try to get out because sitting in manure is familiar, and the alternative carries the risk of the unknown. That sounds drastic but if you've known someone in an abusive relationship, you'll see the comparison. The abused individual stays in the relationship because they know what to expect. Somehow the familiar seems more attractive than the unknown — even when the unknown has got to be better than the familiar. A passionless life cannot generate vision.

For the first twenty years of my life, I lived the ordinary life — I grew up in an ordinary neighborhood in an ordinary suburb, went to an ordinary school, lived with my ordinary family, worked in an ordinary part-time job at an ordinary fast-food restaurant, and went to an ordinary technical school. When I graduated, I did what ordinary people do and married my college sweetheart. My idea of breaking out of the ordinary doldrums was to move to Dallas after graduation — perhaps my life wouldn't be so ordinary if I lived somewhere more exciting.

My twenties were more of the same — doing the ordinary things ordinary young married couples do: we had our only child, bought a house, worked two jobs, and ran up a bunch of debt. We even moved back to Northwest Arkansas to be closer to family. At the time, nothing seemed more ordinary than living in Northwest Arkansas. I was apparently doomed to live an ordinary existence.

As I neared my thirties, I began to wonder if there was something besides "ordinary." I didn't want to shake up my life too much because I liked living in my comfort zone. However, my heart told me I needed to do something to break the cycle of "ordinary." I set some goals to finish my bachelor's degree. For my thirtieth birthday, my husband's secretary threw me a great birthday party. It wasn't long after that I realized my husband and I didn't have the same goals. For instance, one of his goals was to be married to his secretary, and he left three months later to pursue that goal.

That rocked my world and marked the beginning of the greatest learning period in my life. Granted, it was tough because I was drawing a poverty-level wage and living in income-qualified housing. I got my feet underneath me as quickly as I could, bought a house, and finished my bachelor's degree as a single mom and later my master's in business administration. I met and married a man who was confident enough in himself to encourage me to do anything I thought I was big enough to try.

Most of all, I learned that I was capable of being extraordinary if I was willing to work hard enough for it. I learned that it was possible if you make every moment count. Being extraordinary is a choice. It all starts with doing a little more than you thought was possible. Once you experience it, you'll build momentum and then it will eventually fill you with a passion for pursuing the extraordinary. Step out and take a risk. I want you to believe you can be extraordinary too.

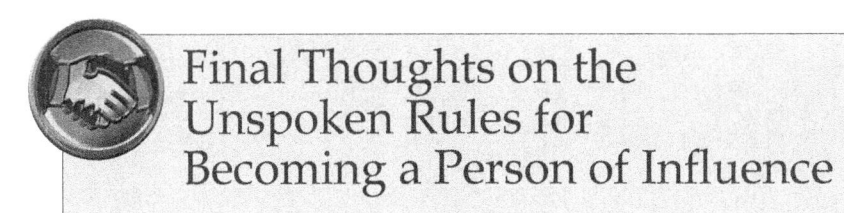

Final Thoughts on the Unspoken Rules for Becoming a Person of Influence

I bet you found many characteristics you already possess and maybe some you took for granted. I challenge you to choose two or three characteristics to develop as an investment in your future. I hope one of those characteristics is living passionately if you currently live a passionless existence at home or work. Life is too short to live without passion.

- No one should work for themselves if they can't stand to sell their company, their product, or themselves.
- Be willing to become the brand for your company. The more you connect your personal brand and your company's image, the more success you will achieve.
- You may need a title to be a manager, but you don't need a title to lead and become a person of influence.
- Difficult situations hone your ability to act quickly. You need to rely on your value system and follow your heart. It might require handling the situation before you have all the information. Waiting often makes the confrontation more difficult and the situation more complicated to correct. Working through difficult experiences teaches you to trust your instincts and defend your values in tough times as well as easy times.
- No matter how private we think we are, our lives, choices, and values are on display for the world. We don't realize that people are watching and learning from our actions every day. It is critical that we be congruent — being the same person in our personal life as we are in our professional life.
- Addressing important requests with a sense of urgency will define you in the eyes of others. When you make things happen because they simply need to be done, you earn the respect you deserve.
- Investing in your professional development will pay dividends in your future.

CHAPTER 14
The Secret to Being Attractive

The day the school yearbooks were distributed was the moment of truth — who was popular that year? The yearbook staff was charged to chronicle the happenings of the school year. That meant they must have attended every activity and thoroughly researched who the "hot items" were, right? If that was the case, you could measure your popularity (or obscurity in my case) by the number of appearances in the yearbook.

That's exactly what I did when I got my yearbook each year. Before anything else, I looked through to see how many times I appeared in the yearbook. Each year, I felt some disappointment that I made it into the yearbook very few times. The only thing that saved me from total obscurity some years was the individual class photo. If you were at school on picture day, you made it in to that section.

The real tragedy was that I let that single measurement determine whether I thought I was important. If I wasn't in the yearbook very much, I figured I must not be very important. I look back at that annual assessment as an adult and realize two things:

- The yearbook committee only photographed the activities that they personally attended, and the members weren't necessarily involved in other extracurricular activities such as band and choir.
- They could only photograph the people who were out there in front. If you were standing in a crowd or, even worse, in the shadows, they couldn't photograph you.

That measure of popularity was very important to me at the time. I equated number of yearbook photos (popularity) to importance (value and purpose). Now that I'm grown up, I've learned that my personal value and purpose are so much more than popularity. When you seek a life of high personal value (value to the world based on what you're doing for it) and purpose (what you feel called to do for the world), you gain something more important — true worth. I have also learned over the years that when you focus on becoming a genuine, interesting, and caring person (the kind of person people are attracted to), popularity will follow.

I was speaking with a large group of high school girls about building relationships. I asked, "How many of you want to be popular?" To my surprise, no one raised her hand. Instantly, the room filled with disapproving faces and nervous chatter. It was if I had asked, "How many of you would like to have acne?"

I immediately struggled for some way to reconnect with them on the topic. After some stammering, I ended up asking, "How many of you want to be the kind of person that people are attracted to?" Finally, hands went up eagerly.

As the parent of an eighteen-year-old at the time, I had never discussed that topic with my daughter. I recall many times where she ranted during the family dinners about "preps" or "cheerleaders" and other types of people who I would have considered "popular."

Thinking back to my painfully shy junior high and high school years, the popular people were the people I admired because everyone knew them. I wanted what they had. At the time, I didn't know how they became popular. I thought they were predestined to be popular. The more I thought popularity eluded me, the more "unpopular" I felt. I was sure that I was insignificant and my life was less meaningful than the popular kids' lives.

What I've come to discover over the years is that our interpersonal skills are what attract people to us. Even in the presidential elections, voters are drawn to the more likeable candidates. Bob Schieffer, chief Washington correspondent for CBS, is known as one of broadcast journalism's most experienced Washington reporters. During an January 2008 discussion with another political analyst about the public's reaction to the Democratic presidential candidates, he made a powerful observation: "Likability is a factor in elections. We're all running for student council."

The presidential election process gives us a grand chance to evaluate the communication skills, intellect, and strategic competence of our candidates, but what provokes us to cast our vote is their interpersonal skills. When you look at the power of interpersonal skills (also known as people skills), it makes the time you'll invest in developing them worth it. Like all skills, we weren't born with them. We develop them through experience and watching others.

Some of us were lucky enough to grow up around people who had great people skills even if we didn't know what made them engaging and attractive. People always wanted to be around them, and they had an ability to get people to do anything. They were the people who others would walk through fire for. The most effective way to pass along values and skills is by modeling them. Just being around them on a daily basis influenced us to adopt their interpersonal techniques.

Others of us grew up in more quiet and reserved families where we didn't get a chance to see interpersonal skills modeled on a daily basis. It's not that the introverts of the world don't do meaningful, valuable work because they do. However, they experience life as a constant, uphill struggle if they are ambitious. Because they lack people skills, they can't overcome the everyday opposition we are all met with. They often wander through their life wondering why they never get a break and why other people won't cooperate with them. Their outlook is more pessimistic, and their life often lacks the reward for a job well done. They don't get to experience the magic that happens for people who can remove roadblocks and create a collaborative environment.

I come from a long line of people who I'm not sure even LIKE to be around other people. I'm pretty sure some of them would have rather been poked in the eye with a stick than meet new people. They are so antisocial. I tried to plan a family reunion one year and NO ONE wanted to come. Some even asked if we could get together by videoconference so they wouldn't have to spend so much time together. I could have screamed. Nothing says family togetherness like looking at each other on a jumpy greenish webcam image where the other person is looking down at the computer screen as they talk. Arrggg!!!

When I was growing up, my parents didn't invite many friends to the house. I never got a chance to see how they made friends and rarely saw what kinds of friends they chose. The only gatherings we had at our house were holiday get-togethers with our relatives. My mom was stressed out by all the meal prep because she was always the hostess. Our family was full of characters with backstories — several struggled with mental illness, and there were the usual conflicts that happen in any family as well. About the only time I saw my dad interact with others was with his dance band when I was very young.

Outside the family gatherings, my introverted parents pretty much stuck to themselves. My dad spent his time inventing things, running a business, and researching. My mom spent her time raising my brother and I, caring for her parents and sister, taking care of the house, and running my dad's office while he handled the service calls. They were both logical and technically gifted people — the kinds of personalities that are not known for being social butterflies.

Because they didn't live their lives in an environment surrounded by others, they didn't push my brother and I into situations where we engaged with other people. I was klutzy and frail so my mom didn't urge me to be involved in sports. In gym class in elementary school, I was ALWAYS one of the last three kids picked when there was a choice. I would go home after school and cry about it. My mom instead pushed me to participate in activities I was skilled at such as crafts, reading, and writing — things you did alone. Even though I would have benefited from the exercise and might have developed enough skills with practice to be a decent athlete, I missed some of the important lessons of sports.

Engagement in sports teaches team members that people are more likely to win when they work well as a team. It gives participants a hands-on opportunity to develop interpersonal skills and be exposed to others' interpersonal skills. It also helps them understand that life isn't fair, people don't always play nice, and that we have to overcome adversity. It also gives us a chance to learn to trust people and encourage others to achieve their potential. Sports are especially important for women because we are culturally geared to avoid conflict, react to emotion, and operate in more one-on-one relationships. Being exposed to the learning experiences of team sports helps them compete more effectively in their career life — companies often depend heavily on the quality of the team culture they foster. The sooner we learn interpersonal skills, the more success we will enjoy.

People with well-developed interpersonal skills are often described as charismatic and influential. This chapter is devoted to the key traits of those skills. This is probably the most important chapter in your ability to build lifelong relationships in all areas of your life. It will not only allow you to create influence, but it will put the finishing touch on all the other skills we've mentioned in this book.

The Law of Attraction

Your life mirrors your physical and mental environment. The Law of Attraction states that you attract into your life what you think about and surround yourself with. When my daughter was in junior high, she had some gothic friends. The gothic culture manifests a feeling of low self-worth. Her friend's feelings of self-hatred attracted other people who were consumed with self-hatred. As a group, they talked about hateful things that attracted more hatred into their life. In a short time, they became outwardly aggressive to others and attracted more animosity and bad feelings into their life. They had some bad experiences because their hateful behavior escalated to activities that were against school rules — bullying, terrorism, and vandalism.

That negative real-life example illustrates that the Law of Attraction can become a powerful tool to use to become the kind of person people are attracted to. When you are negative, you attract more negativity. When you are positive, you attract positive things and people into your life.

The words we choose shape our thoughts. Proverbs 23:7 states, "For as he thinketh in his heart, so is he." If you want to have positive things happen in your life, you have to fill your mind with positive thoughts.

My husband, Tom, can be pessimistic. Some days, it seems that everyone is out to get him. I was concerned that his sourpuss attitude was attracting negativity into my life. I explained the Law of Attraction to him but he didn't really seem to buy in to it. Even though he was negative about so many things in his life, I was determined not to let his negativity affect me. I was also determined to find a better illustration for the Law of Attraction.

We have three female mixed-breed dogs: Speckles, Snappy, and Jazmin. Once you get more than two dogs, you have a pack and the laws of nature dictate a pecking order. Jazmin falls in as number three in the pecking order, but she's always competing for the number-two position when the other two are around. The dogs are just like normal siblings; they fight and play. However, Jazmin just can't behave because she's driven instinctively to attempt to move up in pack order. If she's not barking louder than the other dogs, she's snapping at them and chasing them away from their food bowl. Tom's usual response to her is, "Jazmin, do you have to be such a wiener all the time?" Whenever the dogs are misbehaving, he normally calls them wiener dogs. I should mention that our dogs are black Labrador and Shepherd mixes. There is not one Dachshund in the pack — the breed that you might think of when you hear the term "wiener dog."

Finally, the perfect example of the Law of Attraction came in the form of an orphaned dog my daughter, Darcie, brought home late one night. She was late for curfew and I was waiting up. I greeted her as she walked in and realized she had a black ball of fur in her arms. His name was Midget. His owner was being evicted from her apartment, and she had to give him away. On closer examination, he was really short. In fact, he was a Dachshund mix. Thank you, Tom. He had indeed attracted an actual wiener dog into our lives.

Midget was the example that helped me teach him the Law of Attraction. Once he grasped it, he asked if perhaps we should call our dogs "Million Dollar Dogs" instead so we could attract wealth into our life. Although it was a silly example, he got the idea and it changed his perspective some. I should note that I can't make him change — only he possesses the power to change his attitude and his life. However, I can set a good example and strive to be a ray of light to inspire others. Become a ray of light, and people will want what you have and draw close to you.

Becoming an Attractive Person through Conversation

Being attractive has little to do with personal appearance. Some of the most beautiful people on the inside are not necessarily physically attractive. What attracts us to them is their genuine, interesting, and caring persona. They simply appear more friendly and approachable. Here are four ways to become an attractive person by mastering the art of starting and engaging in conversation.

Approach People and Don't Wait For Them to Come to You

What I didn't realize when I thought I was an unpopular student was that I had total control over changing that. Looking back, I wasn't unpopular, a trait that would indicate that I was disliked. Instead, I was "undiscovered." The bulk of the students didn't realize that I was a loving person because I was off standing in a corner waiting for someone to speak to me. I was hiding myself and my qualities away where no one could discover me.

What I find as I teach adults how to build business relationships is that meeting new people takes them back in time — like that first day of junior high when you are in a new school and you don't know anyone. They stand off in a corner because they are waiting for someone to approach them first — then they are mad because everyone is ignoring them! It's awkward meeting new people. The people who seem like masters at it have simply overcome their fear of it. Some people overcome that earlier than others do.

I'm still not a naturally outgoing person, but I have a rule that I always meet five new people as quickly as possible at a gathering. I attend some gatherings where I know many people but I hold off spending much time with them until I've met my five new people. Sure, it would be more comfortable to spend the time with the people I already know. However, I have learned that I increase the number of interesting people in my life if I will take the initiative to start conversations with new people.

Ask Questions and Take Responsibility for Leading the Conversation

Often, people don't approach new people because they don't know what to say. We all have that fear of saying something that is going to make us look like a goober. I've become a master at leading meaningful conversation, but I still say some dumb things. The remarkable thing is that people aren't nearly as critical of us as we think they will be. Most people are forgiving of our conversational missteps that are bound to happen.

One of the most important things I've learned is that the people standing alone are dying for someone to speak to them. When I go up to them and begin the conversation, I become their hero — I have saved them from the awkwardness of initiating a conversation. Getting the conversation started is as simple as greeting someone and introducing yourself. Generally, when you introduce yourself, the other person will introduce herself in return.

After the initial greeting, it's good to have some prepared questions to ask. Have you ever met someone and then couldn't remember any details because you were trying to think of things to say instead of listening to them? Prepared questions allow you to focus on what the other person is saying instead of what you're going to say next.

Conversation with someone new gives us the chance to see if we would like to get to know that person better. Good initial conversation that allows you to get to know people has three basic components:

- Learn the person's name and where he is in life.
- Find out what he spends his time doing.
- Learn about his family.

These topics help you gather information about that person so you can think of other questions to ask them the next time you see them. The next conversation with that person will be a thousand times easier than the first. Check out the sample questions on the next page for ideas suitable for situations similar to school, parties, or work.

The average initial conversation lasts five to seven minutes. Anything longer may seem uncomfortable. Generally, the conversation will turn around to you and your interests at some point once the other person feels more comfortable. However, if it doesn't, don't worry. Sometimes people are just petrified to ask questions, but they'll be more at ease the next time they see you.

One of the more important benefits of leading the conversation is that it puts the other person at ease. You are also honoring them by placing them at the center of the conversation. It gives the other person a wonderful feeling about the experience. When people feel wonderful about the experience, they will feel wonderful about you.

Listen for Meaning

I spent seven years working at the Wal-Mart corporate headquarters. I was part of their training department for several years. One of the last projects I worked on was a video-based training program that chronicled the twenty-three leadership principles that founder Sam Walton used to lead the company that grew to become a retailing giant.

We interviewed fifty company leaders who had worked with Mr. Sam as he was lovingly known by his employees (which Wal-Mart calls "associates"). Communication was the leadership characteristic that people mentioned most often. When I asked each person why Mr. Sam was such a great communicator, overwhelmingly they noted his ability to ask questions and listen for meaning.

Questions for Each Stage in Life

These are conversation-starter questions. The objective is to ask enough questions to create the threads of information that you can weave into a conversation. With most people, you can find something that will provide enough common ground to build a conversation on. Once these questions create some initial feedback, you can bring up current events that relate to the topic such as recent newspaper articles.

Learn the person's name and where he is in life.

School: Are you the same age as me? Where do you go to school? What neighborhood do you live in? What are you majoring in at college?

Church or Party: Where do you live? How long have you lived there? Where else have you lived? What do you like about your neighborhood?

Work: Where did you grow up? Where did you go to school? Did you go to college? If so, what kinds of activities did you participate in at college?

Find out what he spends his time doing.

School: Do you play sports? Are you in any clubs at school? Do you have a job? Do you have hobbies? What are your favorite bands? Did you go anywhere fun over the summer?

Church or Party: Where do you work? Do you do any charity work? Are you involved in any organizations? What is your favorite restaurant here? Are you planning a vacation this summer? What are your hobbies?

Work: Are you involved in any organizations? Do you do any charity work? Where else have you worked? Do you work out? How do you relax after work? Do you have big plans for the weekend?

Learn about his family.

School: Do you have brothers or sisters? Do you have any pets? Where do your parents work?

Church or Party: Do you have any pets? Do you have children? Are they involved in any sports? Where do your other family members live? How did you meet your spouse/friend?

Work: Do you have children? How old are they? Are they involved in any sports? Do you have any pets? Where do your other family members live? Are you married? What does your spouse do?

For a formula for making meaningful conversation with people you've just met, check out Chapter 4: Leading Meaningful Conversations.

Wow! Sam Walton was a brilliant businessman who said great things, but that wasn't what people remembered most about him. His genius was his ability to listen! Mr. Sam would ask questions about the business when he talked to a Wal-Mart store manager, but he would also ask the customers questions. He walked around the stores and talked with the employees too.

He would ask employees how particular items were selling and how they liked their store manager, but he would also ask about their families. He wasn't just being polite when he asked about an employee's child — he was truly interested. He was known for asking about the child by name again years later. If he had been worried about what he was going to say next, he would never have been able to remember all those details that he learned in conversation.

You've probably heard the old adage, "God gave you two ears and one mouth. You should listen twice as much as you talk." That's a good rule to follow. People love to talk about themselves. When you show a genuine interest in people and allow them the opportunity to speak, they will remember you in a positive way.

Whether it's your first conversation with a person or your ninety-first, remember to ask questions and listen. You'll be known as someone who is caring and genuine, and people will be attracted to you.

Know When to End the Conversation

All good conversations must come to an end. Understanding how to end the conversation gracefully is an art. There are some conversations you never want to end — like when you're talking with someone who's really interesting, important, or attractive! However, you know it has to end because you have run out of things to say.

There are other reasons to end a conversation too. You may need to run because you're late for class or an appointment. Sometimes there are people that you can't wait to get away from. Face it; we're just not compatible with everyone. Maybe they like you but you need your distance from them.

When it's time to end the conversation, just say, "It's been great to talk with you." That sends the signal to the other person that the conversation is ending. At that point, you can take the initiative with the next step. If you have to run for an appointment, say so. If you want to talk with them again, say, "I'd like to talk later. Can I call you?" Above all, be honest. If you don't intend to talk with them again, Just leave it with a simple "See ya!" or "It was nice talking with you."

Make a Powerful, Confident, and Memorable First Impression

Everyone gets the jitters. Even a seasoned salesperson gets nervous when he is making a big sales presentation. Professional speakers get nervous too no matter how many times they step onto the stage. It's okay to have butterflies as long as you keep them flying in formation. If you're not nervous, you are probably over-confident or boring. Both are bad and will kill your image.

Every day, you probably have the opportunity to make a first impression somewhere with someone. You might have a job where you meet the public on a regular basis. There are still people in your daily life who you haven't met yet whose friendship might enrich your life. If you aren't meeting new people because you are afraid of what they will think of you — perhaps you are scared you'll look like a goober — you aren't growing, and your life isn't as full as it could be.

I'm not people-oriented by nature. I could work in front of a computer and be perfectly happy if I didn't talk with anyone all day. Meeting new people makes me anxious. So if my life is going well enough without putting myself through the torture of meeting new people, why bother? I'll tell you why — you never know why you meet the people that you meet, but there is a reason everyone crosses our path. Sometimes they might be our future employer, spouse, or best friend. Simply meeting someone new opens up the possibility to gain knowledge and perspective that you didn't have before because they are broadening your worldview. Other people — particularly the right people — will improve the quality of your life.

You can't attract the right people into your life if you aren't opening the door and inviting them in. A confident first impression is like an open door. There are eight steps you can take to make a confident first impression every time. Use them and you'll be ready whether you are meeting a new friend, a potential client, your future mother-in-law, or your future employer.

One of the great journeys of life is mastering the powerful first impression. It's not just a look though — you have to feel it on the inside. It has to be woven into who you are, and that takes preparation and practice. Embrace being outside your comfort zone because that's where your best growth experiences lie. Here are some ways to look more confident even when you are screaming on the inside.

Smile

A warm, natural smile puts everyone at ease. Even if you don't love your teeth, a warm smile will help you exude a confident first impression. I notice when I smile, the eyes of the other person don't fall below my chin. That means that I don't have to worry about what I'm wearing or if they'll notice the few pounds I've gained or lost since they saw me last. A nice smile will distract people from other things you might perceive negative about you. They can't notice the negative things when they are looking at your glowing smile.

Make Eye Contact

When people look at a photo, the eyes always draw them in. That's not only the best place to look at people; it's the window to other important clues about them. In the American culture, we equate eye contact with trustworthiness and respect. Good eye contact can show you are interested in the person you are speaking with. Just be cautious about gazing at the other person too long — leering at someone makes them feel creepy. Also, try not to look around when people are talking with you or they will wonder if you are interested in talking with them.

Get an Attitude — A Winning Attitude

People like to be around a winner. Be cheerful, upbeat, and interested in the folks you meet. A positive, winning attitude will plant you firmly in their memories.

Have you ever run into someone and asked how she was doing only to be given all the crummy details of her situation? That kind of conversation should be reserved for close friends. When people are bombarded with negativity, they push away. Conversely, people are naturally attracted to a cheerful person because they feel encouraged and uplifted simply by spending time in their positive presence. The world is sometimes a negative place, but you can be a ray of sunshine on a cloudy day.

Mastering the Winning Attitude:
Be Someone People Can't Wait to Be Around

Each day isn't always good. Professional speaker Sarah Victory suggests responding to questions about how business is going with, "Business is incredible!" even if it's incredibly slow. You must look and act as if you are the biggest success story in the world even when you don't feel like one at the moment. People want to be around winners.

One of the best habits to adopt is to avoid saying anything bad about anyone. That's not always easy when your competitors don't play by the same rules. In business, it's crucial to our success. No one likes to hear negative comments about another businessperson, and it only hurts the person who makes the negative comment.

Low self-esteem can kill a winning attitude. When businesspeople don't visibly believe in themselves, their abilities, and their company, no one else does either. Competent people with high self-esteem often rise to the top. People want to do business with confident individuals. Before you can sell anyone on what you have to offer — whether you are looking for a job or selling a product or service — you must believe in what you can do. The first sale you must make is to yourself.

Here are a few tips for people with low self-esteem.

- Never call attention to things you think are negative about yourself. No one notices most of those things.
- Avoid making comments that discredit you such as, "Anyone could do that," "This old thing?" "I'm not a very good public speaker," or "I was running late this morning so I didn't have a chance to prepare."
- Smile, always have something positive to say, and take a genuine interest in anyone you meet.
- Work to overcome low self-esteem. Building knowledge and experience yields confidence and success stories.
- Be passionate. Passion for your business and your customers can cover up a lot of insecurity.
- Demonstrate impeccable attention to detail. Few people practice this impressive skill, and it provides a competitive advantage.
- Work to build your expertise and experience. It will yield confidence and success stories. Investing just thirty minutes every day for a year building your expertise can earn you the respect you desire.
- Finally, build the self-esteem of others around you. It builds your confidence while you are building someone else's self-image.

Extend a Firm, Full-Palm Handshake

I never thought about the power of a handshake until I met a new school bus driver when I was in high school. He shook my hand and told me that my firm handshake would get me far in life. I don't know if I actually had a firm handshake then, but I guarantee every handshake since then was firm and confident. A good handshake consists of a comfortable grip and two or three pumps up and down.

We often judge people by the way they shake hands. When a handshake feels out of the ordinary, it distracts the other person from what you have to say. For instance, what do you think when you get the limp, little-old-lady handshake. Are you thinking that handshake means business? No! Of course not! What about cold, damp hands? For whatever reason they are cold and damp, you probably make some judgments based on the unusual

---

Five Tips for Making an Organized Impression

Your organization skills help you make a powerful first impression. Here are a few ideas to help you present a more organized and professional image.

- **Stash your business cards in an easily accessible place.** A pocket is always best, but that's not always possible in women's clothing. Plan what you wear carefully so you'll have pockets handy.
- **Keep a pen and paper handy.** You often have an opportunity to make notes on someone's business card about their business. Paper is handy if you need to write down a referral as well.
- **Carry a day planner if possible.** When you have the opportunity to give leads or make an appointment, being able to hand off the contact information right then is a huge timesaver. It doesn't matter whether it is a paper-based planner or a personal digital assistant (PDA).
- **Arrive on time.** Whether there is a firm start time or not, you miss valuable networking time if you arrive late.
- **Manage your purse properly, ladies.** Consider leaving your purse in the car. Juggling a purse, your business card case, and a beverage is clumsy. If you must carry your purse, make sure it's an attractive style that closes nicely. Nothing looks worse than a worn-out purse bulging at the seams with papers hanging out of the pockets.

feel. A firm, dry, warm, comfortable handshake feels familiar and friendly and doesn't get in the way of the first impression.

Want the truth about how your handshake feels to others? My friend Tom Jones says you should ask your "broccoli friends" — those people who will be painfully honest and tell you when you have a piece of broccoli stuck in your teeth. We all seem to have them, and they will be honest with us about our handshake.

And ladies, be the first to extend the handshake. The women's movement has created a lot of uncertainty for men about shaking hands. Regardless of your gender, a handshake still means business.

Stand Tall

When you stand up tall, you breathe easier and look more confident. Your clothes hang nicer too. When people are shorter or taller than average, they sometimes feel self-conscious, and it shows in every aspect of their image. It can consume them where they worry about it all the time. It robs them of mental energy they need for other aspects of their image. Embrace your size. If you are shorter than average, stand confidently and comfortably. If you are tall, resist the urge to slouch. Your height is a blessing, and slouching exudes a lack of confidence.

Wear Clothes That Make You Feel Confident

Dress so that you feel comfortable in clothing that is appropriate for the occasion. That doesn't mean the clothes have to be expensive or trendy. Too often, people feel that their self-image depends on their clothing. Once you begin to exhibit a more confident self-image, the superficial components of your image will matter less to others. When you become a confident person on the inside, you'll find that your clothing will become less important.

If your work attire is jeans or khaki pants with a knit, collared shirt with your logo, it's probably appropriate to wear to a chamber of commerce networking mixer. Just make sure you're impeccably clean and pressed. Dress a little nicer if you are attending the chamber's annual banquet. Some people find they need to dress a notch or two above whatever the other attendees wear in order to feel confident. What you wear affects your confidence. Dress so that you have no reason to feel uncomfortable while you are meeting and greeting. And if your clothing doesn't have your company logo on it, wear a name tag with your logo because that helps build name recognition.

Use Your Manners

Nothing looks better on you than a fine set of manners. Good manners make you look better than the most expensive suit. They also make a big impression on those around you. Unfortunately, manners are a rare thing these days, but nothing is too good for your new acquaintances. Roll out the red carpet for them. People notice common courtesies like saying "yes ma'am," "no ma'am," "thank you," and "please." They approve when someone opens a door for them whether they are male or female.

Be respectful but not too stuffy or formal. Prepare to be confident, likeable, and organized, but don't expect everyone to do that. While you mind your manners, make sure you are gracious of others who may not have stellar manners themselves.

Look Organized

If there is one aspect of your personal appearance that is truly important to others, it's your level of organization. You'll run into people who are neat freaks and others who are neutral on the subject. However, someone who is excessively sloppy, rumpled, or disorganized will be trusted with less responsibility than someone who appears organized. People will judge physical appearance as well as the appearance of a purse, backpack, or desk. Whether it's true or not, people will assume a messy person will do a substandard job. If you are organized, embrace it. If you could improve your organized appearance, get to work immediately before chances slip through your fingers.

Presenting an organized business image includes your business cards and marketing materials. Never store them loose in your car, pocket, or purse. In the mind of your potential customer, the quality of your marketing materials reflects the quality of your product or service.

Final Thoughts on Becoming Someone People Are Attracted To

People are attracted to us for all kinds of reasons. We attract people, experiences, and things into our life based on the actions we take, things we believe, and characteristics we embody. If we do our part in a positive way, we attract the positive. Likewise, when we are negative, we attract the negative. Making meaningful conversation and possessing a winning attitude are two of the most important actions you can take to attract the right people, experiences, and things into your life. Regardless of how wonderful or terrible your life is now, positive actions can always improve your future.

- When you seek a life of high personal value (value to the world based on what you're doing for it) and purpose (what you feel called to do for the world) you gain true worth.
- Our interpersonal skills are what attract people to us. Some of the most beautiful people on the inside are not necessarily physically attractive. What attracts us to them is their genuine, interesting, and caring persona. They simply appear more friendly and approachable.
- Those without solid people skills don't get to experience the magic that happens for people who can remove roadblocks and create a collaborative environment.
- The Law of Attraction states that you attract into your life what you think about and surround yourself with. To have positive things happen in your life, you have to fill your mind with positive thoughts.
- Meeting new people takes most of us back in time to that first day of junior high when we are in a new school and we don't know anyone. It's always awkward meeting new people. The people who seem like masters at it have simply overcome their fear of it.
- Having a set of prepared questions to ask anytime you talk with someone allows you to focus on the other person instead of what you're going to say next.
- Whether it's your first conversation with a person or your ninety-first, remember to ask questions and listen. You'll be known as someone who is caring and genuine, and people will be attracted to you.

CHAPTER 15
Getting What You Want, Need, and Deserve

The further you go in life, the more you need to motivate others to act. When we rely on others to carry out their part of a mission, we need to understand how to read their individual needs and preferences. Because we don't live in a perfect world, we are going to encounter challenges, different priorities, challenging personalities, and misunderstandings. We'll address the key areas of making requests with warmth and sincerity, utilizing gratitude, and handling inevitable conflict. These tools will prepare you to handle the situations that threaten our progress as well as the success of our teams and organizations.

Making Requests with Warmth and Sincerity

In his book, *One Minute Millionaire*, Mark Victor Hansen suggests you make your requests with warmth and sincerity: "When you ask, ask from the heart. Important requests are better received when those making them are passionate, friendly, polite, and firm." These four qualities demonstrate the importance of the task. They also position you as the kind of person that the individual would be glad to help.

Here is an example of the right way and the wrong way to make a request:

> **Wrong:** Would you mind to do this if you can find time by the end of the day? If you can't get to that, it's okay; just let me know.

> **Right:** I need your high sense of urgency on this. Would you complete this by the end of the day? I know I can always count on you.

The wrong example will provide variable results depending on the individual. It is definitely polite, but it sounds like it's an option for them if they can fit it in. Some people jump on any request that is made, and others can't ever fit anything in because they are so inflexible. Even a minor change in their plans just seems impossible. They will either begrudgingly perform the task, or they will determine the task is too unimportant to handle before the end of the day.

The right example is direct, specific, and firm but follows with a note that you trust this person to manage this challenge. The person you ask will feel obligated to honor your request or risk losing your trust. Finishing with a positive comment reinforces that you believe they can accomplish this task.

What if the request isn't urgent? Never make a request without a deadline. We live in a world where we consider our e-mail urgent because it sits on our computer workspace and grows throughout the day like a mushrooming to-do list. We are bombarded with information coming in through the Internet, newspaper, and television. As humans, we haven't yet learned to turn that off and re-prioritize. If we don't accompany our requests with a deadline, we'll get put behind those things that seem more urgent even though our request is more important.

What if the person you've asked to help has let you down — how do you finish the request with a comment that says "I know you can do this." Instead of being insincere or lying, opt for a finishing comment such as "This means a lot to our team" or "Your ability to make this happen will really show your worth to our team." Even if you have no evidence that this person will handle your request with a sense of urgency, you can appeal to their willingness to be there for the team.

One last comment on making requests: choose your battles. If you are in the habit of procrastinating until your requests are urgent or treating requests that aren't as important as urgent, you will lose your right to make those requests. When you engage the services of friends, family members, volunteers, or coworkers, treat their time as highly valuable and understand their priorities before you assign a deadline to a request. They won't always tell you if they have something more pressing, so make sure you ask.

Gratitude

When we are racing through life with our to-do list and agenda, we sometimes forget to stop and show appreciation. Gratitude is one of the most powerful leadership tools we have available.

Start Each Day With Five

One of the most basic activities is to practice gratitude in the quiet solitude of the early morning. Begin each morning by listing five things you are thankful for. Even when you are faced with adversity, find a private moment to write down five things you appreciate. This simple activity is a beautiful addition to a prayer time and balances our requests by giving God the recognition He deserves.

Some examples could be very basic such as having enough food to eat or something extravagant such as having a Starbucks Cinnamon Dolce Latte on the way to the office. I'm thankful for a hot shower in a cozy bathroom, a comfortable bed, and my Corvette. Yes, I work hard to earn those things, but none of us are guaranteed that we'll have nice things no matter how hard we work. They could be gone in an instant too, so never take them for granted.

I'm also thankful for the learning experiences that accompany the tough times. I try my hardest to be thankful for the difficult people in my life because it hones my interpersonal skills. Those tough days show me what I'm made of and bring me satisfaction when I overcome the challenges they present. I'm grateful when my friends come to me for help and advice because it helps me remember the real priorities of life.

Appreciating Others

Showing appreciation to everyone in your life pays dividends. Try it with your friends, family members, and coworkers, and watch what happens. It makes them feel valued and needed. They will be more likely to look for ways to help you in the future. You'll discover people who feel appreciated are more willing to honor your requests and more likely to forgive your faults. They will see you model an important skill and learn how to practice it from your example.

Our parents made sure that we said "please" and "thank you" if we wanted anything. They taught us to be grateful when we receive gifts, but proper thanks are in order when we receive help of any kind — even if it is part of someone's job. In fact, if you'd like to make sure you get eager cooperation in the future, a proper show of appreciation is in order regardless of how small the gift or help was.

I mentioned earlier that one of my goals was to brag on other people. This unfortunately doesn't come naturally for me, and I'm not alone. Sure, people have things they are supposed to do because that's their job or role in life. However, it's not always easy for people to carry out the day-to-day tasks even though it's part of their job. They encounter adversity, delays, illness, and other frustrations that make it tough to do the simple things some days. Just a quick note of appreciation as simple as, "I really appreciate that I can always count on you to arrive at work on time." Yes, arriving on time is an expectation and a condition of employment, but it's a feat that isn't always that easy.

I served on the board of the Oklahoma chapter of the National Speakers Association one year. That year, our president was Kristine Sexter. During my entire time as a chapter member, Kristine was always the first to greet me by name with a smile and a hug. It wasn't just me — she greeted everyone with that same aggressive hospitality. It made it easy to say yes when she asked me to serve on her board as a volunteer. It was a big volunteer commitment, but I think I learned something more valuable from her than anyone I had ever volunteered with before — how to show appreciation in sincere ways that motivate the people around you.

Kristine's magic formula for showing sincere appreciation was to present specific instances, explain how they matter to the outcome, and deliver it as quickly as possible.

The best way to teach a behavior is to model it. Kristine showed appreciation for things that I thought were easy and ideas that came naturally. To me, they were no big deal, but she made it seem like they were the most difficult tasks and brilliant ideas ever. And her appreciation was always heartfelt and sincere no matter how "over the top" it seemed at the time.

Most of the chapter officers lived in different cities so Kristine depended on having one good face-to-face board meeting every other month, some phone calls, and lots of e-mail. I'm glad she did because I was able to keep those e-mails as a reminder of how important I was to her.

How many times has someone provided you some information via e-mail and then you simply replied "Thanks." Maybe you even got excited and put an exclamation point on it. Nothing says how little we appreciate people so underwhelmingly as typing six letters and pressing the send button. We

Upgrade Your Appreciation

There are many more creative, heartfelt, and specific way to say thank you. Here are some examples that I pulled from Kristine Sexter's thank you e-mails that she sent to me and to our board members.

Perfect!

Exactly what I was looking for.

Thank you for keeping this fabulous momentum going!

AWESOME! You continue to impress me with your focus, drive, and professionalism.

YOU GUYS ROCK! Thank you for your commitment to our mission.

Incredibly exciting! Let's do it!"

Outstanding display of teamwork, collaboration, and positive attitude!

You make my day.

I don't know what I'd do without you.

live in an age where we rarely receive hand-written thank you notes. When we did, they weren't note cards with just "Thanks" on them — when did we determine that one word was enough to show our appreciation?

When we write note cards, we feel the need to fill the inside space with meaningful comments that relay our sentiments on how much the gift or assistance meant or how it helped us. A typed e-mail intended to convey our appreciation should contain a similar number of words and specific comments as well. Tell the other person how their action or gift helped you.

The Fine Art of Appreciation

One of the big discoveries of my leadership development is that praise is a great motivator for future performance as well as a great way to reward people for their current performance. I also learned that everyone prefers to receive praise in different ways. For instance, some prefer quiet sentiments delivered via a thank you note or private word of thanks. Others appreciate that but really love it when they receive public recognition in front of their peers. Some prefer small gifts, plaques, or cash rewards.

Golden Rule versus Platinum Rule

When most people think of appreciation, they practice something that resembles the Golden Rule: do unto others as you would have them do unto you. That can serve as a good general rule of thumb. However, I've learned that it's more powerful to show appreciation using the Platinum Rule: treat others the way they want to be treated. You probably remember this concept from Chapter 4: Leading Meaningful Conversations or Chapter 8: Creating Meaningful Customer Dialogue. The Platinum Rule is as powerful when applied to appreciation as it is in creating a great customer experience.

The only way to accurately apply the Platinum Rule to the customer experience is to engage customers in communication of some sort that gathers feedback. Face-to-face two-way communication is the most effective way to do that when it is possible. However, some companies use paper, online, or telephone surveys. Using this feedback can help a company make changes to products, services, benefits, policies, and procedures. It's also useful for a salesperson to gather this information with individual prospects and customers so they can tailor their practices to the needs of individual transactions. With large-ticket sales, a customized sales experience can make the difference between getting the sale and getting the boot out the door.

When I do consulting work with work teams, we do a brainstorming exercise on ways to show gratitude. Participants are asked to share how they prefer to receive praise. It's a great springboard for developing an employee appreciation program, but it's also an eye-opener for managers. For many of them, it is the first time that they hear that some team members are mortified by public praise. It's amazing to see how many different ways people prefer to receive their praise.

My first major blunder with delivering appreciation in the way someone prefers was as a young supervisor. I was always a hand-written-thank-you-note kind of person. However, I worked in a company where it seemed to be expected to give public praise — the bigger the accomplishment, the more public the praise. I was pretty introverted, but I was committed to overcoming my fear of speaking in front of groups so that I could provide public praise for my team just like the other managers.

The day came when one of my team members hit her five-year anniversary with the company, and she was doing a great job for our team. It was time for me to recognize her accomplishments in front of our department. The

Ideas for Showing Your Appreciation

Appreciation isn't a one-size-fits-all solution. When you are creating an appreciation program for your organization, design it so you have some flexibility. Make sure that everyone feels their accomplishments are being treated equally. Here are some methods for showing your gratitude for both individual and team appreciation.

- Free food (Take the individual to lunch or give a gift card to a restaurant. When you are providing recognition to the entire team, cater in lunch or take them to a restaurant.)
- Permission to participate in a special activity such as a charity fundraiser or focus group
- Hand-written notes
- Certificates suitable for framing
- Gift cards to a favorite store
- Praise in front of their peers
- One-on-one praise
- Party
- Personal gifts
- Candy
- Flowers
- Paid time off
- Flexible schedule

group would be about forty people. I was really nervous, but I practiced what I was going to say for a couple weeks. It would have been much easier on me to just write her a hand-written note and buy her flowers.

The day of the big meeting came. Visibly nervous, I stood in front of the group and told them how much she meant to our team and gave a couple examples of her contributions to the company. The group applauded, and she blushed and smiled.

Imagine my surprise when I discovered the next day that the public recognition made her furious. I was definitely not expecting that. When she and I talked about it, I found out that she not only preferred to be given quiet one-on-one praise, she was mortified by public praise. You can bet I never made that mistake again.

It was a powerful lesson in knowing how your team members prefer to receive their praise. Everyone needs praise for a job well done, but we need to cater to the needs of individual team members. Just because I may like to receive my praise in a handwritten note doesn't mean that my team members prefer to receive their praise the same way. Take the time to learn the preferences of your team. It's as important as learning how to make requests. Both are key to getting things done through the work of others.

Praise People How and When They Need It

Smart managers know that they need to give praise in ways their people need and desire it. However, some managers only give negative feedback. They are the no-news-is-good-news style of manager. People need to hear positive things every day. Here is an example of how detrimental lack of feedback can be.

Janet is a trainer and content developer in a corporate training department. Her supervisor, Darla, never tells Janet how she thinks she's doing unless something goes wrong. Because Janet only hears the bad things, she assumes her supervisor thinks she only does bad things. The time spent with her supervisor in private or in team meetings focuses on working on issues she needs to improve on.

Janet eventually becomes consumed with all her issues, problems, and failures, and she assumes she can do no right. Over a period of six months, her overall happiness slips into a black hole. She talks often with her friends outside her office about how terrible her supervisor thinks she's doing. Janet is frustrated because she can't seem to improve her performance enough in the key areas her supervisor keeps focusing on.

Janet had even begun having health problems and had missed some work because of it. A coworker had begun to blame Janet for the overload he felt at work because of her absences. Janet's attitude and her health were deteriorating, and she believed she was in a hopeless situation. She became more miserable, and she began to search for a job outside the company. She realized she'd better get out because she was losing her job. She knew it was easier to find a new job when she already had one.

One day, Darla calls Janet into her office. Janet begins to wonder what she's done wrong now. Darla closes the office door, unlocks her desk drawer, and pulls out a legal-sized envelope. Darla reaches into the envelope and pulls out an official-looking sheet of paper. Janet feels her face begin to flush and she starts to sweat. She thinks to herself, "This is it." She is sure she's being reprimanded — maybe even fired. Darla smiles at Janet and tells her, "I've been working on a raise for you for about five months, and I finally got it. It's a 10 percent raise. You really deserve it."

Janet was stunned. All this time, she had worried about how bad her supervisor thought she was doing and how she was probably going to get fired. While Janet was grateful for the raise, what she really craved all those months was some positive feedback and praise for what she was doing right. She was a person who needed more-frequent verbal praise and reinforcement. Her boss would have lost her had she found another job.

Janet and Darla aren't unusual. All people need to hear when they are doing a good job even though they should already know what the standards of a good job are. The world is full of managers, parents, volunteer coordinators, and even companies who forget that people need to hear appreciation and positive feedback. Knowing how to give people the type of positive feedback they need is even more important than providing negative feedback. They need to be thanked because they showed up on time and put in a hard day's work. They need to know how going the extra mile on that report made a difference to the company. They want to know that someone noticed they kept a great attitude when they were under a tough deadline. They deserve the reward that comes with appreciation, but there is something more important than that — positive feedback motivates people to perform to the best of their abilities in the future and strive for success. That future effort is the ultimate outcome for the person, the company, and the customers (internal or external) that person serves.

The Chemistry of Conflict

The art of creating lifelong business relationships includes the ability to handle the inevitable conflicts that come along. Our ability to navigate those with grace, tact, and skill can define us among our peers. The people around us study how we manage disagreements and mistakes to learn whether they can approach us with difficult topics and feedback. They learn whether we are someone they will want to be around in good times and in bad. When they see us at our most challenging times, they see our true character.

Conflict happens in the best relationships. Highly productive, diverse teams experience conflict because everyone brings different ideas, experiences, and expertise to the table. Those in conflict must understand its source and work through it in a positive way. If they don't, the residual effects hang over the individuals like a toxic black cloud that threatens the overall health of the relationship. In the end, everyone must pull together and support the team with a unified front. Even though they didn't agree to start with, they are able to accomplish more together than they could individually.

Conflict normally starts with a small misunderstanding or a poor choice of words. If the individuals involved don't get clarification through meaningful conversation, the misunderstanding commonly escalates into a conflict.

If you study the make-up of the typical conflict, you'll discover a lot of assumptions. A lot of the heat in a conflict is created inside someone's head, and the assumptions cloud the issue. Moving towards resolution requires just one of the individuals engaged in the conflict to muster up the courage to ask a few questions. If you can get some clarification about the subject of the conflict, it can clear the air. As simple as that sounds, it takes an extreme amount of bravery to place yourself on the line to ask the difficult questions. Without those difficult questions, a relationship can be lost forever.

Combustible Verbal Compounds

Words are powerful compounding agents in conflict. Sometimes it's as simple as using particular words that remind someone of a bad memory or a past conflict. You can't always predict how someone is going to react to your choice of words, but it helps to know what words trigger negative feelings in others.

What words make you cringe? One guy told me that when he hated hearing the phrase "No Problem" because someone he knew used to say that and then would disregard his request. Some people are sensitive to hearing the Lord's name used in vain (Jesus! Oh My God!). People who live and work with teenagers hate hearing someone say "Whatever." I get frustrated when I walk into a fast-food restaurant and they say "Next" instead of greeting me or even saying "How may I help you?" When we hear some phrases, it reminds us of something our mom or grandfather used to say. Some words seem totally harmless to one person but trigger a memory of a negative person or bad experience. Choose your words carefully because you don't always know the effect they have on people.

Anyone can say the wrong thing or say something the wrong way. Regardless of how it sounds, assume he or she meant the best possible meaning. Unfortunately, we can't always count on people to take our words the way we meant them. One thing that you can count on is that more words are often better than few words if they provide valuable clarification. Some people pick and choose what they hear. You might say, "This project didn't go as well as I had hoped because of the issues we encountered in the marketplace this year." The individual only hears, "This project didn't go as well as I had hoped," and translates that to mean, "You think I'm a failure."

Some conflicts are caused because someone took your words and twisted them around like a serial killer pastes miscellaneous words together on a ransom note. They don't ask for clarification; they just go with their assumption. If you don't question why they are responding to your words the way they are, you find yourself sitting in the midst of a strange and confusing conflict.

I was working on a photo project for work, and I needed a couple photos of some middle-aged, American Indian men. At the time, very few people fit that demographic in the company. The regional personnel manager referred me to a company facility in New Mexico.

I called the facility's personnel manager and explained what I needed. They had two men that fit the description on the overnight maintenance crew — it was a dirty job in their desert town. I requested that she photograph them at the beginning of their shift so their clothes would be clean and fresh. I asked her if she had any questions and gave her my contact information. She said she would take care of it.

> Some conflicts are caused because someone took your words and twisted them around like a serial killer pastes miscellaneous words together on a ransom note. They don't ask for clarification. They just go with their assumption.

Currency: Striking Networking Gold in a Relationship Economy   247

A couple of days later, my supervisor called me into her office. Our senior vice president of human resources had alerted her that I had implied that American Indians were dirty. The personnel manager in New Mexico assumed I was making a racial slur. She talked to her facility manager about it who contacted her district manager who went directly to the senior vice president. He was leading the company's diversity initiative and discrimination was a highly sensitive topic. How dare I make the assumption that American Indians were dirty people!

I was crushed because I didn't say that and I certainly didn't mean that at all. Furthermore, I was in deep trouble for something that started with a misunderstanding and had traveled up the corporate ladder. I realize now that she probably took what I said and changed the meaning because of her own feelings of discrimination because she was American Indian.

I took a day to calm down and then called her facility manager. I told him my side of the story and apologized for the misunderstanding. I asked him if I could talk to her. He said that she commonly blew things out of proportion, and he thought it would be a good idea for me to talk with her too. I apologized for not communicating more clearly. I assured her that I would never mean something like that because my own great-grandmother was full-blood Cherokee. It was quiet for a moment and then she said, "Oh, I didn't realize that." Suddenly, the meaning was different because I too was American Indian just like her. I think the conversation ended positively, and I followed up with all the individuals involved with the complaint to let them know it was resolved. I received the snapshots I requested about a week later.

The lesson for me was that people have free will to do anything they want with our words — which includes attaching their own meaning to them. I was dealing with someone over the telephone and could not read her body language or facial expressions. Perhaps something in my tone of voice had triggered a bad memory in her head. Had I been face-to-face with her, I might have been able to read her response to my request better. Maybe she was resentful because I was a person from the corporate office asking her to do something that was outside her normal responsibilities. She might have had a very negative opinion of people from the corporate office (definitely not impossible). Whatever the case, she took my words and twisted them into something that triggered a sensitive issue for her. Unfortunately, it meant that I had to look like the bad guy until I could get it straightened out.

A second important lesson to me was the importance of addressing the issue with the individual directly. Some people lack the courage to address misunderstandings and clarify what the offender meant. Instead, they just leave the open wound to fester. In the case of dealing with a difficult personality as the store manager indicated I was, it was important to address the issue at hand. Complainers gripe to anyone who will listen because they think it makes them look like a good guy when they make someone else look like a bad guy. They commonly don't have accurate information about the issue at hand, AND they don't have a solution to the problem they are complaining about.

Susan worked in a volunteer role where she was the leader of the team. She had a great committee, but there was one individual named Don who was a pot-stirrer. Don was charming and funny, and he would tell Susan one thing but go behind her back and do another. Don began to seek out individuals he could stir up about different items or things people had said. Don was so cheerful, they didn't realize what he was doing. In meetings, he would find ways to take the items he was responsible for (or at least concerned about) and monopolize large amounts of time limiting what the team could accomplish. The discussion would end with Don making a commitment to accomplish an action item in his area of responsibility. He would always give it an outrageously close deadline. In the time Susan worked with him, he never met a deadline he committed to, and he rarely finished anything he volunteered to do. He basically just showed up for meetings and shared his opinions. He hadn't even kept up some of the membership requirements necessary for being part of the committee.

Susan ignored it for a while, but it was beginning to cause teamwork issues, and the committee was starting to pull apart. She found that Don was gifted at putting up a smoke screen to cover the tasks he had not accomplished. When she asked Don about his progress, he avoided giving reports. He would claim that Susan asked him to do something different or he wouldn't return her follow-up phone calls or e-mails in a timely manner. Don met with other committee members between the meetings and stirred up trouble and discontent. Susan had joined Don and another committee member for lunch one time. It became a gossip session that made Susan nervous to participate in because of the individuals involved — she felt that she could be guilty because of association. She even had a couple of people come to her concerned about the catty comments they had overheard Don make about fellow committee members. Susan had to do something.

She scheduled a face-to-face meeting with Don away from his usual environment — his comfort zone. They chose a coffee shop, and Susan prepared a list of the items she was going to discuss. Keep in mind that Susan HATES conflict and she REALLY HATES having to address it. It took her several weeks to get up the nerve to do it. This was a volunteer role and she worked far too hard to deal with difficult people OR do something so uncomfortable as deal with a situation like this. Nevertheless, the glamorous job of leader carries with it yucky tasks that help us hone our leadership skills. If you can't stand the heat, get out of the kitchen. While the heat is uncomfortable, in some situations, the heat refines our leadership skills.

Maxie Carpenter (www.mvcinc.org) gives these tips for confronting this type of individual in his book, *Managing Difficult People in the Workplace: A Practical Guide to Confronting Difficult People.*

- Strive to make honesty non-threatening. Provide examples that illustrate how you would have reacted had this person just been honest with you when they had the opportunity.
- Provide specific examples that are indisputable matters of record that clearly identify how this individual behaves away from you compared to how they behave in your presence.
- Be personal when you can, but don't allow unrealistic commitments or statements.
- Be prepared to compromise but only if there is an understanding that matters will be revisited more aggressively if the deceptive behavior continues.
- Listen to their humor; this is their communication vehicle of choice. [Don used his knowledge of the organization's policies to create a diversion instead of using humor.] Be prepared to appreciate it, but also be prepared to let this person know when it is inappropriate, unprofessional, and that it doesn't accomplish what it's intended to. Remember that this type of individual wants to be seen as something other than what they really are.
- This individual does not like follow-up and depends on a supervisor's lack of attention to detail. That's why there is such a willingness to say "yes" in front of you and then to do something entirely different behind your back.

Susan and Don met at the coffee shop and exchanged some rapport-building conversation. Then, Susan pulled out her list of items she wanted to cover. While she had some strong suspicions and second-hand information, she opted to only discuss the indisputable facts such as Don's inability to meet deadlines, not doing what she asked him to do, monopolizing large parts of the meeting, not keeping up his membership requirements to be on the committee. Susan did mention that she felt uncomfortable with some of the conversation the day they ate lunch together. Even though Don presented the information he shared as fact, it construed the details to paint the individuals involved in a negative light. Susan told him that it made her feel very guarded in what she could tell him in the future.

It was a difficult conversation for sure. Don was defensive and assured Susan that she just misunderstood his intentions, but facts don't lie. She encouraged Don to consider leaving the committee if he didn't have the time to complete any of the commitments he made. His role was important, and Susan needed someone who was focused on making a positive difference to their organization. Don ended up finishing his term on the committee. Susan didn't have to address the issues again, but he was never very productive. He had a passion for the organization but that didn't translate into doing anything meaningful on the committee.

We don't always get to select the people we work with. Even when we do, we don't always know their heart and habits until we work alongside them. It pays to know how to address the issues as they happen because the longer you wait, the worse it is to deal with.

Staring Conflict in the Face: What to Do When Conflict Happens

When conflicts happen, we seem to go into "fight or flight" mode. It's a response that all living things were born with. When we are faced with danger, our body takes over based on our ability to overcome the danger. In conflict, we find ourselves faced with the same fight or flight response based on our ability to handle the conflict. The more skilled you become at responding to it, the better you'll be able to face the conflict down and follow it through to resolution.

Not all conflict is resolvable, and not every fight is worth the time, emotion, or effort. You have to choose your battles. Since most conflicts are based in misunderstanding and lack of communication, investing a little effort in creating meaningful conversation will allow you to overcome an above-average number of conflicts. It's not about winning or losing because no one wins if the conflict isn't cleared up. When the light is shed on the situation, it provides clarity to the real issues and truth about the situation.

One Tuesday, the company that picks up Dale's trash forgot one of his yard waste bags. It was a busy week and calling the company to remind them just slipped his mind. The bag sat on the sidewalk decaying. Finally, he called on Friday to let them know that the bag had not been picked up. He didn't think they'd actually pick it up, but he thought he should at least report it. What followed was a comedy of errors.

Dale left a detailed voice mail at the office and asked them to call him if they had any questions. Natalie, the office assistant called him and left a message on his voice mail to call her but didn't tell him what she needed. Dale called her back and once again left her a detailed message. He again asked her specifically to let him know what information she was missing. He was in a meeting when she called back, so she got his voice mail. Dale was puzzled when Natalie simply asked him to call instead of leaving a more detailed message.

Finally, when Dale connected with Natalie, she accused him of not putting the bag close enough to his other trash and not getting it out soon enough. This was not Dale's first time to put out a yard waste bag. He assured her that he did his part, but the pick-up truck driver didn't do his part. Her condescending tone was that of a scorned woman on her last nerve. It seemed to be her goal to prove the pick-up problem was not their fault instead of simply reporting the complaint.

Dale had dealt with this company several times because they've just never been able to handle the city's trash contract with any level of competence. However, they've always been courteous. This woman was obviously someone who had no business talking to anyone on the phone for any company — ever. Dale asked her to transfer him to her supervisor — a normally courteous man who he had spoken with in the past to resolve issues. Dale didn't really think he would get the bag picked up, but he needed to report Natalie's terrible demeanor. The supervisor needed to know how she was treating customers. Natalie abruptly put him on hold, and there was a long wait.

When the supervisor picked up the phone, Dale figured out what the long pause was — Natalie was briefing her supervisor about her view of the issue. When the supervisor picked up the phone, he immediately lit into Dale: "Why did you wait for four days to report it? Why didn't you put it closer to the rest of your trash? Are you sure that you didn't put it out after the trash truck ran?

After the supervisor calmed down, Dale said, "I was talking with your assistant to report the bag left behind so you could address the situation with your driver. I didn't expect to get it picked up. The reason you and I are talking now is because of how Natalie treated me. I've been treated courteously every time I've ever contacted your office. I've never been treated as rudely by anyone as she just treated me."

The supervisor's demeanor changed, and he explained that it had been a stressful week at the office. The supervisor also assumed when Dale called that it was one of his loony neighbors. They lovingly called his neighborhood the "bird cage" — not because the streets are named after birds but because it has so many loony-bird residents with too much time on their hands.

Perhaps part of the office stress was caused by Natalie's explosive demeanor, and she had everyone in the office stirred up. To make matters worse, the supervisor was dealing with incomplete information. If he had simply started the call with some meaningful conversation to clarify the details, he wouldn't have had to apologize for yelling at Dale as soon as he picked up the phone.

Once Dale gained control of the conversation, he clarified that he was simply reporting it. However, he wondered if there was any chance that a truck could pick it up after they finish their normal Friday route. Dale told him that he would understand if that wasn't possible. He reminded the supervisor again that the only reason they were talking was because of his rude office assistant. Dale was able to sympathize with the supervisor about his frustrations at the office and with our crazy neighbors. By the end of the call, the supervisor told Dale he'd personally pick up the yard waste bag which he did just a couple hours later.

What a painful experience that was! It would have been easier to hang up on his crummy excuse for an office assistant and report both issues to the mayor. However, Dale was able to salvage the relationship with the supervisor. It was such a great example for demonstrating the value of using meaningful conversation to diffuse and resolve conflict. By the way, Natalie only lasted a few more weeks.

Resolving Conflict

When I look back on my time in the corporate world, I have to admit that the things I miss the least are the office politics and the inevitable conflicts that arise from normal team interaction. A team that thinks and acts alike provides a pleasant environment. It offers a status quo environment where people who hate change feel very comfortable. On the other hand, it normally doesn't yield innovative ideas and a progressive work ethic like a diverse team will. A progressive and diverse team is usually made up of individuals who have different ideas, backgrounds, skills, and experience.

When there is diversity in an environment where innovation and feedback are inspired and encouraged, there is inherent conflict. The process of working through the conflict is where many ideas are developed. The conflict gives the team members a chance to develop their communication, interpersonal, and conflict-resolution skills. Conflict is normal and healthy but the leader of the team must be skilled in conflict resolution.

Do you remember the story about the angry biker from Chapter 9: The Value of the F Word? Even though he was angry because he didn't agree with a decision that the motorcycle event group made, he had valuable ideas that would help make the event better. We would never have gotten those ideas if we hadn't been able to calm him down enough to get them.

Angry, irrational people can't even access their own ideas, let alone share them. Forget being able to resolve the conflict. The key is to get the individual calmed down enough for rational thought to return. Is there some chance that the person can walk away, stew for a bit, and calm themselves down? Sure there is. However, in many cases, they may calm down, but the thoughts and feelings that escalated their anger are still present. The problem will most likely return if those thoughts and feelings aren't addressed. Worse yet, they could become larger and more distant from the truth if allowed to simmer too long.

In the case of the angry biker, we worked to calm him down. I got him to vent his frustrations by giving him a platform. I simply said, "I understand you're upset with us. Help me understand why you feel that way." He had valid concerns, and it was important that I honor those concerns. I could have gotten defensive about someone not liking our decision, but that would have only added fuel to the fire. Maintaining total control of your emotions is critical when encountering someone who is angry.

Recall that the biker was a participant in our motorcycle poker run. The bikers ride a route to draw cards along the route, and each card has a particular point value. The riders could leave anytime during a ninety-minute period. It began raining that morning right before the first bike was set to leave. The more experienced bikers went out on the route. As the morning wore on, a soft rain continued to fall. We decided to allow the remaining bikers to draw cards at the event without riding the route.

This was popular with the riders who didn't feel comfortable riding in the rain, but it wasn't so popular with the riders who rode the route. Most understood our decision and some used it as an opportunity to tell the war stories of encountering stormy conditions on the open rode. A few grumbled quietly — those are the most dangerous kind because they talk to other people instead of the people in charge. In the short term, that seems better because you don't have to deal with an angry person.

However, they tell their version of the story over and over to anyone who will listen. For a motorcycle event, it creates a network of people who share the story that one angry person perceives as the truth. In just a short time, there are many people who boycott the future events because of the opinion of one person. A happy customer tells three people; an unhappy customer tells thirteen people. Because some people like to pass along negative information, some of those thirteen people will also tell others. It's much better to give the angry person a platform for venting their anger.

Our angry biker fortunately stepped forward and shared his frustrations with us instead. He told me he was angry because he had just ridden the route in the rain when he didn't know there was an option. Given the option, he might have opted just to draw his cards at the event site too. It wasn't fair that all the participants didn't have the same choice.

Once I listened to all the details surrounding his frustration, I explained that we had never had rain before. We made the decision to draw cards at the event site that morning once it looked like the rain would not stop. Part of the value we offered was giving participants a chance to draw cards for prize money. If we didn't draw those cards at the event site, a large number of people wouldn't receive all they paid for. What should I do then — return their money? It was a cancer fund-raiser and with the rain, only a quarter of the people we were expecting showed up.

We didn't make a flawless choice, but it was the best one we could make after we weighed the options. I agreed that it wasn't fair that some had to ride in the rain to draw cards while others didn't. Then I asked, "What would you have done if you were me?" He stopped for a minute and said he didn't know. I assured him that our volunteers had invested hundreds of hours in the event and no one was more disappointed than we were. I asked him to let me know if he thought of any ideas for handling the situation.

I wasn't sure if it was successful, but he wasn't nearly as upset when he walked away as when he started. I asked open-ended questions and listened to his concerns. I listened for understanding and in this case, I agreed that it wasn't a perfect decision. I apologized that he had to ride in the rain when others did not. Once he calmed down, I explained the reason we made the decision. Then, I asked for his suggestions — that made him

Conflict Resolution Formula

Acknowledge their concern or state your concern
+
Add an empathetic statement
+
State your interest in resolution or the reason for the way it is
+
Ask "How can I help?"

Here are some reasons this formula works.
- Giving the other party a listening ear pulls some of the emotion out of the interaction.
- Encouraging them to talk helps them verbalize what they are feeling and rationalize the situation.
- Apologies can move the conflict forward to resolution. Never be afraid to apologize if it will move the situation forward. It shows you are taking responsibility for your participation in resolution.
- All parties involved usually can assume some responsibility in most misunderstandings.

an active participant in addressing the issue should it rise again. It moved the situation from conflict to collaborative problem solving. It was a variation of the Conflict Resolution Formula shown on the previous page.

Sure enough, he came up about an hour later after he had eaten lunch and changed out of his wet clothes. He had an idea. He suggested we include a statement on the entry form: "In the event of rain, poker cards will be drawn at the event site. It was a great idea that became part of our policy for future events."

Here is a scenario that a manager might encounter with an employee who has been passed over for a promotion. The employee was applying for an inventory replenishment manager position. Even though the most-qualified candidate was chosen, the employee still feels angry and frustrated. Left to stew over the situation without using the Conflict Resolution Formula, the employee will share his side of the story with other employees and create an environment of distrust. Using the Conflict Resolution Formula uses a communication platform to inject truth into a situation. If you don't communicate details, the grapevine will inevitably fill in the details for you.

> **Acknowledge their concern or state your concern:** I realize that you wanted that promotion.
>
> **Empathetic statement:** I know that you are disappointed.
>
> **State your interest in resolution or the reason for the way it is:** We chose the other candidate because he had more replenishment experience.
>
> **Ask "How can I help?"** I'd like to mentor you to get you ready for the next available promotion.

Note that the last statement includes an action item that involves both of you. It should be something that you can deliver or you could lose credibility. Make sure you structure this offer in a way that places the responsibility for driving the solution on the other person. The last thing you need is to place yourself in a position to solve someone else's problems. You probably don't have enough time in you day to solve all your own problems. However, if someone is truly interested in resolving this, be willing to offer them feedback and ideas. In many cases, you'll find people are willing to vent their anger but not willing to do what it takes to resolve the issue.

Here is another example where a manager must deal with an employee who has a bad attitude. In many cases, the reason people are angry isn't really the reason they claim it is. Often, something else is going on in someone's life, and he becomes hypersensitive to issues in his environment.

> **Acknowledge their concern or state your concern:** I'm concerned that your attitude is not as positive as it once was.
>
> **Add an empathetic statement:** I realize you are under more stress with work these days. Is that the biggest issue for you?
>
> **State your interest in resolution or the reason for the way it is:** We're going to be extremely busy until this project is finished. However, I'd like to work to resolve this situation because you are important to our team. It affects all of us when you are frustrated.
>
> **Ask "How can I help?"** Is there anything I can do?

It's possible that the employee's attitude is poor because he has an issue with the manager or the organization. While perception weighs in heavily in such a situation, get as much information about the employee's expectations as possible. You have a better chance at resolution if both parties have all their concerns out on the table. Never be too proud to apologize — even if the guilt doesn't fully fall on you. Apologies can move the conflict forward to resolution. It shows you are taking responsibility for your participation in resolution.

Conflict is a huge time-waster for a leader. The objective of the conflict resolution formula is to use meaningful conversation to get to the bottom of the issues or concerns and to create a solution. Not every conflict is solvable and not every individual is mature or rational enough to engage in the process. Likewise, not all people can maintain enough objectivity to distance themselves from the emotions that are triggered in conflict. However, the more you are able to break down the issues at hand and remove the emotion, the more quickly you'll be able to resolve the conflict and get back to the task at hand.

Prayer: Not the Least We Can Do

Despite our best efforts to resolve a situation, some will seem to be out of our control. Why do many people turn to prayer only when nothing else seems to work and the situation feels hopeless? Prayer is one of the most powerful ways to intervene in situations. Even though it seems as though God should know the needs of your life, He also desires to hear the cry of your heart.

If you are challenged by someone difficult in your life, pray for them. I worked with a gentleman named Joe on a training team. No matter what I did, he would avoid me and treat me coldly. It made me feel frustrated and uncomfortable. As we discussed in Chapter 6: Why Don't People Listen, people don't need to have a bad experience with us to be reminded of a past negative experience. Sometimes our mannerisms, appearance, or something we say can take them back to that negative place or feeling. They may not even remember it or realize that it is happening. I was willing to bet that was a factor in my relationship with Joe.

I decided that I would pray for him every day. Even though I admit that I was a bit inclined to pray, "Dear God, please transfer Joe to another department so I don't have to work with him," I decided to pray something different. I prayed for God to bless Joe and draw him closer to Him and help Joe discover his own personal truth.

Almost immediately, I began to feel differently about the situation. The emotional burden of the tense situation with Joe lightened for me. I don't know if it helped him, but it did wonders for me. I worship a big God — I bet he's working in Joe's life too!

Final Thoughts on Getting What You Want, Need, and Deserve

Any place where people work or live together is a breeding ground for conflict. However, it's also a place where we can bring out the best in people by making our requests with warmth and sincerity and showing genuine appreciation. Practicing the Platinum Rule — treating others the way they want to be treated — requires making meaningful conversation and taking a genuine interest in them. When you gather the information you need to treat people properly and overcome conflict, you hold the keys to their heart.

- Important requests are better received when those making them are passionate, friendly, polite, and firm.
- Never make a request without a deadline. If we don't accompany our requests with a deadline, we'll get put behind those things that seem more urgent even though our request is more important.
- Begin each morning by listing five things you are thankful for. Even when you are faced with adversity, find a private moment to find those five things.
- The magic formula for showing sincere appreciation is to present specific instances, explain how they mattered to the overall outcome, and deliver it as quickly as possible.
- When we write note cards, we feel the need to fill the inside space with meaningful comments that relay our sentiments on how much the gift or assistance meant or how it helped us. A typed e-mail intended to convey our appreciation should contain a similar number of words and specific comments as well.
- Apply the Platinum Rule when looking for ways to show your appreciation. Not everyone prefers to receive their praise the same way. Praise people how and when they need it.
- In conflict, we find ourselves faced with a fight or flight response based on our ability to handle the conflict. The more skilled you become at responding to conflict, the better you'll be able to face the conflict down and follow it through to resolution.

CHAPTER 16
Brands and Legacies: Not Such Different Creatures

In the last months of finishing this book, I had many opportunities to explore the reality of leaving a legacy. As I pulled the content together for the closing section, several friends lost parents and other close family members. Then, my father-in-law died — my husband Tom's last parent. As we sifted through the details of the estate and house that Tom's parents shared for fifty-six years, we wondered what they would have wanted us to do with it all. We wondered if we could create a legacy for them?

Because my friends shared this common bond of losing a loved one recently, we engaged in a lot of conversations about the grieving process and the decisions about what to do with everything. When do you give away your father's jacket — the one item you kept because it still smelled like he did after a day spent working at his mechanic shop? If you held it close and shut your eyes, you could still barely smell the pungent combination of transmission fluid, cigarette smoke, and sweat from a hard day's work. Just seeing it hanging in you closet reminded you of the way he gave you a big hug after he came home at the end of the work day.

What do you with your grandmother's tatted handkerchiefs and those gloves she wore on her wedding day? Do you frame them so you can remember her fondly and protect them, or do you pass them on to your daughter to use for her wedding? What would they really have wanted you to do with the leftovers of their estate? Even though they didn't specify any preferences, what would really make them proud of the children they raised — what actions could we take to accurately reflect the values they instilled? What would they want us to remember of the dash on their tombstone?

Build the Right Brand and Your Legacy Will Come

Our memories of our loved ones who have passed on often spark feelings and reactions — some fond and others sad. When we hear one of their favorite songs, see one of their favorite movies, or eat one of their favorite dishes, we are reminded of them. Sometimes we'll catch ourselves an hour later still reminiscing about the times we spent with them. Depending on the individual, we'll be reminded of the values they held dear, the activities they loved, and the things they did for others.

A brand is a lot like a legacy. You build your brand while you are alive; your legacy consists of the things you leave behind. If you strive for the same values and initiatives while you are alive in pursuit of establishing a solid brand, your legacy will be a long-lasting and powerful one. I want that for me. I bet you want that too. Thank God I lived long enough to connect the dots between building a brand and leaving a legacy.

Anyone can leave a legacy. Each person can make a series of choices that defines their legacy — their values, the way they managed their lives and finances, the charities they chose to help by giving time and money to, the friends they called their extended family, and their purpose and calling. The choices that were made intentionally had a greater influence on their legacy.

I do some of my best concept development in the shower. It's also one of my favorite places to solve the world's problems through prayer — maybe that's why I get such great ideas in the shower. One day, I was standing in the shower rinsing the shampoo from my hair, and it hit me — what if we approached the development of our brand as if we were building our legacy? Could we tie the two together? Yes! Of course, we all have the capacity to live an intentional, purpose-led life. The challenge for all of us is determining what brand image will create that lasting legacy.

What Will Your Legacy Be Worth?

For many of us, we harness our competitive spirit and pursue our dreams until we win. Any good brand is based on being a winner, right? And if we pursue the things we were born to do, the race will be easier, correct? But what is the price of winning? And is the race that is easiest for us to run the one we are really *called* to run? Will the race that is easiest to run be the one that grows us the most? I challenge you to choose your legacy not because it is easy but because it is challenging!

Eight Belles: The Price of Winning

Eight Belles, a dark gray filly Thoroughbred with a mighty, competitive spirit, had earned the right to race against a field of colts on that May 3 afternoon in 2008 — running with the big boys in the world's most famous horse race. She was the first filly to run in the fabled Kentucky Derby in nine years. Only thirty-nine fillies had run in the previous 133 years. Veteran *Washington Post* sportswriter Sally Jenkins characterized her best by saying, "She ran with the heart of a locomotive on champagne-glass ankles."

After running the race of her life and crossing the finish line in second place, the unthinkable happened. She snapped one front ankle and then the other, collapsing to the ground and throwing her jockey. Such an injury is catastrophic, and the medical staff saw no choice but to extinguish her life as she lay on the brown dirt track under the late afternoon sun. In a split second, three-year-old Eight Belles became a memory — a life cut short long before her time.

In the days following the race, a flurry of controversy and speculation clouded the sport. Was the racetrack material to blame? Was it wrong to run a filly in a field of colts? Did the jockey fail to read any signs of distress? Was she just too young? Are the bloodlines producing lightning-fast horses with legs too frail to handle the load of a 1,500 pound body thundering around a track? Had racing become a profit-making machine with total disregard to the physical soundness and safety of the horses. Once the dust settles, we'll all agree that it was a horrible tragedy we wish someone could have prevented. Eight Belles won't be remembered so much as the racing legend she should have been. Hopefully, the legacy created by her life cut short will spark a firestorm of change in the horse racing industry. If it doesn't, she will have died in vain.

Amidst the tragedy, I realized how that athletic gray filly symbolized what women today deal with. Eight Belles was doing what she was born and trained to do with power and precision without any thought to the possible consequences. For the chance to compete on an equal playing field against the odds, she won but she also paid the ultimate price.

Come to think of it, I'm not sure the lesson is restricted to the fairer sex. Men and women alike race through life with a Type A pace that threatens to cost them everything they value. What gets measured gets done and often the only thing in our lives that is ever measured, other than our credit score, is our professional performance. The human condition for the performance driven is an out-of-balance focus on something that will matter little when our fire is finally extinguished. The price of winning in the wrong race could rob us of our legacy.

Eight Belles' tragic end symbolizes priceless potential never reached. Perhaps that is really what has captivated the world about her untimely death. Could she be symbolic of the human race putting all our heart and soul into just one great passion and excluding all others until it destroys us? Could we be squandering our lives on activities that are pulling us further and further from what we were really meant to do? Could now be the time when people are reflecting on their life and wondering, "Is this all there is? In the end, will what I'm doing really make a difference? Am I really doing what I'm called to do?" Perhaps Eight Belles reminds us that life is short, and we should spend it doing what we were born to do.

What if we stopped — before it's too late — and asked, "What will be my legacy?" We work and live in a performance-driven culture where today's women feel apologetic if they are "just a stay-at-home mom" and people feel less worthy if they don't make the money that affords the "successful lifestyle." When did we forget that a person's true value isn't about financial net worth but about the strength of their character? When did we determine that winning was about bigger houses or more expensive toys or another rung on the corporate ladder? When did we forget that the best place to teach our young people about leadership, love, and teamwork is at

> ## Reality Check to Test Your Priorities
>
> Here is a simple reality check that will quickly push your life under a microscope.
>
> 1. Make a list of those people or things that mean the most to you.
> 2. Write down all the things that you believe you are called to do — activities that serve something greater than yourself.
> 3. Analyze how you spend your time over the period of a week (e-mail, work, housework, playing with children, etc.)
> 4. Evaluate the amount of time you devote to the items in steps 1 and 2.
> 5. Where changes are needed, plan how you will improve the way you spend your time.

home as a family engaged in meaningful activities? True value is about creating a life that leaves a lasting and profound legacy — a great gift for generations to come.

For a vast number of Americans, they discover their life is critically out of balance. Once we realize we aren't serving our calling because we are running in the wrong race, we can begin to make changes to restore it. It won't happen overnight and sometimes realigning our lives requires drastic measures such as career moves, debt reduction, or relationship changes. Too many people race through life with no direction. They simply move from one payday to the next, prioritizing their activities by what is urgent and not by what is most important.

Some Examples of Lasting Legacies

Trucking giant J.B. Hunt was a large and generous man who spoke his mind and did business on a handshake. When the publisher of the local business journal interviewed him and asked, Mr. Hunt, how do you make a billion dollars?" He said, "Get up a lot of early mornings, son. Work hard, read your Bible, and everything will take care of itself." He believed that all the answers to the world's problems were in the Bible, but you had to pay the price to find them. He also believed that good partners attracted good partners. That's the stuff he built his personal brand on.

When J.B. Hunt passed away after suffering a head injury from a fall on an icy parking lot, a hush fell over the Northwest Arkansas business community. He had been instrumental in not only growing J.B. Hunt Transport Services, Inc. into the number-two trucking company in the United States, he had been a major stakeholder in the growth of the Northwest Arkansas region. At the time, it was the sixth fastest-growing area of the country thanks to him and other visionaries like him. The great news is J.B. Hunt Transport Services continues to thrive, and his business partners and the individuals he mentored and inspired have picked up where he left off. A consistent brand transitioned nicely into a lasting legacy.

Another legacy worth examining is that of retailing visionary Sam Walton, founder of Wal-Mart Stores, Inc. Mr. Sam, as he was known, was an economics major in college. You can see how he used his degree in creating Wal-Mart — a concept built upon economies of scale. He believed in serving his community and listening to his customer and competitors.

Sam Walton passed away in 1992, and Wal-Mart was vastly smaller than it is today. The company was just beginning to explore international markets. Mr. Sam was convinced that Wal-Mart's competitive advantage depended on the use of technology and its logistics strategy. Today, the global company has the best technology infrastructure only second to the United States government. Its logistics network is larger than most trucking and distribution companies and provides them an unparalleled competitive advantage. And, although Wal-Mart doesn't market it widely, they are one of the largest corporate charity donors worldwide and they encourage their employees — they still call them associates — to get involved in their community.

London is a 2,000-year-old city steeped in tradition. It is home to another brand that has endured since 1485 under the reign of Henry VII — Yeomen Warders of Her Majesty's Royal Palace and Fortress the Tower of London.

They are the ceremonial guardians of the Tower of London. You might know them as Beefeaters. Traditionally, their role was to guard prisoners who were detained at the tower as well as safeguarding the British crown jewels and caring for the ravens housed at the Tower of London. The also serve as tour guides to visitors at the tower and have become a popular tourist attraction.

There are thirty-five Yeoman Warders and one Chief Warder. The warders are an elite crew. They are retired from the British Armed Forces and must be former senior non-commissioned officers with at least twenty-two years of service. They must also hold the Long Service and Good Conduct medals. The positions are highly coveted.

The legendary presence of the Beefeaters and their time-honored traditions prove that legacies aren't built overnight.

The Yeoman Warders have executed the Ceremony of the Keys every night just before 10:00 since the fourteenth century. There is a six-month wait for tourists to get tickets to watch the late-evening ceremony. In the brief ceremony, the Chief Yeoman Warder and the Yeoman Warder Watchman walk to the entry of the Tower of London, lock the gates, and then return to recite the same passage they've recited for over half a century.

> Sentry: Who comes there?
> Chief Yeoman Warder: The keys.
> Sentry: Whose keys?
> Chief Yeoman Warder: Queen Elizabeth's keys.
> Sentry: Pass Queen Elizabeth's Keys. All's well.

The tower guard then presents arms. The Chief Yeoman Warder raises his hat and, before he takes the keys to the Queen's House for safekeeping, says, "God preserve Queen Elizabeth." The Sentry replies heartily, "Amen!"

The origin of the name Beefeater is a source of great speculation. However, the Yeoman Warders and their tradition have created a brand that has stood the test of time.

Your Legacy is Your Choice

I hope you read this chapter first AND last. I poured into it so much of what I'm convinced is necessary to create a lasting legacy. We can accumulate wealth, create successful companies, and build big buildings with our names on them. However, none of those things makes much difference when we reflect on our accomplishments at the end of our life.

What will matter is the way we were able to affect people — in one-on-one, face-to-face, two-way communications where we shared our lives, thoughts, and ideas with others. That is where the true magic of business relationships lie. By just stepping out from behind our e-mail, phones, and computers to engage with people, we'll stand the greatest chance of engaging others in a valuable way. That's the way our grandparents and their grandparents did it.

If you have not yet started building your personal brand, begin with the end in mind as Dr. Stephen Covey said in *Seven Habits of Highly Effective People*. Ask yourself what you want to be remembered for or what you'd like to leave behind. Then move toward creating a brand that supports those goals. Don't worry if you don't know what that looks like yet.

Millions of people wander through life every day without knowing even why they exist. As goal-centered and visionary as I am, I'm not even sure I've got it right yet. I just keep looking for guidance from God so I'll serve and glorify Him in the way He chooses. I can't think of a higher calling than running His errands during my time here on earth.

Final Thoughts on Brands and Legacies

What will your legacy be? A planned and intentional legacy will always be rich and full. Life is too short to spend it doing things that just don't make a difference. Don't let your dreams lay lifeless like broken ponies innocently waiting the tragic ending of a calling that will never fully live. Let them run wild, majestic, and free. Follow your heart in search of the legacy you were meant to leave.

- If you strive for the same values and initiatives while you are alive in pursuit of establishing a solid brand, your legacy will be a long-lasting and powerful one.
- What if we stopped — before it's too late — and asked, "What will be my legacy?"
- True value is about creating a life that leaves a lasting and profound legacy — a great gift for generations to come.
- Once we realize we aren't serving our calling because we are running in the wrong race, we can begin to make changes to restore it. It won't happen overnight and sometimes realigning our lives requires drastic measures such as career moves, debt reduction, or relationship changes.

Book Carrie for Your Next Company Meeting or Conference

Carrie Perrien Smith is an expert on building business relationships. She can teach you how to transition your prospects into clients, create a customer base of fans who rave about you to their peers, and create strong professional relationships within your organization. The result is more clients, bigger paydays, and sweeter success. A skilled connector, Carrie is personally responsible for business connections that have resulted in hundreds of thousands of dollars in revenue in the last five years.

She is a publishing, communication, and training industry veteran. Carrie's corporate career spans fifteen years, split between Texas Instruments and Wal-Mart Stores, Inc. Her company, Soar with Eagles, offers training, book publishing, event design, and consulting services as well as a professional speaker bureau.

She publishes an e-zine called *Effective Strategies*. It helps business professionals create strategies that range from finding prospects to transforming existing clients into die-hard fans. She has just introduced an e-zine focused on book publishing for writers and speakers called *The Last Word on Books*. She is the author of *Networking Zone: The Business Referral*

Network Construction Guide and an audio CD called *Maximize Your Network* and is a coauthor of *Wise Words for Smart Teens: The Teenager's Guide to a Great Life.* Her most recent book is *Currency: Striking Networking Gold in a Relationship Economy.*

Carrie is a native of the Tulsa area. She earned her Bachelor of Science and Masters in Business Administration at John Brown University, a private Christian university. After many years in Dallas, Texas, she lives in Rogers, Arkansas with her husband, Tom. They survived their daughter Darcie's teenage years and now share their home with their canine fur children: Snappy, Speckles, Jazmin, and Midget. A self-professed home improvement junkie, she feeds her uncontrollable addiction by starting house projects she knows she can't finish when her husband isn't looking.

Maximize Your Network

Four Techniques That Transform You from Unknown to Top of Mind

38-Minute Audio CD
$12.95

Make every moment count. Carrie reveals four techniques that will help you capture every personal and professional opportunity when you are networking.

- Creating a confident first impression
- Capitalizing on the gold zone
- Leading meaningful conversation
- Follow-up that turns prospects into clients

You can spend hundreds hours a year networking. Like money wasted on ineffective advertising, ineffective networking wastes valuable time you could be spending with your business, family, and home.

If you aren't currently networking, this audio CD gives you the tools and confidence to start. Bottom line, networking is one of the most effective marketing strategies you can employ for your business.

Ready to Get the Most Out of Your Gold Mine?

What it would it mean to your company's success if you could reduce your expenses by maximizing the information, connections, and additional sales in the client base you already have?

Carrie's Bottom Line Business Relationships program can help you dig deeper. Topics in the program include:

- Writing a positioning statement that clarifies your value to your clients.
- Creating customer dialogue that creates lifelong business relationships.
- Transforming every member of your organization into sales consultants.
- Capitalizing on every follow-up opportunity.
- Making a confident and memorable impression on those you meet.
- Building a foundation of trust.

- Defining your target market.
- Building a business referral network that connects you to what you need quickly.
- Showing your value to your organization's leaders.
- Learning how to overcome conflict and negative attitudes.
- Discovering the most powerful communication tool of all.
- Motivating clients and employees to tell their friends about your company.
- Creating a customer experience that your clients will rave about.

When you are ready to take your business relationships and your professional success to a new level, contact Carrie to work with your organization at carrie@soarhigher.com.

- One-on-one coaching
- Team training
- Strategic planning
- Keynotes

BOTTOM LINE BUSINESS RELATIONSHIPS
MORE CLIENT$ BIGGER PAYDAY$ $WEETER $UCCE$$

Do You Know Someone Who Needs to Read this Book?

This book makes a great gift for your clients and Soar with Eagles makes it easy to give. You can order copies at volume discount pricing — the same pricing that the clients who hire Carrie receive. When you order as few as 250 copies, Soar with Eagles will customize your book for an affordable additional charge (see the next page for details).

Take Advantage of Volume Discount Pricing

Order as few as 10 copies of *Currency* and receive discount pricing. The more you order, the bigger the discount.

Discount Pricing Off Cover Price

20%	10-24 books
25%	25-49 books
30%	50-99 books
35%	100-149 books
40%	150-199 books
45%	200-249 books
50%	250 or more books

Get more details on volume discounts, customized copies, or ordering individual sections of the book. Contact Soar with Eagles at 479.636.7627 or carrie@soarhigher.com.

Customize *Currency* to Use as a Client Appreciation Gift or Training Tool for Your Employees

You can customize *Currency* to fit your needs. Include a message for your clients or order a copy for every member of your sales team or your whole organization as a gift or training tool.

- **Personalize this book with your logo, contact info, and message** when you order as few as 250 copies. Add up to four pages of marketing copy about your company in the front of the book for just $1 more per copy you order. Add your logo and contact information to the back cover for $1 more per copy. The book is available in hardcover or paperback.
- **Order any section of this book in hardcover or paperback.** Minimum order of fifty copies required. Pricing based on quantity ordered.
    - Expose Yourself: Building a Solid Business Referral Network through Shameless Self-Promotion
    - Word Power: Using Your Verbal Assets to Accumulate Relationship Capital
    - Transactions: Delivering an Unforgettable Customer Experience
    - Brand Equity: Building a Lasting Brand That Grows in Value and Leaves a Legacy

Three Ways to Order

Online Place your order online at
www.soarhigher.com/currency.htm

Phone Call 479.636.7627 Mon. through Fri. 8 a.m. to 5 p.m. CST

Postal Mail Send your completed order form to
Soar with Eagles
1200 North Mallard Lane, Rogers, AR 72756 USA
479.636.7627

Professional Development Tools

Maximize Your Network: Four Techniques That   38-Minute Audio CD
Transform You from Unknown to Top of Mind   _____ x $12.95 = _____

Currency: Striking Networking   Paperback, 284 pages
Gold in a Relationship Economy   _____ x $24.95 = _____

Wise Words for Smart Teens: Paperback, 264 pages
The Teenager's Guide to a Great Future   _____ x $20.00 = _____

Please add 9.0% sales tax for orders shipped to Arkansas addresses.

Shipping and Handling

USA: Add $4 for the first book and $1 for each additional book.
International: $9 for the first book; $5 for each additional book.

Payment

❏ Check   Credit Card: ❏ Visa ❏ MC ❏ Amex

Card Number _____

Name on Card _____

Exp. Date _____ CSV# (on back of card) _____

Signature _____

Your Information

Name _____

Address _____

City _____ State _____ Zip _____

Telephone _____

E-mail Address _____